T0171007

FORCE OF MIND, SONG OF HEART

Shaping Consciousness, Connection, and Compassionate Cooperation

Lynne D'Amico, Ph.D.

BALBOA.
PRESS

A DIVISION OF HAY HOUSE

Copyright © 2011–2014 Lynne D'Amico, Ph.D.

All rights reserved. No part of this book may be used or reproduced by any means, graphic, electronic, or mechanical, including photocopying, recording, taping or by any information storage retrieval system without the written permission of the publisher except in the case of brief quotations embodied in critical articles and reviews.

Balboa Press books may be ordered through booksellers or by contacting:

Balboa Press
A Division of Hay House
1663 Liberty Drive
Bloomington, IN 47403
www.balboapress.com
1 (877) 407-4847

Because of the dynamic nature of the Internet, any web addresses or links contained in this book may have changed since publication and may no longer be valid. The views expressed in this work are solely those of the author and do not necessarily reflect the views of the publisher, and the publisher hereby disclaims any responsibility for them.

The author of this book does not dispense medical advice or prescribe the use of any technique as a form of treatment for physical, emotional, or medical problems without the advice of a physician, either directly or indirectly. The intent of the author is only to offer information of a general nature to help you in your quest for emotional and spiritual well-being. In the event you use any of the information in this book for yourself, which is your constitutional right, the author and the publisher assume no responsibility for your actions.

Cover illustration by Michał Wręga.

Any people depicted in stock imagery provided by Thinkstock are models, and such images are being used for illustrative purposes only. Certain stock imagery © Thinkstock.

Printed in the United States of America.

ISBN: 978-1-4525-9129-2 (sc)
ISBN: 978-1-4525-9130-8 (e)

Library of Congress Control Number: 2014901252

Balboa Press rev. date: 2/28/2014

Dedication

To Spirit, my muse.

Acknowledgments

I am indebted to every person who has knowingly or unknowingly helped shape my perception and brought me to this current point of understanding: authors, professors, guest speakers, friends, acquaintances, strangers, and family. While it is tempting to think of the ideas in these pages as my own, they belong to every person I have ever read, heard speak, or engaged in interaction. Even ideas I have rejected have helped advance my thinking by provoking me to explore new lines of inquiry and innovation. Undeniably, we are "entangled," inextricably connected to one another in consciousness.

I am grateful for the love of my family, biological and gifted through marriage. I especially thank my parents, Alba and Richard D'Amico, for teaching me by example what it means to accept the responsibility of a relationship. I thank my children, Sari Reisner and Alex D'Amico Reisner, for the privilege of motherhood and their constant support and inspiration. I thank my husband, Marek Wrega, for his capacity to love selflessly and share me. I thank my former husband, Darrell Reisner, for helping me prove how the guidance described in these pages really does work.

I am grateful for my friends. I especially thank Marjorie Bernardi, Isabelle Blanco, Pam Fahr, Steve Finucane, Hope Gibbs, Nora Grubbs, Gay Harrington, Gary Bivings, Valerie Johnston, Gina Manlove, Felicia Montineri, Bonnie Rae, Bill Rogers, and Linda Roth for ongoing support and encouragement. Isabelle and Gay read and commented on an earlier version of *Force of Mind, Song of Heart*, and Gay has been my constant companion over the years on our willful journey to lead a more consciously connected life. I also thank Jeff Wilkinson and Ceal Hayes for reading an earlier version of Force of Mind, Song of Heart, and am grateful to Ceal for informally piloting the original exercise section.

I thank those who have participated in the Prince Street Practicum for Conscious Living, especially Hope Gibbs, who lent me her personal copy of A Course in Miracles and helped me organize the original course study group from which the practicum grew. Were it not for the practicum, which led me to pursue yogic studies and develop a deep commitment to meditative practice, I might not have been inspired to write *Force of Mind, Song of Heart*. I am grateful to

Eileen Elgin, Gay Harrington, Carolyn Marsh Halachoff, Ann Matikan, Maryann Picone, Bill Rogers, Irene Stephanski, and Valentina Stamenova for their contributions.

I am indebted to the late Dell Hymes and Nessa Wolfson, my mentors at the University of Pennsylvania, who first inspired me to study expressions of disapproval.

I am grateful to Maria O. Pryshlak and Andrzej Kaminski for the privilege of working in East Central and Southern Europe on behalf of the Georgetown University's Center for Intercultural Education and Development, years that have had a profound impact on my process of self and consciousness.

I thank Corinne Licckett of Smith Publicity and Dan Gerstein of Gotham Ghostwriters for their time and willingness to help me in my search for sage advice on book publishing. Dan referred me to Jane Wesman of Wesman Public Relations, who generously provided the advice I was seeking.

I am grateful to the professionals at Balboa Press for guidance with publishing and marketing, especially Melinda Herrington, Stephanie Cornthwaite, Emma Gliessman, David Bernardi and Richard L. Robertson.

I am grateful to those who have helped me advance interdisciplinary connections. I feel especially privileged, as a linguist, to have been accepted as a member of the American Psychological Association, and the Association for the Scientific Study of Consciousness. I thank Natasha Hennessy for the opportunity to teach a three-month workshop at Pure Prana yoga studio on *Mindtuning to the Perfect Pitch of Heart Connection*. I thank Bonnie Rae for inviting me to speak on the same topic at the National Association of Professional Women, Naples chapter. I grateful to Debra Riggs, Executive Director of the National Association of Social Workers, Virginia chapter, for inviting me to be keynote speaker on the *Language of Healing* at the NASWVA pre-conference Institute. I am grateful to Maurizio and Zaya Benazzo for welcoming me into the Science and Nonduality community as a SAND13 presenter. I also thank Marilyn Turkovich for including Knowledge-Shaping Solutions as an organizational partner with the Charter for Compassion.

I am honored and grateful to Michal "Sepe" Wrega for creating the cover illustration for *Force of Mind, Song of Heart*. Michal is an award-winning urban street artist, graphic designer, and illustrator who paints and exhibits around the world. You can see more of Michal's work online at www.sepeusz.com.

Finally, I thank those in government contracting who paved the path for me to step away from intelligence education to write Force of Mind, Song of Heart.

Contents

Acknowledgments. vii

Preface xi

Introduction xiii

Part 1 – Background
Consciousness and Perception: Understanding Your Self

1   What You "See"—Limits and Opportunities 1

2   Obstacles to Connection: Perceptual Inattention & Passive Participant-Observation . . . 25

Part 2 – Guidance
Compassionate Cooperation: Removing the Obstacles to Connection

3   Mind-Set and Force of Mind: Musical Score for Your Relationships and Your
     Emerging Process of Self-Seeing. 45

4   Symbols, Strategies, and Techniques: Tools for Shaping Compassionate Cooperation. . . 73

5   Conclusion. 121

Part 3 – Applying the Guidance
Shaping Relationships, Self, Consciousness, and Connection

6   Exercises: Relationship Scenarios. 125

Bibliography 187

There's an explosive potential for a higher level for human evolution and creative capacity. And this is not just a spontaneous emergence, but something that is consciously created and consciously directed. This happens when you are participating in the evolutionary process with all of your self.[1]

—Andrew Cohen

1   "Human Emergence," http://www.humanemergence.org/programs.html.

Preface

Inter-dependence ... is a fundamental law of nature. Not only higher forms of life but also many of the smallest insects are social beings who, without any religion, law or education, survive by mutual cooperation based on an innate recognition of their interconnectedness ... All phenomena from the planet we inhabit to the oceans, clouds, forests and flowers that surround us, arise in dependence upon subtle patterns of energy. Without their proper interaction, they dissolve and decay.[2]   —His Holiness the Fourteenth Dalai Lama of Tibet

Do you wish your relationship with your husband, mother, or some someone else in your life were different? Do you find yourself thinking, *"If only he would ... If only she wouldn't ...?"*

Did you know that your brain keeps you from feeling "happy," genuinely satisfied with people and life? That your every moment of existence is an opportunity for better relationships, more purposeful living, and self-actualization? That the people who frustrate you most are your greatest opportunity for personal growth, empowerment, and more conscious living?

Force of Mind, Song of Heart provides an extraordinary look at ordinary personal relationships. It challenges you to improve the relationships you have with the most important people in your life, and to see your "self" as a mind, not a brain, with limitless creative potential to invite and support connection with every person in your life, be it a spouse, parent, or other family member.

Force of Mind, Song of Heart reveals how every personal relationship is a dynamic tension between merging and separating, which you evolve in your consciousness through your thoughts, recollections, and imaginings, and through social interaction with others. Revealing how you shape this dynamic jointly with others using an instrumental force of mind and drawing on

---

2   His Holiness the 14th Dalai Lama of Tibet, "Message on Compassion and the Individual," http://www.dalailama.com/messages/compassion.

emotional symbols, *Force of Mind, Song of Heart* teaches how to actively restore balance to the negative and polarizing dynamic that inhibits connection and causes you to push others away.

Force of Mind, Song of Heart is testimony to the emerging process of self and consciousness that is mirrored in every relationship, and to human "inter-dependence" and interconnectedness. If you are struggling with a personal relationship in your life right now, and want to understand how to improve it, this book is for you.

Force of Mind, Song of Heart shows you how to "rewire" you brain for more genuinely satisfying relationships, and more joyful and purposeful living. Revealing how to improve a personal relationship beyond what it looks like "on the surface" in your interaction with others, it shows you how to

- Recognize and eliminate the obstacles to connection in your interaction with your self and others that interfere with your ability to invite and support connection
- Use perceptual reinterpretation to generate the positive and unifying force of mind that causes connection with a relationship partner and reflects a balanced relationship dynamic
- Rebalance a negative and polarizing relationship dynamic by restoring power-sharing and positive reciprocity

Improving a personal relationship requires you to develop self and consciousness to serve collective wellness, to balance your personal needs and interests with those of others. I have not always understood this. For many years, I had no idea how I was preventing myself from connecting with some of the most important people in my life, or how my emerging process of self and consciousness was tied to the people who caused me the most angst. While I was always polite in interaction with others, I also saw myself as accommodating and blameless. As a young adult I received a civic award, where I was described as "fluent in three languages but unable to say 'no' in any of them." It was intended as a compliment, but it foreshadowed the lifetime of study, inquiry, teaching, and learning I would follow in trying to come to this transdisciplinary point of understanding that is the subject of *Force of Mind, Song of Heart.*

I have been practicing the guidance in *Force of Mind, Song of Heart* for more than a decade, and have been able to dramatically improve the quality, authenticity, and outcomes of some of the most important relationships in my life. Through professional talks, workshops, and coaching, I have also been teaching others how to apply the guidance in this book to their own relationships and lives. If I can help you understand how your every thought, recollection, and imagining shapes "you," your consciousness, and your relationships and guide you to use your mind as a unifying instrumental force to change lives, writing this book will have been worth the effort.

Introduction

Emotions are not just reactions to events. Different emotions can change the ways we think and influence how we respond to others. Emotions are intensely social in that they can draw us closer or push us farther apart.[3]

—James W. Pennebaker

Who is *that one person* in your life who knows exactly how to push your buttons? That one person who agitates you, frustrates you, or causes you resistance? Is it your husband? Your mother? Your mother-in-law? Your brother? *"If only he would ..." " If only she wouldn't ..." "Why can't she ..." "How could he ..." "Why won't she ..." "Why does she ..."*

What comes to your mind when you think about that one person? *"He wasn't like that when I married him ..." "Why won't she listen ..." "He's a jerk ..." "She's controlling ..." "He's annoying ..." "She drives me crazy ..."* Maybe you feel overwhelming resentment, or focus specifically on the fragments of a hurtful memory, reliving in exquisite detail a situation from years ago. Does your mood shift when you bring that person to mind? Does your body tense? What are you thinking about that person right now?

You may not know it, but you just created your future.

Whatever thoughts, recollections, or imaginings you just had—or are having at this instant—predispose your brain to producing more thoughts, recollections, and imaginings based on the same assumptions and premises. In any given moment, whatever you give attention to, and the kind of attention you give it, reinforces or adjusts your brain's neurological network, how your brain is "wired," learning that determines how you will experience people and situations in your future.

Your brain works like a supercomputer that is programmed to respond nonstop to internal and external signals. Just as it responds automatically to an external temperature change by adjusting

3   James W. Pennebaker, *The Secret Life of Pronouns* (NY: Bloomsbury Press, 2011).

the body's regulatory systems, it responds to other stimuli in the same reactive way. Whether you are aware of it or not, whether you give it attention or not, your brain is continuously teaching you what to think, remember, and feel about your husband, mother, father-in-law, and every other person and relationship situation in your life.

No thought, recollection, or imagining you have is an isolated representation in consciousness, with value and meaning only to itself. Each is tied to every other thought, recollection, and imagining, and it is also tied to the experience that initially triggered your brain to react. Whether you are aware of it or not, whether you give it attention or not, your brain draws from a storehouse of biased and subjective data to shape the attitudinal and emotional patterns it teaches you.

The attitudinal and emotional response patterns your brain teaches you are derived from the inferences and premises it rotely extends from your experiences, witnessed or imagined. Through a continuous process of assumption and deduction, you tell your self biased and subjective stories about a relationship partner, based on the emotional patterns you've learned. These stories, and the thoughts, recollections, and imaginings tied to them in your consciousness, cause you to feel satisfied and fulfilled with the most important people in your personal life—or frustrated and dissatisfied with them.

This happens because the attitudinal and emotional patterns your brain uses as the basis for the meaning of the stories you tell yourself are "intensely social." They generate an instrumental *force of mind* that postures you either to draw others closer or push them away. Moment by moment, whether you are aware of it or not, the stories you tell yourself, and sometimes share with others, about a relationship partner generate a force of mind that influences the quality, authenticity, and outcomes of your relationships. Force of mind shapes the dynamic tension between merging and separating that is every personal relationship, and it accounts for why you can't wait to see your best friend as well as why you loathe to visit your mother-in-law or resent your husband.

The relationship dynamic you shape jointly with a partner, be it your husband, mother, or someone else, reflects your attempt to balance the tension between merging your *self* with another person and staying separate. It reflects an emerging process of self, who "you" are at any given instant, which also reflects an evolving process of consciousness. This dynamic process unfolds largely outside your awareness because your brain is constantly and automatically deciding for you how to interpret and assign emotional value and directing you to use its instrumental force.

The force of mind you generate in any given instant postures you for specific kinds of relationship experiences and outcomes because it affects the dynamic of a relationship. On the one hand, you draw others closer to you when you generate the unifying force of mind that is compassionate cooperation, the force produced by positive attitudes and emotions such as love, peace, forgiveness, gratitude, and service. On the other, you push others away from you when you generate the polarizing force of mind that is opposition, the force produced by negative attitudes and emotions such as fear, anger, resentment, criticism, and entitlement.

A balanced relationship dynamic produces *connection*. It enables you to draw others closer to you without losing your own uniqueness or causing others to lose theirs and is characterized by power-sharing and positive reciprocity. Connection is the basis for every genuinely satisfying and positive human relationship.

Paradoxically, your human nature is to seek connection with others while your brain is predisposed to inhibiting it.

Force of Mind, Song of Heart is a sincere effort to explain this paradox in practical terms and show you how to use the creative potential of your mind to accommodate it and improve any personal relationship in your life, be it one with a spouse, parent, in-law, or other family member.

Demystifying connection and relationship satisfaction, *Force of Mind, Song of Heart* shows you how to redirect the force of mind that is opposition as compassionate cooperation when your brain postures you to push others away. It is by using the unlimited creative potential of your mind to redirect opposition, in spite of what your brain is telling you to do, that you can restore balance to a relationship dynamic, which has been disrupted by the negative and polarizing values of opposition.

How can you redirect opposition as compassionate cooperation? By drawing on positive and unifying emotional symbols, you cause your self to generate the force of mind that is compassionate cooperation, which is how you draw others closer and take an active role in shaping your relationships, your emerging process of self and consciousness, and your life.

Force of Mind, Song of Heart is divided into three parts:

Part 1: Background explains foundational assumptions and serves as the backdrop for part 2. It suggests how you come to "see" others as you do and emphasizes the subjective and unreliable nature of perception that causes you to believe what you "see," however self-deceptive and damaging to your relationships and life. It explains the obstacles to connection and the force of mind that is opposition that invites and supports the negative and polarizing *me-against-you* dynamic that causes separation and disturbs the balance of a relationship dynamic.

Part 2: Guidance teaches you how to take willful and active steps to eliminate the obstacles to connection and generate the force of mind that is compassionate cooperation, the unifying me-and-you dynamic that invites and supports the balanced relationship dynamic that is connection. It contains three components. First, it introduces the perceptual paradigm for compassionate cooperation and the attitudes and emotions of thought and expression that generate the force of mind that shapes connection. Then, it explains the process of perceptual reinterpretation, and how to use reframing and re-scripting to reshape the negative and polarizing stories you tell yourself and others about a relationship partner, a process that rebalances the tension between merging and separating in a relationship dynamic. Lastly, it details language and other emotional symbols along with strategies and techniques to help you redirect opposition as compassionate cooperation when your brain postures you to do otherwise.

Part 3: Practice provides you with scenario exercises so you can practice applying the guidance in part 2. Each exercise contains a scenario, a series of inductive problem-solving and decision-making challenges, and discussion input.

Interdisciplinary Grounding

Most generally, *Force of Mind, Song of Heart* has been influenced by my study and teaching of *A Course in Miracles,* where I learned how to "see differently" and dramatically alter my understanding of "reality," self, and consciousness, which radically changed my assumptions about the world and my place in it. Also, were it not for the course, I would not have organized the Prince Street Practicum for Conscious Living, where I have been evolving the ideas explained in this book for more than a decade.

A fundamental assumption made in *Force of Mind, Song of Heart* is that the universe, and our relationship to it, is beyond human understanding, an assumption echoed by quantum physicists. This assumption opens us to limitless possibilities, because we no longer restrict ourselves to currently accepted thought paradigms. We free ourselves to consider alternative thought paradigms. In the practical "real" world, the value of a paradigm is in its capacity to produce a specific and desired result. I have written *Force of Mind, Song of Heart* to detail a thought paradigm that produces connection.

To use this paradigm, it is not important to "believe in" anything, but it is necessary to see collective wellness as a worthy goal. However you self-identify, whether you think of yourself as religious, spiritual, agnostic, atheist, straight, gay, bisexual, transgender, black, white, Asian, Moslem, Christian, or Jewish, directing your relationship outcomes toward collective wellness empowers you to see how you can embrace you own individual uniqueness and the uniqueness of others without having to push others away and experience conflict. Concern for the physical and mental wellness of every relationship partner is a goal that ultimately benefits you, others, and humanity. It also serves peace-building and is an antidote to the extreme and violent expressions of an oppositional force of mind that are rippling through the world.

Force of Mind, Song of Heart is tied to the notions that human nature is adaptive and you emerge and "grow" as you expand awareness of *self* in response to the stimuli of circumstances and conditions in life. *Force of Mind* reflects many of the ideas familiar to the spiral dynamics model of human development and integral psychology. While it is recognized that genetics and other factors affect your individual capacity for change, it is also recognized that you are capable of reshaping the neural pathways of your brain to accommodate new experience. Neuroscientific studies show how neuroplasticity allows the brain to reshape itself in response to new learning *throughout your life*, not just until adolescence as was previously thought. Brain scientists now understand that the brain can even reshape itself to compensate for dead and damaged areas caused by stroke, Parkinson's disease, and other medical conditions. Current studies at the Stanford School of Medicine, for example, use brain stimulation to address circuit disruptions in the brains of Parkinson patients that cause tremors and other problems.

Most specifically, *Force of Mind, Song of Heart* is rooted in discourse analysis research in the "ethnography of speaking" participant-observation tradition I began as a doctoral student at the University of Pennsylvania.[4] It considers study evidence of how unwritten and invisible social rules drive human behavior, including speech behavior, tying families and other communities of individuals together. It is based on research evidence that shows how different types of relationship partners in several educated American English communities of practice jointly create the speech action of expressing disapproval. It also draws on study evidence showing how expressions of disapproval, over time, shape larger conflict themes and dynamics in family relationships.

Force of Mind, Song of Heart assumes an intimate and interdependent relationship between perception and language, a relationship well established in the linguistics and psychology literatures.

Force of Mind, Song of Heart assumes a strong link between genuinely positive relationships and physical and mental wellness, an idea that is central to the discipline of positive psychology and suggested by neuroscientific and psychological study evidence. It considers evidence that negative feelings cause stress that places wellness at risk by alerting the nervous system to flood the blood with a surge of chemicals that place the body in a heightened state of physiological arousal. Although a temporary surge of chemicals can be protective, providing you with the extra

---

4   Lynne D'Amico-Reisner, "An Analysis of the Surface Structure of Disapproval Exchanges." In Wolfson and Judd, eds., *Sociolinguistics and Language Acquisition* (Rowley, Mass: Newbury House, 1983). *An Ethnolinguistic Study of Disapproval Exchanges* (Philadelphia, PA: University of Pennsylvania, 1985). *Avoiding Direct Conflict through the Co-construction of Narratives about Absent Others*, Presented at the American Association for Applied Linguistics (AAAL), Stanford, Connecticut, 1999; *Power and Solidarity in Disapproval Exchanges between Intimates: A Gender Issue?* Presented at the International Association of Applied Linguistics (AILA, Amsterdam, 1993) and, at the American Association for Applied Linguistics (AAAL, Atlanta, 1993). *That Same Old Song and Dance: Repetition as a Critical Discourse Feature in Disapproval Exchanges between Intimates*, Presented at the American Association for Applied Linguistics (AAAL, Atlanta, GA: 1993) and the International Association of Applied Linguistics (AILA, Amsterdam: 1993).

strength and energy needed to survive a physically dangerous situation, extended exposure to an "activated" state can lead to chronic stress, causing physical and mental "wear and tear," which is recognized universally as a serious public health concern.

It considers how negative feelings have been directly linked to health risks. For instance, among married couples, there is study evidence showing that verbal arguments inhibit proper immune system functioning.[5] The evidence is especially strong for women, who have been found to hold on to negative feelings more than men and report higher levels of marital dissatisfaction than their partners. This suggests that if you are a married woman, you are at increased risk for lowered immune system functioning as well as for feeling dissatisfied with your husband, because you are likely to hold on to negative feelings.

It also takes into account research findings suggesting how marital partners begin their life together feeling satisfied with one another, but end up feeling dissatisfied within the first three years of marriage,[6] a feeling that is likely to persist throughout a marriage once it is established.[7] While you don't need to stay in a dissatisfying marriage, the higher divorce rate for second marriages in the United States suggests that trading in your spouse isn't necessarily the answer to creating satisfying marital relationships.

Based on an assumption cognitive-behavioral psychologists have long recognized, *Force of Mind, Song of Heart* is based on the assumption that there is value in using the mind to create in the reality you want to see, a successful pathway for helping clients make adjustments to improve their experience of life. This assumption reflects the well-established view that you can empower yourself by harnessing control of the mind and your behaviors to effect changes in your personal lives, communities, and the world.[8]

Grounded in evidence-based psychological science, *Force of Mind, Song of Heart* is consistent with cognitive-behavioral therapy (CBT), an evidence-based psychotherapeutic approach. This approach assumes the mind plays a critical role in shaping relationship behaviors, improving

---

5   J. K. Kiecolt-Glaser, C. Bane, Glaser, R. et al., *Love, Marriage, and Divorce: Newlyweds' Stress Hormones Foreshadow Relationship Changes,* Journal of Consulting and Clinical Psychology 71: 176–188; and, Kiecolt-Glaser, J. K., W. Malarkey, M. Chee, et al., *Negative Behavior during Marital Conflict is Associated with Immunological Down-Regulation,* Psychosomatic Medicine (1993): 395–409.

6   Ibid.

7   K. L. Heffner, J. Kielcolt-Glaser, T. Loving, et al., "Spousal Support Satisfaction as a Modifier of Physiological Responses to Marital Conflict in Younger and Older Couples," *Journal of Behavioral Medicine* 27: 233–254.

8   Consistent with *empowerment theory,* the multidimensional social process through which it has been proven people can take control of and change their lives.

mental health, and promoting life fulfillment.[9] It advances the idea that you make moment-by-moment choices that dramatically affect your own relationships and influence the lives of others and your communities. Based on the CBT premises that change happens in the mind and that you project what we believe, *Force of Mind Song of Heart* promotes willful action as a core requirement for empowerment and genuinely positive change that shapes relationship growth and renewal to serve collective wellness and peace-building.

9   The need to deliver evidence-based psychosocial interventions is acknowledged and CBT is identified as having the strongest research base for effectiveness: Graeme Whitfield and Chris Williams, "The Evidence Base for Cognitive-Behavioral Therapy in Depression – Delivery in Busy Clinical Settings," *Advances in Psychiatric Treatment* 9 (2003): 21–30, http://apt.rcpsych.org/content/9/1/21.full.

PART 1 – BACKGROUND

CONSCIOUSNESS AND PERCEPTION: UNDERSTANDING YOUR SELF

Part 1 of *Force of Mind, Song of Heart* explains foundational assumptions and serves as the backdrop for part 2.

Part 2 suggests how you come to "see" others as you do and emphasizes the subjective and unreliable nature of perception that causes you to believe what you "see," however self-deceptive and damaging to your relationships and life. It explains the obstacles to connection and the force of mind that is opposition that invites and supports the negative and polarizing *me-against-you* dynamic that causes separation and disturbs the balance of a relationship dynamic.

CHAPTER 1

What You "See"—Limits and Opportunities

Although we ascribe our actions to reason, man in fact operates primarily out of pattern recognition; the logical arrangement of data serves mainly to enhance a pattern-recognition system that then becomes "truth." But nothing is ever "true," except under certain circumstances, and then only from a particular viewpoint, characteristically unstated.

—David R. Hawkins[10]

Imagine as you get off the metro one evening, you pass a couple and hear the man shouting at the woman:

> *What are you fucking nuts? Don't you tell me what to do! You don't know what the fuck you're talking about.*

How would you react? Would you feel yourself tensing up and your heart beating faster? Would you hardly notice? Would you ignore the shouting and the words? Would you take the shouting seriously or dismiss it?

Your reaction would depend on how you "see" the experience, your perception, a conditioned and nonconscious reaction, a result of your brain's predisposition to neurological patterning that is tied to your language of feeling, the emotional symbols your brain uses to construct meaning. If, for instance, you grew up in a family where your parents routinely screamed vulgarities at each other and acted out anger, you would have a different reaction to the man's shouting than if you grew up in family where you never heard your parents raise their voices or intimidate each other or you. Your reaction to the man's shouting would be determined by how your brain values the shouting, an emotional response pattern it extends from your past experiences that causes you

---

10 David R. Hawkins, *Power versus Force,* 27, 28. Permission to quote given by Veritas Publishing.

to value your thoughts, recollections, and imaginings in any present instant as you do. What you "see," your perception of people and situations is highly constrained and biased by your past emotional experiences.

The evolving interplay between perception and the emotional symbols you use to shape experience affects everything you "see," think, remember, or imagine as well as what you neglect to "see," think, remember, or imagine. It both enables and limits your experiences and accounts for what you value, reject, tolerate, expect, desire, and anticipate from others. It affects your experiences of your self, people, and life, and it explains your preferences, judgments, opinions, and views. It also accounts for why some people measure up to your standards and others don't, and why your standards are what they are.

What you "see" is an illusion because it is *different from what you think it is.*[11] What you think you "see" is a subjective experience where you derive meaning from the "qualia of consciousness,"[12] the attitudes and emotions affecting the interplay between perception and language. The qualia of consciousness are what give meaning to your thoughts, recollections, and imaginings.

What You "See"

You have a brain, but you are a mind. You are consciousness, the product of your interplay with the world, your awareness of *self* that is "you." "You" shape your experiences and your *self* using a repertoire of emotional symbols—such as words, images, and gestures—that you draw on generally without much awareness or attention.

Neuroscientists show how your mind has a "life of its own," how it is an independent entity with "mental force" that shapes and controls the functioning of the physical brain, offering convincing evidence of your human free will to choose.[13] The potential you have to willfully direct your *force of mind* and shape it through the emotional symbols of feeling to produce more satisfying personal relationships is the focus of *Force of Mind, Song of Heart.*

Your brain is like a supercomputer, the most complex organ of your body and the control center for all your other organs and functions. The largest part of the brain, the cerebral cortex, contains billions of neurons that are connected by synapses and other neurons to cells. While scientists know that neurons produce electrical signals and cause chemicals to be released into the body in response to internal and external stimuli, they don't know exactly how the brain works.

---

11   Deepak Chopra, "Neuroscience of Enlightenment," Preconference Workshop, Science and Nonduality Conference (SAND 13), October 24, 2013, San Jose, CA.

12   Ibid.

13   Jeffrey M. Schwartz, Sharon Begley, *The Mind and The Brain* (NY: Regan Books, Harper Collins: 2009), 256.

With supercomputer efficiency, your brain rotely engages in a continuous and ongoing interaction with internal and external stimuli as it engages with the different levels of mind awareness: *conscious,* inside your awareness and control, *nonconscious,* outside your awareness and control, and *superconscious,* from intuition and revelation. From these different levels of awareness, your brain interprets information, extends assumptions, draws conclusions, and creates meaning, inferring and generalizing in an ongoing and evolving representation of emotional values, which your brain uses to direct your thoughts, recollections, and imaginings.

Your brain is astonishing in its processing capacity, but it is precisely this capacity that causes the processing errors that make all thought and expression biased, unreliable, and subjective.

Your brain automatically and continuously produces and extends meaning based on an overgeneralization of attitudinal and emotional conclusions and inferences. Whether you are aware of it or not, whether you give it attention or not, your brain carries on the business of "wiring" you to experience people and relationship situations in specific ways. Since the brain's neural pathways and synapses are highly responsive to changes in behavior and environment, a quality called "neuroplasticity,"[14] your every experience, witnessed or imagined, affects your brain's circuitry and the way you evolve meaning through your thoughts, recollections, and imaginings. Through an ongoing and evolving deepening or reshaping of its neural circuitry, your brain positions you for experiencing others and your self as you do.

Consider how the *nonconscious* and *conscious* levels of awareness appear to interact.

The *nonconscious* is *outside your awareness and control,* and represents your entire storehouse of subjectively processed experience, the master repository of your "emotional take" on everything you have ever witnessed or imagined. Your brain automatically draws and extends inferences from this highly subjective and biased master repository of nonconscious awareness as it responds to the internal and external stimuli of conscious awareness.

The relationship between nonconscious and conscious awareness becomes clearer when you consider how you learn a new skill, such as playing a musical instrument. When you first try to play an unfamiliar song, it is challenging. You have to fully concentrate on what you're doing. You probably hit some wrong notes, misread the music, and struggle to get your hands to coordinate and play the music. But over time and with practice, it becomes easier to play the song, and your performance improves. You no longer have to concentrate, you don't hit the wrong notes, and your hands easily coordinate to play the music. Your nonconscious mind has started to take over. Eventually, if you continue practicing, you'll probably be able to play the song effortlessly even

---

14 Norman Doidge, *The Brain That Changes Itself: Stories of Personal Triumph from the Frontiers of Brain Science* (New York: Penguin Books, 2007), 35.

without the music, and without bringing any conscious attention to what you are doing. You might even notice how you can easily play the song while you're thinking about other things, such as the dress you plan to buy or how you felt about last night's dinner.

Nonconscious awareness is *reactive*. It will always be enabled as well as limited by your brain's capacity to interact automatically with the mastery repository of conscious and nonconscious experience to produce what you "see" in any instant of conscious experience. *Post-Traumatic stress disorder* is an extreme example of how nonconscious awareness causes the brain to respond automatically and negatively to stimuli in thoughts, recollections, and imaginings with ingrained and resistant negative emotional response patterns. To a less dramatic extent, but in the same way, nonconscious awareness affects you and your relationship experiences.

The opportunity you have to shape your relationships, your *self,* your consciousness, and your life lies in your capacity for *self-directed neuroplasticity,*[15] your willful commitment to redirect force of mind. Understanding how you come to "see" as you do and use what you "see" to generate force of mind is a first step to understanding how to redirect it.

Culture, Family, and the Biases of Perception

Two core influences, culture and family, shape how you come to "see" as you do and how you come to acquire the symbols of feeling you use to shape your *self,* your awareness, and your relationships. Two influences largely shape your most basic values, expectations, desires, intentions, and beliefs: (a) where you were born and raised in the world and (b) your early childhood experiences with the people closest to you. They account for your most general perceptual tendencies, which are rooted in how you come to conceptualize and react to the emotional symbols you draw on to shape meaning and make sense of the world.

Culture and family largely explain your assumptions about your *self,* who "you" are, who you want to be, what makes you happy, and your expectations of others.

The broadest influence on "seeing" is culture. Guided by parents and other caretakers and authorities, you develop subjective ways of looking at the world and understanding who you are in relation to others, views that are shared by other "insiders," people in the same group and place where you were born and raised. Through the process of socialization, you come to hold and embody values according to the biased and subjective values and expectations of the people around you, the social *norms* that tie together your group.[16] Generally, you come to assume that

---

15   Jeffrey M. Schwartz, Sharon Begley, *The Mind and The Brain,* 256.

16   That we can be "brainwashed" or "radicalized" suggests that perception is *subjective,* and that we can change and be influenced to change what we "see."

your own values and expectations are more important and "correct" than those of others. When you feel threatened by values and expectations that are different from yours, especially when they threaten who you believe your *self* to be, as often happens with political and religious issues, your human nature is to justify and defend your own values as the "right" ones.

Culture is one of the most significant ways you distinguish yourself from others. It accounts for your broadest thought paradigm and shapes your general perception of people and life, your "worldview." To better appreciate the influence of culture, consider three very different traditions: Western, Eastern, and Islamic. While the different cultures associated with each of these traditions is unique, it can be helpful to consider how the roots of cultural tradition influence how we see life differently from one another and how we embody those differences.

Western culture grew out of Greco-Roman tradition and is most often associated with North America and Western Europe. The United States and Canada are examples of cultures rooted in Western worldview. Eastern cultures associate with the ancient traditions of Buddhism, Jainism, and Hinduism. Examples of cultures connected to Eastern worldview are India, Japan, and China. Islamic cultures are associated with ancient traditions based on Muslim values and beliefs. Afghanistan, Iraq, and Pakistan are examples of cultures connected to Islamic worldview. Different cultures that associate with the same worldview develop their own unique sets of biased and subjective values and beliefs. For instance, while the United States and Canada both have Greco-Roman roots, each culture has its own distinctive tendencies for thought and expression. Canadians believe government should play a role in people's lives and well-being, whereas Americans value non-interference by government in their lives." As a result, attitudes and emotions about life and relationships are significantly different in the two cultures.

Cultural tradition associates with different beliefs about matter. In the Western worldview, matter is largely seen as *physical*. Generally, if you are American, you probably believe "if you can't see it, it doesn't exist." A physical view of matter accounts for viewing disease in biological terms. Although Americans recognize the role of consciousness and its effects on physical and mental wellness, the tendency to believe that matter is physical results in a traditional Western medicine focus on curing disease. The idea that the mind and consciousness are central to wellness is still largely considered alternative or complementary to mainstream American views, which are based on a different paradigm of assumptions. However, recent neuroscientific advances suggesting that you can use the invisible force of your mind to control the functioning of the physical brain are already causing adjustments to the current paradigm.

Eastern worldview, by contrast, is strongly grounded in the idea that matter is *vitalistic*, that there is something "immaterial" that distinguishes living from inanimate matter. Within this worldview, the role of mind and consciousness are seen as critical to physical and mental wellness.

It is foundational to the Eastern mind-set that a vital flow of invisible *qi* from ancient Chinese culture, and *prana* from ancient Hindu culture, sustains and unifies all of life. While we have our own versions of *qi* and *prana* in American culture, the complexity of meaning associated with these notions in Eastern tradition is largely outside our Western experience. In the United States, *prana,* largely understood as "breath," is generally viewed as a way to advance "mindfulness," relaxation, and release from stress. In the Eastern tradition, it plays an important role in practice of Ayurvedic and traditional Chinese medicines. These traditions are associated with the belief that the complementary life forces of *yin* and *yang* are interdependent in the natural world and affect *balance*, the prerequisite for high-level wellness. Both practice areas are regarded in the Eastern tradition as reliable and effective in creating and sustaining high-level wellness.

Another broad distinction between Eastern and Western worldview has to do with how you conceptualize *self* in relation to *other*, your *I-perspective*, which is related to the different views of matter just described. In the Western worldview, where matter is considered physical, the relationship between self and other tends to be "dualistic," where individuals tend to see themselves as separate from others and the larger whole of life. Dualism tends to result in a more egocentric (self-centered) view of self because individual needs and interests are seen as separate from and more important than the needs and desires of others. In American culture, for example, individual freedom is a core value that affects personal choices and decision-making as well as domestic lawmaking and international posturing where winning is a valued outcome. The desire to win reflects a desire for power-holding, which is disruptive to balance in a personal relationship dynamic and causes polarization.

In the Eastern worldview, where matter is seen as an invisible life force and believed to sustain and connect the "whole of life," the relationship between self and other tends to be "nondualistic." The self is generally seen as part of a larger whole, and responsibility, loyalty, and obligation to group affiliations tend to trump individual needs and desires. Interconnectedness is a foundational value, and the notions of cause and effect often drive relationship problem-solving and decision-making. In nondualistic cultures, individual needs and desires tend to be seen as less important than those of the family, clan, tribe, and community. As a result, there is a tendency to solve problems collaboratively and to an extent where humility, self-sacrifice, and honor drive social interaction.

In the Islamic view, the self is also oriented toward larger interests in relationship problem-solving and decision-making, which is often led by elders with group authority. As in the Eastern worldview, personal needs and interests tend to be less important in the Islamic tradition than those of the family, clan, tribe, and community. Because groups are often nomadic and live in desolate areas that are isolated from each other, people have strong dependencies on one another that dramatically impact social interaction and personal relationships as well as attitudes and emotions toward "outsiders."

Culture influences your broadest mind-set, your tendencies for conceptualizing your *I-perspective* and the emotional symbols you understand and draw on to shape meaning in your experiences and life. It predisposes you to understanding and using language symbols to embody the values you share with other "insiders" of your group. It makes it more or less likely that you will sacrifice your own needs and interests for the good of a relationship partner or group, such as family or community. It influences the degree of solidarity you feel with family members and others in your culture, the degree your individual choices are influenced by society, your feelings of responsibility for others, and your self-perceived position in relation to authority.[17] If you are American, for example, you are likely to value your individual freedom and see other adult members of your family or community as responsible for themselves. You are likely to raise your children to value independence as well and to do as they choose when they are adults without feeling obligated to sacrifice their personal interests for you, as children raised in China are more likely to do.[18]

Culture also influences your expectations about how direct and explicit you expect people to be when you interact with them. If you are American, you are likely to value explicit explanations and details rather than implied and inferred ones. You are also likely to be more verbose and use less precise words than if you were raised in Japan, where people use implication and inference to communicate without compromising understanding. You also probably understand that it is impolite to ask an acquaintance how much she weighs or earns in the course of ordinary conversation.

Culture also orients you toward a particular purpose and meaning in life. In ancient cultures, the central meaning of life tends to be procreation, and kinship relationships as well as patriarchal authority are important because life is organized to serve the needs and interests of the group rather than any single individual in it. In such cultures, "who you are" is often connected to "who came before you," your lineage, and sometimes a tribal or clan association. By contrast, if you are American, you probably value thinking for yourself, showing a competitive spirit, and winning. "Who came before you" is probably not critical to who you are today. You may have not even know or care exactly where your grandparents were born and raised. You are likely to value independence and self-reliance above all. Some Americans, like John Robbins, heir apparent to

---

17 Mary Douglas and Aaron Wildavsky, *Risk and Culture: An Essay on the Selection of Technical and Environmental Dangers* (Berkeley: University of California Press, 1982).

18 Kimberly Crider, "Strategic Implications of Culture: Historical Analysis of China's Culture and Implications for United States Policy," 1999, http://www.au.af.mil/au/awc/awcgate/wright/wf08.pdf.

the Baskin-Robbins ice cream empire, even give away their family fortunes to prove that they can make it on their own.

Whichever tradition you come from, it is your human nature to tend to see your own ways as the "right" ones or "better" ones, an indication of how emotional values shape perception. Consider some research findings by the Pew Research Center's Global Attitudes Project, which reveal how two groups of people who have a tendency to oppose each other, Muslims and Westerners, hold similarly critical views of one another:[19]

> Many in the West see Muslims as fanatical and violent, while … Muslims in the Middle East and Asia generally see Westerners … as violent and fanatical.[20] And, while many in the West believe Muslims are not respectful of women, [H]alf or more in four of the five Muslim publics surveyed say the same thing about people in the West.[21]

In spite of their dramatically different cultural Islamic and Western traditions, the respondents in the Pew project reported equally biased and negative perceptions of one another. The similarly negative views they express about one another suggest how their respective perceptions are shaped by attitudinal and emotional values. The example is also telling because it shows how you mirror your *self* in *other*, limiting your own capacity to "see" by limiting how you see others, which is a barrier to developing your *self* and consciousness in ways that serve collective wellness.

Every human engages a language of feeling using the same range of values, but the way you come to conceptualize, react, and respond to different attitudinal and emotional values is largely driven by culture.

To get an idea of how the same value can be interpreted differently, largely based on where you are born and raised in the world works, consider *anger*.

A comparison of East Asian and American views of anger reveals two very different conceptualizations of the same value. If you were born and raised in the United States, you come from a tradition where anger often directs relationship problem-solving and decision-making, a tradition that is uncommon in the East Asian cultures of China and Japan. In fact, when anger has been used in an attempt to direct change in Chinese and Japanese contexts, it has been shown to

---

19   The Pew Research Center's Global Attitudes Project, July 21, 2011, http://www.pewglobal.org/2011/07/21/muslim-western-tensions-persist/.

20   The Pew Research Center's Global Attitudes Project.

21   The Pew Research Center's Global Attitudes Project, July 18, 2011, http://www.pewglobal.org/2006/07/18/islam-and-the-west-searching-for-common-ground/.

be much less effective, and even to make matters worse.[22] Although the embodiment of anger is common among Americans, even its violent extremes are tolerated, it is considered inappropriate and undesirable among East Asians. Americans are largely much more tolerant of anger in social interaction than East Asians are.[23]

Attitudes about anger in Chinese and Japanese cultures, as compared to American culture, relate to very different ideas about self-control and balance. In Chinese culture, the notion of anger, *nu*, is tied to the concept of *qi*, the energy that flows through the body and relates to the concepts of *yin* and *yang*.[24] The Chinese believe that the body's oppositional forces of *yin* and *yang* need to be in balance in order for the harmony of the universe to be maintained. They believe that anger disrupts the balance. The Japanese view of anger is similar.

In the Japanese belief system, anger is viewed to originate in the stomach area before rising to the chest and continuing to the head.[25] The Japanese believe that if anger is allowed to reach the head, this demonstrates a person's inability to control it.[26] According to Japanese folk theory[27], anger can interfere with a person's normal mental functioning.

By contrast, in American culture, anger is tolerated and encouraged, figuring prominently into problem-solving. There is evidence of it everywhere, on television, in advertising, in sports competitions, and in service encounters. Anger, and the aggression and polarization that go along with it, "sells" in American culture.[28] American culture thrives on the "adversarial atmosphere" that is so familiar in public discourse.[29] News anchors, journalists, interviewers, politicians, and other public figures routinely express anger. Although many of us wish it weren't so, even extreme expressions of anger and violence are routinely modeled in American social interaction, both in reality television[30] and real life. Bullying, physical fighting, homicides, drive-by shootings, mass

---

22 Hajo Adam, Aiwa Shirako, and William Maddux, "Cultural Variance in the Human Effects of Anger in Negotiations," Psychological Science 21, no. 6 (June 2010): 882–889, http://faculty.insead.edu/maddux/personal/documents/PsychScienceCultureAngerandNegotiations.pdf.

23 Adam, *Cultural Variance in the Human Effects of Anger in Negotiations*, 882–889.

24 Zoltan Kovesces, "The Concept of Anger: Universal or Culture Specific?" http://www.asc.upenn.edu/courses/comm360/anger1.pdf.

25 Kovesces, *The Concept of Anger*.

26 Kovesces, *The Concept of Anger*.

27 Kovesces, *The Concept of Anger*.

28 Deborah Tannen, *The Argument Culture* (NY: Random House, 1998), 30.

29 Tannen, *The Argument Culture*.

30 "Black Women on Reality TV," *The Root*, March 3, 2011, http://www.theroot.com/views/fight-night-black-women-reality-tv.

shootings, "road rage," and other types of violent and extreme expressions of anger are pervasive in American culture and society.

The types of outward expressions of anger that are commonplace in American culture are not likely events in countries like Japan, with their grounding in Eastern tradition. This is because the way a culture conditions people to conceptualize and respond to anger influences how they will react to biological and genetic predispositions, such as depression and anxiety. In cases of extreme and violent expressions of anger, if you are American, you are likely to turn that anger outward to harm others, while if you are Asian, you are likely to turn your anger inward to harm yourself. While it is not impossible for a Japanese person to "go postal"[31] in response to feelings of extreme anger, turning anger inward and committing suicide is a much more likely response. An investigative study explored suicide rates in Japan in the late 1990s,[32] when there was a doubling of unemployment. As unemployment increased, suicide rates also increased. Along with Japan's low crime rate for murder and robbery,[33] this suggests a cultural predisposition away from the outward expression of anger.

The high tolerance in American culture for the outward expression of anger is strengthened by a persistent focus on self-interests in advertising on radio, television, and the Internet. If you are American, you have probably come to identify with slogans that promote the myth of entitlement as a birthright: *"Because I'm worth it," "You deserve a break," "Just do it," "Indulge yourself," "Have it your way."* There's a good chance you've been conditioned to see your personal needs and interests as of foremost importance. While you probably can't and wouldn't want to detach completely from your cultural roots, you can benefit from being on the lookout for cultural value patterns that interfere with your ability to create and sustain genuinely satisfying personal relationships. If you are American, your assumptions about anger and the way you see your self in relationship to others significantly affect how you shape your personal relationships. These assumption also predispose you to experiencing frustration and dissatisfaction, especially with the people in your life who are most important to you.

As you are socialized into broad cultural value patterns, you also inherit ways of "seeing" from your parents and other caretakers that tie the biased ways you think and express to a biased "family system of values" where you develop your own role in the complex family of origin relationship dynamic. Consistent with or responsive to parental ways, you come to mimic or resist

31   "Go postal" was coined in the 1980's to refer to killings caused by uncontrollable workplace rage that after the first incidents killed US Postal coworkers, managers, and others.

32   May 19, 2011, http://www.medscape.com/viewarticle/743024.

33   David Kopel, "Japan: Gun Control and People Control," http://www.davekopel.com/2A/Foreign/Japan-Gun-Control-and-People-Control.htm.

the attitudinal and emotional response patterns modeled in your family of origin as you develop your own individual role and style within the family system.

You develop your own way of reacting and responding to family circumstances and dynamics. If your father is an alcoholic who becomes violent when he drinks, you may hide in the closet while your sibling tries to sedate him. As an adult, you may end up mimicking your father's alcoholic behavior while your sibling may end up as an obsessive workaholic who holds others to impossible standards. Genetics, resilience, personality, desire, will, and other factors combine to play a part in how your personal story unfolds.

Later in life, you extend the attitudinal and emotional response patterns you learn in your family of origin into other relationships. Whatever causes you to create emotional distance with a relationship partner, how strongly or weakly you posture your mind for emotional struggle, and how you are apt to react when others don't comply with your expectations are conditioned by past learning within the family system, the output of the qualia of consciousness. The attitudinal and emotional value patterns your brain infers and uses to shape perception at any given instant influences your tendency to engage in or refrain from speaking when you feel provoked, the level of assertion or aggression you display, the degree of directness or passivity you default to, and how polite or disrespectful you feel obligated to be when you interact with different kinds of relationship partners, such as a parent or in-law.

You may be nothing like the parent who angers quickly and lashes out, but you may have developed an equally unproductive pattern of withdrawing from anger or passive-aggressively instigating a relationship partner to explode without realizing what you are doing. While you may think of yourself as blameless, your quiet way of pushing others away or baiting a relationship partner can be as damaging to connection and relationship satisfaction as a parent's angry outbursts. Look more closely, and you may find that you bait your spouse to react so you can recreate familiar childhood drama.

The role and strategies you develop in your family of origin system predispose you toward inviting and supporting personal relationships in predictable ways. You may take on a parent's anger and frustration with life and the world, or their joy and hope. As study evidence shows, there is an association between the emotions and behaviors of parents and the attitudes and emotions of their children, particularly in the way the children are affected by the marital conflicts of their parents.[34]

You probably recognize how easily you can take on your parents' feelings or react to them.

---

34 Alice C. Schermerhorn, Sy-Miin Chow, and E. Mark Cummings, *Developmental Family Processes and Interparental Conflict: Patterns of Micro-level Influences*, Dev Psychol 46 No. 4: 869-885, July 2010.

Maybe you mimic a parent's passive-aggressive ways of dealing with frustration by skirting around feelings, engaging in sarcasm, or withdrawing. Or maybe you snap aggressively at an intimate relationship partner every time she fails to meet one of your expectations.

Your brain develops attitudinal and emotional response habits that bias you toward specific kinds of relationship experiences. This is how you can come to "see" everything a spouse, sibling, parent, or in-law says or does as a threat or offense. It is how you come to limit your options in relationship problem-solving.

The Unreliability of Perception

Perception is unreliable because your brain limits and biases what you can "see."

Visual illusions are commonly used to show your brain's perceptual limitations. They can help you appreciate how your brain misleads you into making unreliable conclusions and inferences. By experiencing how your brain fools you into "seeing what isn't there," you can get a glimpse of how your brain deceives you.

Consider an example. When you look at the image below[35], if you are like most people, you probably "see" a white equilateral triangle in the center of the image:

Seeing What Isn't There

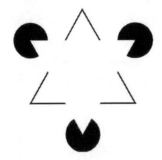

The white triangle you "see" isn't what you think it is. It's an illusion, a conclusion your brain makes without your conscious awareness that is based on the experiences you've had with shapes and lines. You "see" a white triangle because your brain biases you to "see" lines and shapes in a specific way, based on your experiences with them.

---

35   Kendra Cherry, *The Kanizsa Triangle Illusion*, Optical Illusions, About Psychology: psychology.about.com/od/sensationandperception/ig/Optical-Illusions/Kanizsa-Triangle-Illusion.htm.

Your brain routinely makes inferences, engaging in a complex thought process that produces highly unreliable results that are limited by the biases of your master repository of conscious and nonconscious awareness. In the example just given, you "see" the edges of a white triangle even though there are no edges because your brain infers them. Your brain can decide meaning only by creating and extending patterns.

Visual illusions show you how your brain deceives you with shapes and lines, but unless a particular configuration of shapes and lines triggers your brain to feel a pain you'd like to forget or joyful memory that gives you pleasure, they don't help you experience the "feeling illusions" your brain routinely produces.

In the same way your brain causes you to "see the white triangle that isn't there" by extending conclusions and inferences about shapes and lines, it routinely fools you into making conclusions and inferences based on its subjective and biased attitudinal and emotional conclusions and inferences. This makes you prone to *feeling bias,* where you believe what you feel, and you shape the stories you tell yourself and others about a relationship partner or situation accordingly. When feeling bias is positive, it doesn't cause you to push others away, so it isn't problematic to creating genuinely satisfying and positive relationships. In fact, if you train your brain to draw others closer, positive feeling bias can be helpful. But when your brain predisposes you to negative feeling bias, you end up pushing people away, even when you don't really want to.

Interplaying with dozens of other biases shown consistently in heuristics and biases research and experimental studies to affect perception, feeling bias influences your perceptions of others and relationship situations and events, causing you to "see what really isn't there" as you consciously and nonconsciously shape your thoughts, recollections, and imaginings about a relationship partner and embody them in social interaction.

Some common biases are summarized in the chart below to give you a general idea of how they interact with feeling bias to affect "seeing" and bias how you shape meaning in a relationship.

Common Biases	
Bias type	**Effect**
Feeling	Shapes all understanding and interpretation, determines whether and what you think, remember, and imagine
Memory	Leads to feeling bias and explains why you remember and value experiences and information differently

Common Biases	
Bias type	**Effect**
Negativity	Leads you to give more weight to negative experiences and information than to positive experiences and information
Availability	Narrows the scope of information you use to draw conclusions
Cause and effect	Predisposes you to finding causes for random or accidental phenomena
Introspection	Causes you to believe your own insights are more reliable than those of others
Blind spot	Predisposes you to believing you are less biased than others
Confirmation	Causes you to seek or interpret information consistent with your own preconceptions and assumptions
Selective perception	Predisposes you to seeing what you expect to see
Anchoring	Causes you to weigh a single factor too heavily in decision-making
Status quo	Predisposes you to resist change and stay with what is familiar
Groupthink	Skews your collaborative outcomes and feelings toward the views and interests of those who hold the most power and influence in group
Hindsight	Causes you to look back and be able to predict an outcome after knowing the outcome

Feeling bias influences *memory bias,* why you recall experiences that are important to you more easily than those that are not, what you remember about them, and how easily you bring them to mind. You can probably recall experiences where others have remembered differently than you. When your recollection of an experience is dramatically different from what others remember, memory bias causes you tend to trust your own memory more. Consider the following example where Mike and his mother have different recollections of Lindsay from a holiday event:

Mike

You met Lindsay. You met her last year at Christmas.

Mother

No, I didn't, I never met her.

Mike

You *did*. You met her last year at Christmas.

Mother

I did *not*. I don't care what you say. I was there, and I didn't meet her.

In the example, Mike's mother believes her own memory of the holiday experience is more accurate than Mike's. Maybe Lindsay didn't make an impression on her, or she was more focused on Mike than she was on the girl he brought along with him to the holiday event. Maybe the only girl his mother associates with him is his former girlfriend, whom she adores and also saw at the event. Whatever feelings bias her memory, Mike's mother is certain she never met Lindsay. The example suggests how feeling bias interplays with memory bias, affecting what you "see."

Feeling and memory biases interplay with *negativity bias.* You are predisposed to negative feelings and to giving more weight to negative experiences and information than to positive ones, a tendency that greatly affects relationship experiences and outcomes. This predisposition is self-protective. As far as your brain is concerned, it reacts to protect your boundaries of *self* whether the threat it perceives is physical or emotional by readying you to defend yourself victoriously.

Consider the Shana's comments below about her sister. The story she creates about her sister reflects her own *negatively biased* feelings, symbolized by the inherently negative words she uses to express herself, which are underlined:

My sister is very <u>needy</u>. She <u>has to have all the attention</u>. <u>Nauseating</u>. I find it very <u>difficult to be around</u> her. I hate listening to her. <u>She goes on and on and on</u>. <u>Drives me crazy</u>. If I get like that, shoot me!

"Needy," "having to have all the attention," "nauseating," "difficult to be around," "she goes on and on," "Drives me crazy." Negativity bias affects how Shana "sees" her sister, what she thinks, recollects, and imagines about her, and how she interacts with her and others in social interactions.

Leading you to cling stubbornly to your positions and beliefs in an effort to prove yourself "right" and others "wrong," negativity bias influences you to ignore your own role in a relationship dynamic. In the example just given, Shana freely criticizes her sister while she completely overlooks how she might be swaying her sister into helping her evolve an unproductive relationship dynamic with her.

Feeling, memory, and negativity bias also interplay with *availability bias*. When this happens, you should narrow the scope of information you use to draw negative conclusions. You may conclude that your brother's wife is spending your brother's money without pulling her weight because she doesn't have a job. Your conclusion may be incorrect because you are basing it on what you "see," which excludes information that is not readily available to you, such as whether she helps your brother with his business, takes care of the children, cleans the house, or completes other tasks that give him time and space to work more efficiently. If you allow yourself to shape your stories about your sister-in-law in ways to reflect your erroneous and negative conclusions, you will affect not only the quality, authenticity, and outcome of your relationship with your sister-in-law but also with your brother and others involved. Whether you share your negative perceptions with your brother or not, you would embody them in your interaction with him. He would certainly understand you have an issue with his wife, even if he didn't know exactly what it was.

Availability bias has been shown to affect estimates of risk and risk probability. It might cause you to believe your partner is being unfaithful to you while you're away from home because you repeatedly tried phoning him but couldn't reach him.

Cause-and-effect bias, on the other hand, inclines you to find causes for random or accidental phenomena that justify what you "see." You "see" exactly what you expect to see, and you feel exactly as you expect to feel. Cause-and-effect bias accounts for how you seek and find causes to defend and argue based on your own biased feelings, blaming and accusing others for inferred causes. In the example below, Tina justifies her negative feelings about an acquaintance to a friend at a community event. By identifying negative causes and making the acquaintance she's talking about the object of her criticism in her story, Tina supports her own negatively biased feelings:

> She's a whore. Did you see the way she came on to him? All she's interested in is his money anyway. I don't care what anybody says, she's a gold digger. I'm not sitting with her.

In the example, Tina finds negative causes to justify her own biased attitude toward the woman she judges. She identifies a negative cause for not wanting to sit with the woman at the community event. Based on her own subjective analysis, Tina finds personal qualities about the woman to justify her own antagonistic feelings. When you infer the causes of another person's behavior, cause-and-effect bias accounts for how you overestimate your own importance, both as a cause and as a target.

Cause-and-effect bias relates to *introspection bias*, where you tend to believe your own insights are more reliable than the insights of others. You trust your own introspections more than those of others, which creates the illusion of superiority where you think you are less biased and conformist than others, an effect known as *blind spot bias*. You may, for instance, routinely think of your sister as manipulative without recognizing how different aspects of your own controlling self interplay with hers and affect the negative relationship dynamic you create together. Blind spot bias supports the egocentric view of *self,* where there you place more interest in your own needs and interests than on those important to others.

Confirmation bias accounts for your tendency to seek or interpret information that is consistent with your own negative preconceptions and assumptions. For example, if you believe your mother-in-law is controlling, you will see everything she says or does as an attempt to control. You will have the tendency to block out any positive interpretation of her, and if you talk about her with your friends, you will be apt do so in a way that reflects your own biased and negative perception of her.

Selective perception bias ensures that you "see" negatively when you expect to see negatively. If you don't feel secure in your relationship with your boyfriend and feel threatened by his continued interaction with his ex-wife, you are likely to see his ex-wife in a negative light and convey your negative thoughts about her to your friends. Cause-and-effect bias might also affect your tendency to associate negative qualities with her, as Kim has done:

> She's such a princess! He's too stupid to see what's going on. I just hate that he has anything to do with her. I don't care if they have kids or not. They're divorced! Move on! Get a life! I want her OUT of the picture!

Anchoring bias causes you to weigh a single factor too heavily in decision-making in order to justify your own negative perception. If you don't want to go to your in-laws' house for the weekend, for instance, you may focus on your mother-in-law's comments about your food preferences, which you have given a negative spin. Every time you discuss a possible visit with to your in-laws' with your spouse, you may end up arguing about how his mother makes negative comments about your eating habits, as Jill does:

> **Jill:** She knows I don't eat like that, and she's got to keep saying it.
> **Josh**: She doesn't mean anything by it. She just doesn't understand it.
> **Jill:** She's just trying to make me feel bad.

Availability bias and cause-and-effect bias often work together. Using the example just given, you might latch onto the way your mother-in-law makes you feel about the food issue as an available excuse and indirectly blame her, making her the reason you don't want to go visit her.

Status quo bias causes you to resist change and stay with what is familiar, a tendency that explains why you are apt to continue thinking in the same negative ways, even if they interfere with your relationship goals. Status quo bias combined with negativity bias explains why you may draw on the same negative emotional pattern with your husband when he does something to irritate you, knowing you will end up creating the same arguments together and producing the same negative outcomes.

Groupthink bias skews your collaborative outcomes and feelings toward the views and interests of those who hold the most power and influence in your groups. Combined with negativity bias, it can lead to negative venting and bullying, where power-holders in the group shape damaging and negative alignments against others.

Hindsight bias, combined with negativity bias, accounts for how easily you can look back and predict a negative outcome after knowing what the outcome is. If your fiancé cheats on you, for instance, you can look back and easily see all the warning signs that point to defects in his character, or other red flags that suggest how you should have known and how untrustworthy he is.

Negativity bias, interacting with other biases, can lead to *extremes in negative perception* because it becomes a habitual and nonconscious reaction. Extremes in negative perception often cause recalcitrant response patterns. For example, your husband may usually come home from work to a clean and organized house, dinner on the table, and bathed children but inevitably find some reason to criticize you. Your elderly mother may assume you don't want to help her because you can't be available to help on one specific day. Your wife may interpret a single mistake you made as something you *always* say or do. Or, you may refer to your stepmother as "Idiot" instead of using her given name, boxing her into a negative role.

You are prone to "seeing what isn't there" and defending the illusion you see in your interaction with your self, and sometimes with others. The next time you find yourself being insistent, resistant, or unyielding, consider how negativity bias, along with other biases, might be causing you to defend your views and beliefs. Maybe your husband left the kitchen faucet dripping, your mother neglected to volunteer to babysit, or your sister's very presence made the hair on your back bristle. Whatever the trigger, when negativity bias engages with other biases, your superefficient brain automatically begins to accumulate evidence to support unreliable emotional conclusions, "seeing" that is limited by conclusions and inferences based on the emotional response patterns of your thoughts, recollections, and imaginings about a relationship partner or situation.

The Relationship Dynamic

Every personal relationship reflects a dynamic tension between and among relationship partners. This tension is collaboratively shaped, evolves in consciousness, and is embodied and adjusted in social interaction.

This process, which is a "relationship dynamic," reflects the emerging interplay between your own force of mind and that of others. When the tension is balanced, it produces the harmony of a balanced relationship dynamic, the positive and unifying dynamic shaping connection and genuinely satisfying and positive relationship experiences. When the tension is out of balance, it produces the dissonance of an imbalanced relationship dynamic, the negative and polarizing dynamic that interferes with connection and shapes separation. The more of an imbalance you shape, the greater the experience of separation.

A balanced relationship dynamic is characterized by power-sharing and positive reciprocity, where individuals in a relationship, or tied to you, are not invested in trying to control how others think or behave, and are postured to extend kindnesses to one another. Power-sharing and positive reciprocity are necessary elements in adult relationships aimed at producing connection and genuinely satisfying and positive outcomes.

Relative power and reciprocity in a relationship dynamic reflect how people tend to respond to each other in similar ways. "Like" tends to invite "like." When you extend a kindness in a relationship dynamic, the tendency is for a relationship partner to respond similarly. When you withhold a kindness or extend unkindness, you encourage a relationship partner to do the same. Because your invitation to restore balance to a polarizing relationship dynamic encourages a partner to respond similarly, you have tremendous potential for redirecting a dynamic that isn't working or is causing you frustration. Similarly, if you invite a polarizing dynamic, you invite a partner to respond similarly, making negative reciprocity likely. Because you use force of mind to shape your thoughts, recollections, and imaginings about a relationship partner, negative reciprocity easily extends across consciousness.

In an imbalanced dynamic, there is a temporary or more extensive interruption across thoughts, recollections, and imaginings in power-sharing and positive reciprocity. When this happens, you or others in a relationship feel entitled to coerce, manipulate, or otherwise attempt to control what you expect others to be, think, or do. The attitudes and emotions you generate in response to the stimulus that triggered the imbalance interplay with feeling symbols, such as words or images, causing you to create thoughts, recollections, and imaginings about a relationship partner, stories you sometimes share with others, to support and strengthen a imbalanced dynamic.

Learning how to invite and sustain a balanced relationship dynamic is core to being able to improve an adult personal relationship, and it is also a key to self-actualization, because it involves learning how to actively shape your emerging process of *self*, which is consciousness.

Every thought, recollection, and imagining you have produces an instrumental mental force[36], positive or negative, unifying or polarizing, that invites and sustains a balanced dynamic or causes imbalance. You shape a relationship dynamic through this instrumental mental force that is your force of mind.

As your brain interacts continuously with internal and external stimuli, it automatically derives and assigns attitudinal and emotional value to everything it "sees" and interprets, a constant interplay between input and output. Your brain uses these values to shape the emotionally symbolic stories you tell yourself about a relationship partner. The emotional symbols of your stories invite and support the positive and unifying relationship dynamic that causes connection or the negative and polarizing one that interferes with it. Because your brain causes you to "see what isn't there," and because your brain "believes" whatever you "see," it responds to the emotional symbols of your stories.

Force of mind is meaningful in any single instant of thought or embodiment of thought. It also affects the overall dynamic of a relationship as a whole, its "melody" or general quality. When the tension of a relationship as a whole is balanced, its melody is harmonious, and it produces the "song of heart" that is connection. When the tension of a relationship as a whole is imbalanced, its melody is dissonant, and relationship partners experience a lack of connection. For example, Caroline and Meg are domestic partners who both feel genuinely satisfied with their relationship. Its overall melody is harmonious even though they occasionally experience an instant of imbalance when they struggle over Caroline's exercise habits. But since their occasional and brief struggles are neither intense nor extended, and since Meg likes to be playful when they struggle, they are able to rebalance the tension in their dynamic quickly and easily.

A positive and unifying force of mind is shaped by positive and unifying attitudinal and emotional symbols, such as *love, peace, forgiveness, gratitude,* and *service,* that invite and support

---

36 Recent advances in neuroscience show how your brain actually changes shape physically in response to input, suggesting the impacts of force of mind. Also, Jeffrey M. Schwartz, with Sharon Begley in *The Mind and the Brain,* NY: HarperCollins, 2002, talks about using mental force to help his patients overcome obsessive-compulsive disorder, providing evidence of force of mind. More controversial is David R. Hawkins' proposed *Map of Consciousness,* an outcome of applied kinesiology, muscle testing used to measure the force of commonly recognized attitudes and emotions, such as shame, guilt, grief, fear, anger, pride, love, joy, and peace. Using a logarithmic scale, and organizing values into numerical sequence, he identified a "critical point" of 200 as the dividing line between negative and positive force where love, joy, and peace calibrated at the highest levels and shame at the lowest: *Power versus Force: The Hidden Determinants of Human Behavior,* Carlsbad, CA: Hayhouse, 2002/Veritas Publishing.

compassionate cooperation, the *me-and-you* dynamic that causes connection. A negative and polarizing force of mind is shaped by negative and polarizing attitudinal and emotional symbols, such as *fear, anger, resentment, criticism*, and *entitlement*, that invite and support *opposition*, the *me-against-you* dynamic that causes separation.

Shaping a Relationship Dynamic		
Force of mind	**Orientation**	**Outcome**
[+] Compassionate cooperation	Unifying: *me-and-you*	Connection (closeness)
[-] Opposition	Polarizing: *me-against-you*	Separation (distance)

The force of mind that is opposition will always polarize and encourage some degree of separation between self and other in a relationship dynamic while the force of mind that is compassionate cooperation will always unify and encourage some degree of connection. While a polarizing relationship dynamic may be helpful and desired in some situations, such as when you want to discourage a pesky admirer who won't take "no" for an answer, it cannot encourage connection because the forces of polarization and unification are mutually exclusive.

Whether you are aware of it or not, whether you give it attention or not, the force of mind you generate at any given instant through your thoughts, recollections, and imagining affects the way you shape a relationship dynamic jointly with others. It affects the constellation of lives and the communities to which you are tied. If, for instance, you are having a secret affair with a coworker, the dynamic you create impacts your relationship with your self, spouse, children, parents, in-laws, friends, and other coworkers. Whether others know about your relationship or not, it affects how you shape your thoughts, recollections, and imaginings about your lover and the stories you tell yourself about others.

This is so because no single thought, recollection, or imagining in consciousness is an isolated experience. It is both object and input in the emerging process of consciousness that is *self*. Every single moment of consciousness derives emotional meaning from consciousness as a whole, the repertoire of conscious and nonconscious experiences comprising your internal world. It affects how you prioritize your thoughts, recollections, and imaginings, and what kind of impact they have on you, which is why your relationship with a favorite teacher can have far-reaching affects on who you believe yourself to be, even if you haven't seen the teacher for twenty years, and even if you interacted with each other for only a short time.

The Emerging Process of Consciousness and *Self*

Consciousness is an emerging process of *self* that takes shape through your personal relationships and is mirrored in your every relationship dynamic. If you were to map out the dynamic of every relationship in your life, from the moment you were born, you would have a master representation of your evolving process of consciousness and *self*.

Your *I-perspective*, how you posture your self toward others and the world, is an ongoing process of formation and reorganization. In any given instant, it is a representation of who "you" are. It directly and dramatically affects your capacity to invite and support a balanced a relationship dynamic.

The way you posture your self in a relationship dynamic reflects the biases of culture, family, and other influences. Although not every person from the same culture defines their *I-perspective* the same way, "insiders" in any cultural group do share some common assumptions that affect their notion of self. For instance, if you were born and raised in American culture, you are likely to tend toward an *I-perspective* that reflects "vertical individualism,"[37] a strong focus on personal needs and interests, where values such as self-reliance, competition, "winning," personal freedom, and personal gain affect how you shape your emerging process of self and consciousness.

You can think of *I-perspective* as a continuum, with posturing reflecting *small you* values at one extreme and *Big You* values at the other. *Small you* posturing aims to satisfy the needs and interests of the individual to create boundaries, advance self-focus, and maintain separateness. *Big You* posturing aims to eliminate individual boundaries and merging. *Big You* can be thought of as "pure consciousness" where no boundaries between self and other exist.

A balanced *I-perspective* enables you to shape a balanced relationship dynamic because it affects power-sharing and positive reciprocity, elements important to your capacity to invite and support compassionate cooperation and collective wellness. *I-perspective* balance is key because it discourages the *small you* "seeing" that causes self-centered problem-solving and decision-making and the *Big You* "seeing" that causes lack of healthy boundaries. It enables you to give attention to your individual needs and interests and the needs and interests of others.

I-Perspective Continuum
small you/egocentric seeing <————midpoint = balance————> *Big You*/altruistic seeing

---

37   Henry C. Triandis, Xiao Ping Chen, K-S Darius, *Scenarios for the measurement of collectivism and individualism*, Journal of Cross-Cultural Psychology, March 1, 1998.

I-perspective balance is critical to your capacity to shape the positive and unifying force of mind that enables connection. If you have been born and raised in the United States and have been socialized into American cultural values, you are at risk for egocentric *I-perspective* posturing, because you are influenced by core cultural values such as self-reliance, independence, competition, personal freedom, and personal rights. While these values can be helpful and productive, they can also cause extremes of *small you* seeing, such as self-centeredness and narcissism, which inhibit inclusive problem-solving and decision-making and place genuinely satisfying and positive relationship experiences and wellness at risk.

Relationship Authenticity

Relationship Authenticity		
Force of Mind	**Quality of Relationship Experience**	**Outcome**
[+] Compassionate Cooperation	Genuinely Positive	Connection
[-] Opposition	Inauthentically Positive	Separation
[-] Opposition	Authentically Negative	Separation

You can be polite and appropriate in your interaction with others but disingenuous. In fact, certain social situations and relationships require you to be *inauthentically positive*. This often happens in hierarchal networks, such as workplaces and family systems, where your role gives you more or less power and affects reciprocity in your relationships. For example, a parent may yell at a young child, while the child may be expected to apologize for doing something "wrong." Whether or not the child agrees, and however resentful she might be, compliance is required. The mismatch between the child's apology and her resentment produces an inauthentically positive relationship experience.

In everyday adult personal relationships, you may find yourself creating inauthentically positive relationship experiences as a way to avoid confrontation or conflict. If you do, you're likely to so with the people with whom you most want to "preserve face" (positive image),[38] theirs or yours. While you are likely to avoid confrontation or conflict by trying to camouflage an oppositional force of mind, you will always embody it to some degree.

In contrast, with the people you feel most comfortable with and entitled to control, you are likely to create *authentically negative* relationship experiences. Authentically negative relationship

---

38 D'Amico-Reisner, 1983, 1985, 1999.

experiences result when you act out an oppositional force of mind with others in your interaction with them.

Neither inauthentically positive nor authentically negative relationship experiences support connection because you cannot shape connection with the force of mind that is opposition. To shape connection, you have to generate the force of mind that is compassionate cooperation.

CHAPTER 2

Obstacles to Connection: Perceptual Inattention & Passive Participant-Observation

> Quantum theory tells us that all the properties that create reality are contextual; they depend on the acts of observation. As such, quantum theory has opened the door to a noetic, mind-based universe. Reality, we would infer, is mind-made.[39]
> —Deepak Chopra, Menas Kafatos, and Rudolf E. Tanzi

The greatest obstacles to connection are perceptual inattention and your willingness to play the role of a passive participant-observer in the "mind-based universe" of consciousness, where your thoughts, recollections, and imaginings shape your every momentary experience of your "mind-made reality."

Perceptual inattention is a quality of nonconscious awareness as well as conscious awareness. If you've ever left home without remembering if you turned off the coffeepot or locked the door, you've experienced nonconscious awareness, how your brain acts according to habit, without your attention and outside your control. Being able to "act without thinking" is often helpful and productive because it allows you to function efficiently and quickly, and to multitask. For example, if you've learned to play Beethoven's *Für Elise* on the piano, you can probably play it without much conscious attention, focusing instead on what you'd like to have for dinner or on a conversation you had earlier in the day with a friend.

Your brain acts the same automatic way in all situations, because it works tirelessly, adjusting emotional response patterns responses based on its continuous internal and external interactions, an ongoing interplay between stimulus and response. While it is helpful to be able to act without

---

39 Deepak Chopra, Menas Kafatos, and Rudolf E. Tanzi, *From Quanta to Qualia: The Mystery of Reality (Part 3)*, The Huffington Post, October 12, 2012, http://www.huffingtonpost.com/deepak-chopra/from-quanta-to-qualia-the_b_2038207.html.

thinking in many situations, allowing your brain to control your relationship experiences and outcomes is not always productive to relationship goals.

Where your goal is to create genuinely satisfying and positive personal relationships, perceptual inattention is an obstruction. It reflects your tacit acceptance to assume a passive participant-observer role in shaping your relationships and your life. Because your brain is prone to making processing errors and is predisposed to giving negative attention to the thoughts, recollections, and imaginings you use to shape the stories you tell yourself about others, perceptual inattention places you at risk for generating the force of mind that is opposition.

By accepting your brain's automatic and emotionally negative meanings, you relinquish control to your brain and allow it to shape your emerging process of *self* and consciousness as it interferes with your capacity to connect with a relationship partner. How this happens, and what exactly happens when you allow perceptual inattention to persist and accept a passive participant-observer role in the interaction you have with your self and others, is explained below.

The Force of Mind That Is Opposition

The force of mind that is opposition is thought to be evolutionary in origin and related to natural selection. Because our ancestors needed to be highly responsive in life-threatening situations, the fight-or-flight mechanism was essential for self-protection in response to physical threats. It readied the mind and body to fight off predators, releasing hormones into the bloodstream to enable defense and attack. Generating the force of mind that is opposition is still helpful in everyday life today. It allows you to muster up extraordinary physical strength to avert a physical catastrophe, which is how a mother is able to lift the end of a car up to free her child's trapped foot. It also allows you to create emotional distance when you intentionally want to keep a person away. The force of mind that is opposition is only an obstacle in personal relationships when you accept your brain's automatic fight-or-flight posturing by default. This happens as a result of perceptual inattention, when you allow yourself to take the role of a passive participant-observer in the private world of your mind and mistakenly assume that "you" are your brain instead of your mind.

Just as your brain is conditioned to react to visible stimuli, such as the shapes and lines that cause you to experience visual illusions, it is conditioned to react to invisible emotional stimuli, triggers that similarly fool you into "feeling what isn't there" and giving negative attention to your illusions. When your brain perceives a threat or offense, it reacts automatically by generating the force of mind that is opposition, which invites and supports the negative and polarizing *me-against-you* relationship dynamic that causes you to push a person away.

Anything another person says, does, thinks, represents (or neglects to say, do, think, or represent) can trigger your brain to "feel what isn't there" and posture for fight-or-flight. It might be that your husband left his shoes in the living room, your mother-in-law dropped by unexpectedly, or your stepmother didn't invite you over for dinner. Anything perceived as inconsistent with your own expectations, desires, intentions, or beliefs will trigger your brain to react automatically and negatively with the force of mind that is opposition, posturing you to disrupt the balance of a relationship dynamic and biasing you toward an egocentric *I-perspective* that causes you to feel entitled to control others or prove them wrong or unworthy through the stories you tell yourself about them, and sometimes in interaction with them and others.

The strength of an oppositional force of mind in a *me-against-you* dynamic is directly related to how significant and extensive your brain perceives a threat or offense to be, the depth and extensiveness of your negative perception, and how you jointly mold the dynamic you create with a relationship partner. The polarizing force of mind that is opposition positions you for directly, indirectly, covertly, or overtly disempowering, coercing, manipulating, punishing, or rejecting a relationship partner through the thoughts, recollections, and imaginings your create in your interaction with your self and others.

By accepting the default role of passive participant-observer in your internal world, the universe of your mind, you allow a relationship dynamic to evolve according to past habits of negative feeling. This causes you to relinquish control and allow negative perception to deepen and perpetuate resistance across a relationship and the lives tied to it, and unknowingly to form a habit of creating distance with the people in your personal life who pose the greatest threat to your sense of self. It is also how you can end up more generally experiencing life as dissatisfying and unfulfilling.

Negative Emotional Symbols – The Language of Negative Feeling

Your brain is predisposed to generating the force of mind that is opposition with the people in your personal life you problem-solve and make decisions with most, typically a spouse or other family member. These are the people you expect most from and feel most entitled to control. They are also the people your brain perceives as a greatest threat to your personal needs and desires, which is why your brain reacts to more threat stimuli with these individuals than with others.

In the evolving tension that is a relationship dynamic, your brain is conditioned to react automatically to protect your boundaries and personal needs and interests. When your brain is triggered by a threat stimulus to react, it signals the autonomic nervous system to prepare for fight-or-flight, a physiological reaction that positions you for challenge and defense. In your "mind-made" universe, your brain reacts in the same negative way to a new threat experience as it does to existing thoughts, recollections, or imaginings it perceives as threatening, which is to generate the force of mind that readies you for attack and defense.

This explains how you end up giving negative attention to a person or relationship situation for days, weeks, months, or forever, in some cases without ever having a conversation with the person. You essentially cause yourself to intensify opposition by aligning the emotional significance of your thoughts, recollections, and imaginings to support it. When this happens, you bias your internal universe of consciousness, and your emerging process of self toward opposition and separation.

You create negative meaning using negative emotional symbols to tell yourself stories about others. These negative values generate the force of mind that is opposition, and they are represented by negative emotional symbols such as fear, anger, resentment, criticism, and entitlement. Whatever negative and polarizing symbols you use to shape the thoughts, recollections, and imaginings of your internal "mind-made" universe, they can only generate the force of mind that is opposition, cause imbalance in a relationship dynamic, and inhibit connection.

Negative emotional values disrupt power-sharing and reciprocity in a relationship dynamic. When you draw on them to shape the stories you tell yourself about others, they always reflect egocentric "seeing," which causes imbalance to a relationship dynamic: When your stories symbolize *fear,* a "flight" emotion, you see yourself as less than equal to a relationship partner, recoil and relinquish control, act passive-aggressively, or assume aggressive posturing. When they symbolize *anger,* a "fight" emotion, you might create stories that aggressively aim to show others than you are more powerful, more "right," and justified to feel as you do. When they represent *criticism,* they might be less aggressive but still aimed at proving others wrong and assigning blame. When they symbolize *resentment,* they reflect a dull but persistent negativity that more indirectly pushes others away. When they symbolize *entitlement,* they provide testimony to your belief that you are more deserving or worthy than others.

The degree of imbalance you cause to a relationship dynamic depends on many factors, including the amount and type of negative attention you give to your thoughts, recollections, and imaginings. The more negative attention you give a person, the stronger and more extensive the force of opposition, and the more you "wire" your brain to deepen and extend negative attention across a relationship and your life.

The Negative Stories You Tell Your Self

The negative attention you give to a relationship partner in your interaction with your self causes your brain to create the habit of negative perception. A single critical thought, recollection, or imagining, such as *"He's a jerk," "I hate the way he dresses,"* or *"She's always ignoring me,"* deepens negative perception and affects the story you tell your self and others about a person. It also affects how you posture yourself in interaction with others and how others come to see a person. A single criticism or other negative story is never an isolated instance, because it is connected to your universe of consciousness, your database of thoughts, recollections, and imaginings that are your emerging process of self. There is no reality other than the illusions you create in your "mind-made" universe.

The more you negative attention you give to a relationship in your interaction with your self, the more likely you are to deepen the polarization of a negative relationship dynamic and extend negative perception across a relationship and the constellation of lives tied to it. Just as continuously playing the same song over again on the piano eventually allows you to perform the song without thinking, you become conditioned to producing an oppositional force of mind. Before long, you can easily make every thought, recollection, or imagining you have about a person negative, and every association you make with the person a negative one. Over time, you can intensify the polarizing force of mind that is opposition to the point where you see your differences with others as irreconcilable. In marriages, this often leads to divorce. In other family relationships, it may limit social interaction or cause resentment and anger.

As the force of mind that is opposition strengthens, you become more defensive and inflexible in the stories you tell your self about others, clinging to your own values, beliefs, desires and expectations, blaming others and trying to make them "wrong" and yourself "right" as you justify your own biased perceptions. This is how you end up driving yourself into a state of agitation and frustration over something as seemingly insignificant as your husband's request to pick up his shirts from the dry cleaners, just as Meredith does when her husband John asks her, "*Can you pick up my shirts at the cleaners later before they close?*"

Meredith's brain perceives John's request as a threat. Even before he finishes his question, she's thinking to herself, *There he goes again. Here it comes.* She can feel her body begin to tense up as he asks the question. Even before he's finished asking it, Meredith's brain reacts with the fight-or-flight attitudes and emotions that posture her for resistance and struggle. While she feels heavily invested in her negative feelings, which give her a "rush," Meredith accepts the role of a passive participant-observer in her interaction with her self, following her brain's unreliable and negatively biased lead. When this happens, the parts of her *small self* that are used to coming to the forefront to fight her battles will engage automatically and sway her toward egocentric "seeing," which will cause her to shape the story she tells herself about John and the situation to reflect her *me-against-you* posturing.

Without her help or permission, Meredith's brain shapes the story she tells herself, using negative emotional symbols that tie her thoughts, recollections, and imaginings together to generate and support the force of mind that is opposition:

Why doesn't he pick up his own shirts? I'm tired of doing his errands. There's never any place to park. It pisses me off that he expects me to do it. He thinks I'm his maid!

Meredith's story symbolizes *resentment* and *anger*, negative and polarizing attitudes and emotions that generate the force of mind causing her *me-against-you* posturing. Whether she shares her story in her interaction with John or with others about John, her story will interfere to some extent and intensity with her capacity to connect with him.

Even if Meredith agrees to pick up the shirts from the cleaners, if she accepts this story about John, it will shape how she feels about him, their relationship, and her life. Even worse, if she is deeply invested in her negative perception, she will generalize her negative reactions about picking up the shirts to other experiences in her relationship with John, extending her story to other issues, which will intensify her more general feelings of anger and resentment toward John. Maybe she'll begin to feel resentment and anger about making dinner or cleaning the house, blaming John for not doing enough to help out. Eventually, she may even come to see everything John does as proof that he doesn't care about her. Her brain will work tirelessly to prove she is "right" and John is "wrong" because it is programmed to do so.

Similarly, Sarah and her husband struggle over a seemingly petty issue, taking out the trash:

Sarah: Are you gonna take the trash out or not?
Robert: I said, "Yes," but I need to finish what I'm doing first.

Before Sarah confronts Robert on the trash issue, she's already firmly accepted the negative story she tells her self about him:

How long is it going take him to take the trash out this time? He is so incredibly slow. It drives me crazy! I should just take the trash out myself. It would be faster, that's for sure. It's like talking to the wall. If I want something done around here, I need to do it myself!

In fact, Sarah is so conditioned to creating negative stories about Robert, using negative emotional symbols of *criticism, anger,* and *resentment,* that almost all the stories she tells her self about him are similarly symbolic. They jointly sustain an imbalanced relationship dynamic, where Sarah has the habit of trying to control Robert's behavior, and he withdraws in reaction to it. Robert's own negative story about Sarah intensifies his own *me-against-you* posturing:

I wish she would just *shut up*! I already said I would take the trash out. Why does she have to nag? No way I'm going to get up and take the trash out now. She'll have to wait!

Robert's story shows the imbalance in their dynamic, the clear lack of power-sharing, when he tells himself, *No way I'm going to get up and take the trash out now. She'll have to wait.* It also shows negative reciprocity, his retaliatory reaction to Sarah's nagging, which is an expression of her power-grabbing and feelings of entitlement toward controlling Robert's behavior.

As with any dynamic you evolve with others, the negative stories Sarah and Robert tell themselves about one another are emotionally symbolic and can cause dramatic and extensive imbalance to their relationship. The matter of the trash becomes a negative emotional symbol in Sarah and Robert's relationship, which they respectively draw on in their thoughts, recollections, and imaginings about one another as they deepen the imbalance of their relationship dynamic.

Sarah and Robert each shape *criticism, anger, and resentment,* which eventually cause them to feel disconnected and dissatisfied in their relationship. The topics of the negative stories they tell themselves about one another are not important. Whether about the trash or something else, such as paying a bill, cleaning the house, dropping the kids off at school, or hiring a painter, the *emotionally symbolic meaning* of the negative stories they tell themselves will affect how they evolve their dynamic together.

Whether or not you share the negative stories you tell your self about a relationship partner in interaction with others, they will shape how you posture your self in a relationship, what you will expect from it, and the outcome you will create. When Don decides to leave his domestic partner Annie after ten years because he's met Holly, he's probably convinced himself that Annie's got issues, isn't upbeat enough, and is making too many demands on him. He probably sees Holly as sweet, upbeat, and easy to get along with, even though she and her husband are divorced. Don overlooks the fact that he felt exactly the same way about Annie ten years ago and ignores the role the negative stories he's been telling himself about Annie have played in the relationship dynamic they jointly shape.

The Perceptual Inattention Trap (PIT)

Your brain postures you for opposition automatically and without your permission. While you can bring awareness and attention to nonconscious negative perception once you learn how to watch for it, you probably can't stop yourself from ever having negative thoughts, recollections, and imaginings because your brain is "wired" to produce them.

Your brain extends the force of mind that is opposition by automatically engaging a mind-set that can be thought of as the *perceptual inattention trap* (PIT), the domain of negative perception. When your brain engages the PIT perceptual paradigm, the various aspects of your *small self* step forward to do emotional battle, causing you to shape the stories you tell your self to symbolize negative and polarizing emotional values such as *fear, anger, resentment, criticism,* and *entitlement.* It is when this happens that you are most vulnerable to allowing your brain to mold your "mind-made" reality by accepting the role of passive participant-observer. When you allow your thoughts, recollections, and imaginings to develop within the PIT mind-set, you give up your control over your brain, your relationships, your emerging process of self and consciousness, and your life.

Over time, you can condition your self to engage the PIT mind-set in whatever thoughts, recollections, or imaginings you generate about a certain person or relationship situation. This is how you can easily come to the point where you see everything a person says or does as "wrong" and your entire relationship as dissatisfying. Your brain will always bias you toward more negative perceptions as it extends existing neurological patterns.

The Negative Stories You Tell Others

Many different factors affect whether you are likely to share the negative stories you tell your self about a relationship partner with others, and what you are likely to say if you do. The type of relationship you have with a person and where your interaction takes place are two of them.

The type of relationship you have with someone affects how you see your rights and privileges in the relationship and what you expect from the other person. Relationships with a spouse or domestic partner are typically the ones where you feel you have the most rights. As a result, you are more predisposed to sharing the negative stories you tell yourself about these types of relationship partners directly with them, which causes you to experience more authentically negative relationship experiences with these partners than with others. For instance, if your wife dragged dirt all over the kitchen floor you just cleaned, you would probably react differently than you would if a friend did it. Similarly, while you might be quick to blame your husband for dirtying the tablecloth at dinner, you probably wouldn't say anything to a neighbor who came as a guest and did the same thing. It's more probable that you would try to be polite and appropriate in conversation with the neighbor, complaining to your spouse about the tablecloth after the neighbor goes home.

Situational factors also affect whether you're likely to share your negative stories with others or not. For example, you might share a negative story about a neighbor with your spouse only if you are alone but keep your story to your self if there are others present.

Not every husband, wife, mother, mother-in-law, friend, or other relationship partner will shape the stories they tell themselves and others in the same way. But the way you come to understand your options for storytelling and sharing has much to do with the culture and family values into which you have been socialized. These values account for the way you come to use emotional symbols to shape and embody opposition in the stories you tell your self about others, and they constrain and shape the stories you share with others. They explain why you tend to create authentically negative relationship experiences with a spouse or domestic partner and inauthentically positive ones with others.

Inauthentically positive relationship experiences, where you keep the negative stories you create about a relationship partner to your self or share them with people other than the person-object of your opposition, allow you to avoid confrontation and conflict. But they don't allow you to balance a relationship dynamic or heal separation.

This explains why improving communication in your interaction with others doesn't always improve a relationship. You can learn to be clearer, more precise, and more direct in your interaction with a relationship partner, but if you generate the force of mind that is opposition, you will nevertheless invite or sustain a negative and polarizing relationship dynamic.

There is nothing unclear or imprecise in Dee's interaction with her mother-in-law at dinner as her mother-begins to serve her a piece of fish. While Dee does nothing to cause overt confrontation or conflict with her mother-in-law in their interaction together, she shapes the story she tells herself about her mother-in-law with *criticism* and *resentment*. In her interaction with her self, Dee is saying, *Yes, I like fish, but I don't like YOUR fish, and I don't like YOU.* But she refrains from sharing her negative story directly in her interaction with her mother-in-law at dinner:

> **Mother-in-Law:** [Begins to serve Dee a piece of fish]
> **Dee:** No, no, that's okay. I'm good.
> **Mother-in-Law:** I thought you liked fish.
> **Dee:** No, it's okay. I'm good.

Dee may be appropriate and polite enough in her interaction with her mother-in-law to avoid confrontation or conflict, but she won't be able to invite connection with her mother-in-law because the polarizing force of mind she generates can only inhibit it and support separation.

Authentically Negative Relationship Experiences

Study evidence suggests that you are most likely to engage in *authentically negative* relationship experiences with a spouse or domestic partner, evidenced by patterns of "attack-and-defense" in your interactions with these partners, which give visibility to an imbalanced relationship dynamic.

Consider an exchange between Mark and Erica, a husband and wife. Mark is angry because Erica committed him to going over to her brother's house on his day off from work. He reacts automatically and negatively, defaulting to the PIT perceptual paradigm, when he learns that she's committed him to help her brother, but his reaction in this instant is intensified by the other negative stories he tells himself about Erica in the thoughts, recollections, and imaginings of his "mind-made" universe of consciousness.

Mark fails to recognize how he assumes the role of passive participant-observer in his internal world of consciousness. Instead, he uses the situation to justify his negative feelings and use them to intensify his own emotional story about Erica as he invites her to help him embody the *me-against-you* dynamic he shapes in his mind. He does this by pointing out his subjective and negative perception of what she did wrong (*"Why did you ...?"*) Together, Mark and Erica create an oppositional dynamic, shaped by a predictable pattern of "attack-and-defense":

> **Mark:** Why did you tell your brother I'd help him on Saturday. I told you I don't want to go over there this week. [Attack]
> **Erica:** Sorry. I thought you could just go for an hour. [Defense]
> **Mark:** No, I can't. It's my one free afternoon, and I don't want to spend it over there. [Defense]
> **Erica**: Sorr-y. You don't have to get all mad about it. [Defense]

Mark is not looking for an answer to his question, *"Why did you tell your brother ...?"* He is *criticizing* Erica for not complying with his expectation, which he emphasizes when he says, *"I told you I don't want to go over there this week."* He clearly expresses his opposition, inviting Erica to support the *me-against-you* dynamic he makes visible in their interaction together by pointing out his perception of what she's done wrong. Although Erica tries to apologize when she says, *"Sorry. I thought you could just go for an hour,"* Mark doesn't accept her apology, choosing instead to continue with his own defensive response: *"No, I can't. It's my one free afternoon and I don't want to spend it over there."* Erica tries to apologize a second time, more strongly and a bit sarcastically, tagging on her own criticism of Mark when she says, *"You don't have to get all mad about it."*

Mark acts out the negative story he tells himself about Erica's decision to commit him to helping her brother on Saturday. While his feelings are valid, his decision to use them to shape a negative story about Erica postures him to push her away and also prevents him not getting his real need met, which is to have a quiet afternoon at home on his day off. Erica ends up feeling blamed, rejected, taken for granted, and unloved, feelings her brain will extend and intensify as she gathers more negative evidence to justify her own negative perceptions about Mark.

Consider another interaction where Jeff has just returned from a long day at work. Of all the many conversations that he could have started with his wife Elizabeth, he allows himself to default to the PIT and become a passive participant-observer in his "mind-made" universe. Perceptual inattention causes him to stay in the space of negative perception, and share the negative story he creates that symbolizes the *criticism* and *anger* he feels when he sits down on the couch and notices it's dirty:

Jeff: That thing is filthy. [Attack]
Elizabeth: I know. I tried to clean it, but it just won't come clean. [Defense]
Jeff: You didn't use the right stuff. [Attack]
Elizabeth: Why are criticizing me as soon as you get home from work? [Attack]
Jeff: I'm not criticizing you. [Defense]
Elizabeth: You are, and you don't even realize it. [Attack]
Jeff: [Gets up from the couch and walks out the room in a huff] [Attack]

Jeff overtly but indirectly criticizes Erica for not cleaning the couch when he says, "*That thing is filthy,*" implying that the couch is filthy because she hasn't cleaned it. Erica recognizes his words as a criticism of her, triggering her to react in the same automatic and negative way with a counterattack: "*Why are you criticizing me as soon as you get home from work?*" The polarizing *me-against-you* dynamic they shape spirals them away from each other, clear evidence of negative reciprocity and retaliation: He denies his intention, she calls him on it, and he counterattacks, clearly taking his power by getting up and leaving the room "in a huff." While Jeff denies his criticism, he sets an overt emotional struggle into motion, which means that Erica has understood and responded to his oppositional force of mind by sustaining the negative dynamic he initiates, positioning herself for defense.

The exchange just described would probably not have occurred between the couple early on in their relationship, before they were married. The adage "love is blind" reflects a nonconscious desire to "see" everything a relationship partner does and says as "right" and positive. Because of a desire to make their relationship work, relationship partners in the early stage of a relationship bias perception positively and automatically so they see one another in the light of perfection. Phrases like "*He wasn't like that when I married him*" and "*She wasn't like that when I first met her*" suggest how shifts in perception change from positive to negative in a relationship.

While the force of opposition can deepen and extend the negative melody of a relationship as a whole, it can also dissipate when relationship partners redefine their roles and the rights and responsibilities they assume in their relationship with one another change. Lauren's comment to a friend about her ex-husband is telling:

My ex is a great guy. I have no idea how we ended up fighting so much about every little thing. I just don't understand why we couldn't we give each other what we needed. We both wanted the same thing.

Self-Defensive *small you*

The force of mind that is opposition reflects egocentric, *small you* "seeing" that causes you to sustain *me-against-you* posturing and an imbalanced relationship dynamic.

You may recognize familiar ways of *small you* "seeing," the way your *small self* habitually and automatically engages when you feel threatened, annoyed, angry, irritated, or offended. You might even be able to label a familiar habit of perception. You may recognize a *spoiled child, doubting Thomas, drama queen, victim forever, negative Nellie, control freak, people pleaser, angry bully,* or some other way of "seeing" your *small you* self, which tends to engage automatically in response to experiences, thoughts, recollections, or imaginings that disrupt your peace of mind. While it is important to embrace the different aspects of *small you* that make you who you are, as well as recognize that these aspects of your self are helpful and necessary in some circumstances, it is also important to learn to recognize when they interfere with your relationship goals.

Small You Perception
Spoiled child wants everything her way and everyone to accommodate her needs
Doubting Thomas doesn't have confidence in her decisions or in what others tell her
Drama queen reacts with excessively negative emotional performances
Victim forever sees herself as an object of adversity and abuse
Negative Nellie views every situation and circumstance with opposition
Control freak tries to direct and manage everything and everyone
People pleaser says and does what she thinks others want or need, often disingenuously
Angry bully engages extreme performances of opposition to intimidate and coerce others

Small you perception causes imbalance to relationship dynamic because it generates the force of mind that is opposition. When you feel irritated or frustrated with a person and allow the stories you tell your self to distract you from feeling loving and joyful, you are experiencing the power and impact of a *small you* perception on your life. Where you choose to engage overtly and directly in struggle with a relationship partner, *small you* will always try to get you to push others away, aggressively or passive-aggressively.

In your interaction with others, when you embody opposition and invite a relationship partner to engage directly and overtly, *small you* can quickly cause a struggle to spiral out of control. *Small you* will always try to defend the boundaries of your individual self and work to keep you separated. It will always cause you to "see" through the veil of negative perception and to shape your experiences, thoughts, recollections, and imaginings with language of negative feeling that symbolizes negative and polarizing values such as fear, anger, resentment, criticism, and entitlement. The more you allow *small you* perception to shape how you "see," the more you relinquish control over your relationships and life.

Consider how Audrey and Bill habitually allow their respective *small selves* to engage and negatively affect their relationship. Audrey and Bill have been married for five years. They have complementary personalities, which is what attracted them to one another when they first met. Audrey is highly energetic, organized, detail oriented, and proactive. Her take-charge attitude makes her a valued employee at work and an excellent supervisor. While Bill is responsible and dependable, he takes things as they come and is laid back. Audrey routinely takes care of almost everything around the house, including the cats, the bills, the kids, service appointments, cleaning, and organizing. The frustration and anger she feels toward Bill, feeling that he always leaves everything for her to do, has contaminated how she feels about him as a person and their relationship. It also plays into how Bill feels about Audrey and his view of the relationship. Their antagonistic attitudes and emotions toward one another have intensified over the five years they have been married.

Audrey and Bill have settled into a predictable pattern of emotional struggle in their life together, a familiar negative relationship dynamic that has come to define their relationship. It shapes their individual thoughts, recollections, and imaginings about one another, and their experiences in their interaction together. While they each have a role in how the dynamic they shape together, Audrey blames Bill and Bill blames Audrey. Neither of them sees their own role in the dynamic how it interplays with the other's role. Ironically, Audrey and Bill have come to dislike the very qualities in one another that attracted them to each other in the first place.

Consider what's going on between Audrey and Bill. Audrey and Bill have always had different needs and interests. They work at very different paces, and their expectations about how to spend their free time are different. They have different priorities, and different approaches to almost everything. Every little thing seems to bother Audrey, who routinely takes the lead in inviting Bill to engage in the *me-against-you* dynamic they jointly evolve. Time after time, Bill accepts Audrey's invitation in his own passive-aggressive way, which provokes the familiar pattern of attack-and-defense that always unfolds in the conversation between them.

Both Audrey and Bill are passive participant-observers in respective worlds of consciousness. Audrey doesn't accept responsibility for the *control freak* aspect of her self that wants everything done her way and isn't satisfied with the way others do things. She doesn't recognize how she is so proactive in getting things done at home that she doesn't give Bill a chance to step in and help. She also doesn't see how her *control freak* self causes her to evaluate everything Bill does as "wrong" or inadequate. Bill, on the other hand, has a *doubting Thomas* aspect that engages automatically in response to Audrey's *control freak*. The more Audrey tries to control, the more Bill doubts his own abilities, a familiar push-pull in their relationship together. Bill's view is that no matter what he does around the house, it's never enough, or it's never done well enough for Audrey. Because he feels he can never do anything "right" in Audrey's eyes, and because he feels she nags and bosses him around, he has given up trying to please her. When he withdraws, it only annoys Audrey more. The result of their struggle is that both Bill and Audrey feel disconnected from one another and deeply dissatisfied in their relationship together.

You are most likely to allow *small you* perspective to engage openly in interactions with a spouse or domestic partner, but it's becoming increasingly common to see *small you* struggles in public between strangers, probably because they don't expect to each other again. The entitlement many people feel when they drive makes the road a place where *small you* expressions between strangers can be commonly observed. Drivers commonly mouth obscenities, use vulgar gesturing, or shout at the "offender" through an open window. In extreme cases, they justify their "road rage." Consider an example where a man driving a car approaches a biker who is traveling parallel to his car but at a much slower pace. Because the driver doesn't expect to have to share the road with the biker, his *small self* postures him for opposition. Through his open car window, he yells at the biker, "Why don't you get the hell off the road."

Balanced Tension and Imbalance

Any *small you* perception generates the force of mind that is opposition and invites imbalance to a relationship dynamic. Because *small you* perception causes polarization, it disrupts power-shaping and positive reciprocity, disturbing the balanced tension between merging and separating, the human need to draw others close but not so close they you lose your self. You invite and sustain imbalance to a relationship dynamic through your experiences with other and through your thoughts, recollections, and imaginings about them. The more negative attention you give others in the universe of your mind, and in social interaction, the greater the risk for imbalance and disconnection.

Reflecting egocentric "seeing" and a self-centered *I-perspective, small you* perception causes you to see through the veil of negative feeling, and justify and defend what you see in the stories you tell your self about others and sometimes share in social interaction. Negative perception symbolizing *entitlement* will cause you to think and express as if you "have the right," are more deserving or worthy than others, or others owe you. It can cause you to react with *fear* when you think you are not getting what you deserve or to *criticize* and blame others for your perceived lack of abundance. More generally, any negative perception can cause you to experience *anger* and *resentment* and to justify your negative thoughts, recollections, and imaginings about your husband, mother, or other relationship partner.

Small you perception reinforces *me-against-you* posturing that biases you to see yourself as "right" and others as "wrong." It prevents you from developing an emerging awareness of *self* that serves collective wellness and relationship satisfaction.

Extending Harm with Negative Alignments

Your *small you* perception and oppositional force of mind affects your entire web of personal relationships and, by extension, the communities to which you are tied. While you may refrain from direct and overt struggle in your interaction with a relationship partner, when you allow the force of opposition to persist in your consciousness, you tend to create negative alignments with others against the person-object of your negative perception. Very cleverly, you "make your case" against the person-object of your opposition in a way that causes connection with the people you draw into your own negative "seeing."

Subtly and not so subtly, you create negative alignments against the person-object that cause others to give similarly negative attention to the person, consistent with your own negatively biased and subjective "seeing." Others get pulled into your own *small you* perception, where their own thoughts, recollections, and imaginings concerning a person they may not have even ever met become aligned with yours.

Two types of negative alignments are common in American social interaction, *negative venting,* and *bullying.*

Negative venting is pervasive in talk between spouses, domestic partners, family members, and friends. Women are especially vulnerable to the complaining, blaming, and criticizing of an absent person-object that typically characterizes negative venting. Typically, one person baits others into a conversation about an absent person-object, shaping opposition through negative language symbols reflecting fear, anger, resentment, criticism, entitlement, or other negative values. The person inviting the negative alignment against the absent person-object typically invites others to support their own biased and subjective negative perceptions. Frequently, the person who invites negative venting criticizes or blames the person-object in an attempt to coerce others to agree and offer support for the biased, subjective, and negative perceptions targeted at the person-object.

A misguided strategy for connection with those being brought into negative alignment against the absent person-object, negative venting unfairly biases others to join and strengthen a negative relationship dynamic, enhancing separation with the absent person-object. In so doing, those who are drawn into a negative alignment shape their own stories to be consistent with the negatively biased ones they have been drawn into. Without much awareness, they limit their own awareness, harming themselves and others by generating the force of opposition that shapes unfair realities about others and creates additional barriers to connection.

Consider how Rae criticizes her friend Kate to her friend Beth, who doesn't know Kate personally, only through Rae's talk about her:

> **Rae:** The only thing I don't like about Kate is that she always invites us without the kids.
> **Beth:** Really? That's weird.
> **Rae**: Her kids are always running around when we're over there, but our kids can't come. I don't see the point. If she doesn't want kids around, she should get a sitter. The last thing I want is somebody else's kids running around when mine are home.
> **Beth:** Strange. I wouldn't go without the kids. What's her problem?

Rae's criticism of Kate to Beth is overt and direct. While it provides Rae with a way to bond with Beth by confiding in her, it does so at Kate's expense, because it makes Kate the person-object of biased and negative perceptions. Rae's criticism of Kate distances her emotionally from Kate while it connects her to Beth. It also inhibits Beth from connecting with Kate, because Rae's negative story about Kate will negatively affect how Beth sees Kate.

Rae's criticism of Kate to Beth encourages Beth to align her view of Kate with her own negative and subjective story. Beth's picture of Kate becomes colored by Rae's criticism while circumstances that present Beth in a different light are ignored. Maybe Kate is trying to keep grocery expenses down by not including Rae's children as guests. Or she might feel Rae's children influence her own children to misbehave and cause chaos. Whatever the other possible interpretations, Rae puts forth a single subjective and negative picture of Kate for Beth.

The negative alignment against Kate that Rae invites and Beth accepts in this single conversation affects her relationship with both Beth and Kate in the present as well as the future. It also shapes Rae's relationship with Kate because it intensifies Rae's opposition toward Kate and encourages her hold on to her negative story. In addition, it shapes Beth's own emerging process of self, because it influences how she positions herself toward Kate in her thoughts, recollections, imaginings, and in interaction with her, if they ever meet in person. Beth may even share her negatively biased story of Kate with other people later on other interactions, even if she never meets Kate.

Negative alignments like the one described allow you to release your negative feelings, but not in a productive way. When you make another person the object of your negative stories, even if you draw others closer to you in the process, you create a critical, judgmental, and egocentric representation of your self and unfairly portray a subjective and harmful negative representation of others, based on your own biased perceptions.

A more extreme example of harmful negative alignments is *bullying,* where multiple people overtly and directly strengthen negative perceptions, which they embody against a single individual in the presence of the person, who is the negative object. While there are many kinds of bullying, all are harmful, intimating, and sometimes even violent.

Commonly, a group of friends engage in bullying a stranger or acquaintance, someone who represents values they reject. The force of opposition might be triggered by an individual's physical appearance (such as weight, height, shape, or physical features), sexual preference (gay or lesbian), gender orientation (transgender), race (such as black, Asian), ethnicity (such as Mexican), or religion (such as Islamic or Jewish).

Bullying illustrates how negative perceptions can intensify an oppositional force of mind to an extent that, when embodied in interaction with others, it invites coercive, controlling, and abusive behaviors that place the physical safety of the person-object at risk.

Intensity of Overt Opposition	
Weaker	**Stronger**
Indirect/implicit negativity < … … … … … … … … … … … > Direct/explicit negativity	

Consider what happens when three young adult men board a crowded city metro car and approach a young woman who is standing by the door waiting to get off at the next stop. One of the men grabs and lifts the hem of her skirt, acting out entitlement and criticism:

> Mother fucker! Get your big, fat ass out 'a here! [Pushes on her back as he walks away] You big, fat, ugly mother fucker!

The woman's physical appearance causes the man to generate the force of mind that is opposition, which he allows himself to act out directly and explicitly. His negative reaction is threatening, abuse, and insulting to the woman who is the object of his biased and negative perception of her.

Bullying can be even more intimidating, violent, and extreme than the example just given, but there are also many more subtle expressions. In the following situation, as several young female friends huddle together at a storefront in the mall, one of them says in earshot of a classmate they routinely talk about, who happens to be passing by:

> **Bully:** Somebody ought to clue her in about how to dress. Did you see that skirt?
> **Friends:** [Giggle and laugh]

The negative alignment the bully establishes with her friends, baiting them to strengthen her own oppositional force of mind toward the girl who is the object of her criticism, causes her friends to also push the girl-object away. The bully invites her friends to reject the girl-object's uniqueness because it is not consistent with her own values. Taking her power in the exchange, the bully makes her own negative force of mind visible, and influences how her friends will think about, remember, and imagine the girl-object in their own minds and how they will relate to her and to the bully in the future. The "ripple effect" of this single interaction has the potential to extend and intensify *me-against-you* posturing across the constellation of lives tied to it, also interfering with cohesiveness of the school community to which the girls belong.

PART 2 – GUIDANCE

COMPASSIONATE COOPERATION: REMOVING THE OBSTACLES TO CONNECTION

Part 2 of *Force of Mind, Song of Heart* teaches you how to take willful and active steps to eliminate the obstacles to connection and generate the force of mind that is compassionate cooperation, the unifying me-and-you dynamic that invites and supports the balanced relationship dynamic that is connection. It contains three components. First, it introduces the perceptual paradigm for compassionate cooperation and the attitudes and emotions of thought and expression that generate the force of mind that shapes connection. Then it explains the process of perceptual reinterpretation and how to use reframing and re-scripting to reshape the negative and polarizing stories you tell yourself and others about a relationship partner, a process that rebalances the tension between merging and separating in a relationship dynamic. Lastly, it details language and other emotional symbols along with strategies and techniques to help you redirect opposition as compassionate cooperation when your brain postures you to do otherwise.

CHAPTER 3

Mind-Set and Force of Mind: Musical Score for Your Relationships and Your Emerging Process of Self-Seeing

We might say that the whole of life lies in that verb—if not ultimately, at least essentially. Fuller being is closer union ... union increases only through an increase in consciousness, that is to say in vision ... [40]

—Pierre Teilhard de Chardin

The opportunity to improve a personal relationship lies in "seeing," in your willingness and commitment to *see differently* in your "mind-made" universe of consciousness, where you shape your emerging process of self. This is where your limitless creative potential for transformational relationship change lies.

By opening your mind to the boundless possibilities you have for reinterpreting your thoughts, recollections, and imaginings to invite and support the positive and unifying relationship dynamic that is *compassionate cooperation*, you can take steps to restore balance to a negative and polarizing *me-against-you* dynamic that inhibits connection and disrupts power-sharing and positive reciprocity. This is how you can take an active role in shaping your relationships, your emerging process of self, and your life. It is the *only way* to advance genuinely satisfying and positive personal relationships, and experience more joyful, purposeful living.

Adjusting how you "see" requires you to understand your self as *a mind*, a dynamic and emerging process of consciousness, and to actively intercept the automatic responses produced by your brain when you notice they are interfering with your relationship goals. Your brain "believes" the emotional value of what your mind knowingly or unknowingly tells it. By allowing your

---

40 Pierre Teilhard de Chardin, *The Phenomenon of Man* (NY: Harper Perennial Modern Thought, 2008), 31. Originally published in French as *Le Phénomene Humain* by Editions du Seuil, Paris, 1955.

brain to use the emotional value of its own creations, which are predisposed to negative bias and processing errors, you give up control over your relationships and life.

Your opportunity for empowerment lies in your potential to *use your mind* to fabricate your own creations. This opportunity is limitless because consciousness is limitless.

You can unleash your creative potential through perceptual reinterpretation, the process through which you can redirect the negative and polarizing force of mind that is opposition, and restore balance to a relationship dynamic when your brain positions you to push others away. This is the path to relationship growth and renewal. It is also the way to self-actualization, because it requires you to an active role in shaping your emerging process of self, who you are in your thoughts, recollections, and imaginings of others, and also in your interaction with them.

Moment by moment, you "are." Every instant of thought is an opportunity to "be" different, to shape your self in a way that serves collective wellness. When you make the choice to *see differently*, you open yourself to the limitless possibilities of "being" that support collective wellness, an adjustment in *I-perspective* that reflects a wider view of self and consciousness.

Mind-Set – The Paradigm for "Seeing"

Consider an analogy. If you wanted to play a violin solo with an orchestra, you'd probably want to become familiar with the musical score to get a "big picture" understanding of your solo. The notes, tempo markings, and metronome markings on the music would serve as performance indicators and guide you to play your solo so it evolves harmoniously and in balance with the playing of the other performers in the orchestra. You would also probably want to practice specific techniques on your own, such as vibrato and pizzicato, to help you execute your part of the performance to the fullest expression of the musical score and as a important part of a unified performance with the orchestra as a whole.

Mind-set is the musical score for your relationships and life. It is the perceptual paradigm that guides "seeing" and accounts for how you feel about inviting your in-laws over for dinner, what you think about your sister's plans to go to Hawaii, and what you imagine your mother will say about your kitchen floor.

Generally, you engage a mind-set without thinking. When you become "comfortable" in a relationship, your brain tends to act in "automatic ways," habits extended and inferred from consciousness that are an outcome of repetition. This is only problematic when you allow yourself to be a passive participant-observer to negative perception in interaction with your self or others. When this happens, you generate the force of mind that is opposition, posturing yourself to invite and support the negative and polarizing relationship dynamic that inhibits your capacity to shape connection.

Consider an example of how mind-set causes two women, Monique and Jennifer, to shape very different relationship dynamics in spite of their very similar relationship situations.

Monique's husband left her last year for another woman, but he still wants to play an active role in their three-year old daughter's life. Monique despises her husband's girlfriend and doesn't want her daughter near her, but she is legally obligated to share custody with her ex-husband. Monique spends most of her time thinking about how she doesn't want to share her daughter with her ex-husband and how she doesn't want his girlfriend near her daughter. When she thinks of her ex and his girlfriend, she feels gut-wrenching anger and resentment as her mind pulls her to new lows with negative scripts that give her no space to think about anything else. When she's with her friends, Monique is constantly blaming and criticizing her ex and his girlfriend for her own current situation, as she emphasizes her own victimization and overlooks her role in the relationship dynamic she evolves with her ex-husband and his girlfriend. Her interaction with her self reflects resentment and envy most of the time, regardless of what she's doing, even when she is involved with activities she used to enjoy and even when she is pretending as if she's having a good time in the company of friends and family. She wakes up and goes to bed feeling angry and resentful and wastes a lot of time being distracted by negative thoughts, recollections, and imaginings about her ex-husband and his girlfriend.

Monique is typical in that she blames her frustration and unhappiness on someone else. She sees her ex-husband and his girlfriend as responsible for ruining her life (*"If only he didn't …,"* *"If only she would …"*). Monique sees external circumstances as the cause of her negative feelings and her decision to allow them to seep across her life in general as an unfortunate consequence of "what has happened to her." She clings to the belief that her ex-husband and his girlfriend are the cause of her present situation, that they robbed her of her right to be happy and ruined her life. She promotes that belief as the new backdrop for her future.

Monique allows herself to become a victim, accepting her brain's predisposition to negative patterning, and overlooking her mind's potential to "rewire" her brain. She accepts and deepens her negative thoughts, recollections, and imaginings about her ex-husband and his girlfriend in her interaction with her self, justifying and defending the *me-against-you* orientation she has toward her ex-husband, his girlfriend, and life. By accepting the giving attention to the negative stories that unfold in her interaction with her self, she relinquishes her creative potential to engage more productively in her relationships and life. While the negative stories she tells her self sometimes give her a "rush," especially when she feels she's "won" by punishing or rejecting her ex-husband, as when she refuses to allow him to switch visitation weekends just to be spiteful, they also leave her little room for being an effective co-parent in an oppositional relationship dynamic that distracts her thoughts, recollections, and imaginings most of the time.

Jennifer's husband also left her last year for another woman. Her situation is almost identical to Monique's. But, unlike Monique, Jennifer does not blame her ex-husband and his girlfriend for ruining her life. While she initially felt anger and resentment toward them, she decided to use the situation as a learning experience. Instead of letting herself continuously spin negative stories in her thoughts, recollections, and imaginings about her ex-husband and his girlfriend, Jennifer understands the potential she has to use her mind to "rewire" her brain. She is committed to taking an active participant-observer role in her interaction with her self and using her creative potential to redirect her brain's responses to serve her more productively in her relationship and life.

Jennifer strives to understand her own role in her former marriage, and the part of her *small self* that habitually interfered with her efforts to sustain a positive and unifying relationship dynamic with her ex-husband so she won't recreate the same dynamic with another husband. She dedicates herself to actively watching for negative perceptions in her thoughts, recollections, and imaginings about her ex-husband and his girlfriend so she can reinterpret them to serve her emerging consciousness of self and capacity for joyful living. Jennifer is also committed to ensuring that her daughter does not feel as though she needs to choose between her parents or that she is being disloyal to her mother by loving her father or spending time with him.

Jennifer is actively committed to shaping her thoughts, recollections, and imaginings to produce a genuinely satisfying and positive relationship with her ex-husband and his girlfriend for her own sake as well as her daughter's. She does not want her daughter to experience the influence of negative alignments or the stress and tension that results from the negative and polarizing relationship dynamic of opposition. While Jennifer does have momentary setbacks where she loses her emotional footing in her interaction with her self, she has become very masterful at redirecting opposition and taking an active role in re-patterning her brain to be consistent with her relationship goals and desire for a joyful life.

The Mind-Set of Positive Perception

Just as Jennifer and Monique make different choices about their respective relationships and lives, your capacity to *see differently*, in a way that supports connection, is directly related to the your willingness and commitment to actively engage a mind-set capable of producing the positive and unifying force of mind that is *compassionate cooperation*, the "song of heart" that produces connection. If your goal were to play a Vivaldi solo with an orchestra, it wouldn't be helpful to study and play the musical score for a different piece. In the same way, if you want to create connection, it isn't helpful to engage a mind-set that *cannot* produce it. The PIT mind-set from which you generate the force of mind that is opposition, the negative and polarizing dynamic causing separation, cannot produce connection.

The choice to *see differently* is directly dependent on your willingness and commitment to actively engage a perceptual paradigm capable of allowing you to produce the positive and unifying force of mind that is *compassionate cooperation*. In the same way you might use a musical score to help you prepare and perform a violin solo with attention to playing cooperatively and in balance with an orchestra, you can use the *mind-set of positive perception* to redirect opposition as *compassionate cooperation*, which will allow you to shape a relationship dynamic to produce the song of heart that is connection.

The *mind-set of positive perception* provides the perceptual scaffolding for shaping your relationships, your self, and your life to serve you, others, and your communities. Reflecting the most basic set of assumptions for perceptual reinterpretation, it empowers you to drive meaning in your thoughts, recollections, and imaginings about a person or relationship situation in ways that produce connection and collective wellness.

Reflecting the emotional symbols of positive perception, represented by values such as *love, peace, forgiveness, gratitude,* and *service,* the mind-set of positive perception allows you to produce the force of mind that is *compassionate cooperation*.

Mind-Set of Positive Perception	
Perceptual Values	[+] Positive and unifying values, such as love, peace, forgiveness, gratitude, service [+] Positive and unifying thoughts, recollections, imaginings, interactions
Impacts	Positive and unifying force of mind that is *compassionate cooperation* Relationship *balance*, evidenced by power-sharing and positive reciprocity
Outcomes	Connection, genuinely satisfying and positive relationships, collective wellness, joyful living, self-actualization

The potential you have for improving the personal relationships in your life lies in your capacity to engage creatively and actively in generating thoughts, recollections, and imaginings about a relationship partner or situation that are consistent with the mind-set of positive perception. Your every instant of thought provides you with an opportunity to use your potential for relationship growth and change, and for more joyful and purposeful living.

Reframing – The Process of Perceptual Reinterpretation

Being watchful for negative perception in your thoughts, recollections, and imagining is crucial. You can't change what you neglect to recognize. By actively watching your mind for stories with negative emotional value and recognizing how emotional symbols of polarizing values such as fear, anger, resentment, criticism, and entitlement generate the force of mind that opposition, you may become an active participant-observer in within your internal universe of consciousness.

By being watchful for negative perception, you can identify opportunities for improving your relationships and your life. These are your greatest moments for relationship growth and self-actualization. Every moment of negative perception is an opportunity for you to *see differently* and refuse to accept your brain's predisposition to negative bias and errors in mental processing.

Your creative potential to shape genuinely satisfying and positive personal relationships lies in your creative potential to shape consciousness and your emerging process of *self* through the process of perceptual reinterpretation, or *reframing*.

Reframing enables you to actively shift away from the default PIT mind-set, which your brain automatically engages to build and intensify the negative stories you tell your self across your thoughts, recollections, and imaginings, and interactions about a relationship partner, to the mind-set of positive perception. Through the process of reframing, you can intentionally reinterpret your thoughts, recollections, and imaginings to symbolize the positive and unifying values of positive perception that generate the force of mind that is *compassionate cooperation,* which is how you restore balance to a relationship dynamic.

Reframing is like "choosing your own adventure" in the world of fan fiction, because it similarly empowers you to create your own emotional story about a relationship partner or situation. Guided by the positive and unifying values of a positive perceptual mind-set, you can learn how to redirect the polarizing *me-against-you* relationship dynamic produced by the force of mind that is opposition. By giving positive and active attention to you negative stories, you can generate the force of mind that is *compassionate cooperation*, which produces the balanced and unifying *me-and-you* relationship dynamic. By learning how to restore power-sharing and positive reciprocity to an imbalanced dynamic, elements critical to genuinely satisfying and positive relationships and collective wellness, you take steps to use your limitless potential for relationship growth and more joyful living.

Guidance for Reframing	
1	Identify and *rationally* explain your negative feelings to yourself. Remember: *You* are not your brain.
2	Shift from an egocentric *I-perspective* to an inclusive *I-Perspective*.
3	Revalue the negative story you tell yourself so it reflects the emotional values of a positive perceptual mind-set, values such as *love, peace, forgiveness, gratitude,* and *service*.

You can use the reframing guidance to help you reinterpret the story you tell yourself about a relationship partner or situation. Through prompting, you can work to clarify and understand your negative story so you can retell it in a way that reflects the emotional values of a positive perceptual mind-set:

> We can learn to clarify … what emotions we are feeling, what values we want to live by, and what we want to ask of ourselves and others. We will no longer need to use the language of blame, judgment or domination. We can experience the deep pleasure of contributing to each others' well being … even under trying conditions.[41]

Reframing can help you clarify what initially triggered your brain to push a person away and why you are postured for fight-or-flight in the negative stories you are telling your self about a relationship partner or situation in your thoughts, recollections, or imaginings. By bringing attention and clarity to the need or issue underlying opposition, you take responsibility for your feelings without having to make others wrong or diminish their worth through blame. This is how you assume the role of an active participant-observer in your interaction with your self and others without sacrificing your personal needs and interests. It is what frees you to create alternative interpretations of people, circumstances, and events and to "see" in a way that includes others, embraces their uniqueness, and sustains connection. Making others "wrong" and proving your self "right" is not the road to more genuinely satisfying and positive relationships.

---

41   Marshall B. Rosenberg, *Center for Nonviolent Communication*, http://www.cnvc.org/about/what-is-nvc.html.

You can learn to use your negative feelings productively and in a way that helps others understand you and draws them you closer to you. Although it is important for you to embrace all the different parts of your self, it is also important for you to challenge yourself to learn how to use your feelings productively to shape your relationship experiences. By taking an honest look at yourself, you can learn to recognize and rationally explain your feelings to your self. This is how you distance your self enough from your brain's learned patterns of negative response enough to open the door to change.

The reframing guidance can prompt you to distance yourself from the automatic and negatively biased response patterns your brain produces, which can help you move away from a self-centered *I-perspective* that prioritizes your own needs and interests at the exclusion of the needs and interests of others.

As you strive to reframe a negative story you tell you self, you can prompt yourself to consider how it reflects the negative and polarizing emotional values of the PIT mind-set that interfere with connection and a balanced relationship dynamic: Is your negative story rooted in *fear*? If so, what is your fear about? Does your negative story reflect *anger* or *resentment*? If so, why? Does it represent *criticism*? If so, what is causing it? Do you feel a sense of *entitlement*? If so, why? Guiding yourself to think about how your negative story reflects negative emotional values such as fear, anger, resentment, and entitlement can draw attention to the negative assumptions underpinning a story that generates the force of mind that is opposition.

Consider how Julie's negative and polarizing story causes her to keep her mother-in-law at an emotional distance. Although she sees her mother-in-law only a few times a year, Julie spends a lot of time in her internal world of consciousness allowing herself to be distracted by the negative story she tells herself about her mother-in-law. Every time Julie's husband gets a phone call from his mother, which happens about once every two weeks, Julie's brain deepens her fight-or-flight reaction and causes her to cling stubbornly to the negative story she tells herself:

Why is she constantly calling him? Why doesn't she just stay away and take care of her own stuff. I can't stand it when she does this! Why does she have to call *him*. She is *so needy*!

The adrenaline rush she feels at these times is predictable and more intense every time her mother-in-law calls. She also feels the rush whenever she thinks about her mother-in-law during the weeks when her mother-in-law doesn't call. Although Julie doesn't say anything directly to her husband about being resentful or angry about the calls, her attitude and body language clearly imply her feelings. They also cause her husband to see her as selfish and self-centered. Both Julie and her husband have begun to extend their respective negative views to other issues about one another that have nothing to do with the phone calls. The mother-in-law, on the other hand, feels that Julie is off-putting toward her but doesn't understand if she's done something wrong or if Julie and her son are having marital problems. She finds the situation difficult because she and her son were always so close before he got married, and she feels shut out from his life with Julie.

As time goes on, Julie's resentment and anger intensify to the point where she is generally angry and resentful of her mother-in-law and also with her husband for taking the phone calls from his mother. She doesn't want to be feeling the way she does, and she knows she is alienating her husband over the issue. But she doesn't recognize how her oppositional force of mind is causing her resistance toward her mother-in-law and creating distance between her and her husband.

What if Julie decided to watch her mind and be vigilant for negative thoughts, recollections, and imaginings about her mother-in-law and the situation?

She could begin by reminding herself that she is not her brain. Remembering that her brain reacts automatically and without her permission to a threat or offense stimulus, and that these reactions are what make her human and fallible, she can begin the process of reframing. By being willing to take an honest and rational look at her self to identify and confront her irrational feelings, she can loosen the grip her brain has on her.

She doesn't need to change her feelings about the situation or her mother-in-law, which she may not be able to do, but she does need to distance herself enough from them enough to talk rationally about them to herself. If she doesn't, the negative story she tells herself about her mother-in-law and the phone calls will continue to sustain the imbalanced relationship dynamic she evolves with her mother-in-law, and also with her husband on the issue. It will also continue to impact the relationship dynamic her husband has with his mother and cause all of them to feel generally less satisfied with their lives than they could be.

Where can Julie begin? By bringing to mind negative emotional symbols of the PIT mindset, such as *fear, anger, resentment,* and *entitlement,* she can prompt herself to recognize what she is feeling and begin to clarify what is causing the biases of her negative perception. First *fear.* If Julie asks herself, *What am I afraid of in this situation?* she might realize that she feels threatened by her mother-in-law because she's fearful that her husband might love his mother more than he loves her. Julie rarely spends time with her mother-in-law but still perceives her mother-in-law as a threat, which is irrational. Maybe she's afraid her mother-in-law will get more of her husband's attention, which means less attention for her. Her fear causes her to feel *anger, resentment,* and *entitlement.* Her perception is that she has "more of a right" to her husband's attention than his mother does. Her sense of entitlement strongly affects how she positions her self toward her mother-in-law, reflecting her assumption that she has a right to control the situation and what her mother-in-law as well as her husband *should* or *shouldn't do.* Her assumption that she is more deserving than her mother-in-law causes imbalance in the dynamic she shapes with her mother-in-law, and also affects the one she jointly shapes with her husband, causing the lack of power-sharing and reciprocity that inhibits connection.

Julie might be able to recognize that the *spoiled child* part of her self always engages when she feels threatened or offended. If she can admit to herself that this aspect of her engages when see she feels fearful that her husband will love her less or give her less attention than his mother, she will be taking steps to understand her real underlying emotional need in the situation. Once she reminds herself how she is not being helpful to herself or others when this happens, she can strive to rebalance the relationship dynamic she shapes, willfully giving attention to shifting her *I-perspective* in her negative story to reflect "inclusive seeing" rather than egocentric (self-centered) seeing.

To help herself move to more inclusive seeing, Julie can use the creative potential of her mind. She might imagine herself in her mother-in-law's situation and her mother-in-law's need to talk to her son, along with her own need to feel important to her husband and have his attention. If she allows herself to think about it rationally, she can come to understand that her needs and her mother-in-law's needs are not mutually exclusive. She can come to recognize that she can accommodate both sets of needs, a solution that serves her, her relationship with her mother-in-law, and her relationship with her husband.

Once Julie can rationally explain her negative story to herself, she can strive to reframe it using positive and unifying emotional values such as *love, peace, forgiveness, gratitude,* and *service* to guide her reinterpretation. These positive and unifying attitudes and emotions generate the force of mind that is *compassionate cooperation.* By retelling the negative story she tells herself to reflect these values, she will restore balance to the relationship dynamic she evolves with her mother-in-law, an outcome that will also affect the dynamic she evolves with her husband.

To reframe her story, Julie can re-script the negative narrative she spins through her thoughts, recollections, or imaginings about her mother-in-law once she recognizes she is "seeing" through the veil of negative perception. The interaction with her self might look something like this:

> Why is she constantly calling him? Why doesn't she just stay away and take care of her own stuff? Okay, I'm doing it again. I'm feeling like there isn't enough love to go around and I'm taking it out on his mother. I'm going to turn my thoughts around. Let me start by imagining her perspective … She lives alone and has no one to talk to all day. He is the closest person to her. He's her son. It makes sense for her to want to check in with him regularly, and I'm sure he wants to know she's okay.

In the example, Julie's recognition, *"Okay, I'm doing it again"* is a turning point for Julie. Rationally explaining to herself what's true for her will allow her to distance from a familiar negative response pattern.

There is no limit to how imaginative Julie can be in reframing the negative story she tells herself about her mother-in-law. As long as she actively imagines *positive and unifying reinterpretations* symbolizing positive values such as *love, peace, gratitude, forgiveness,* and *service,* she will redirect her force of mind to serve her productively in her relationship with her mother-in-law and her husband.

You can prompt yourself to create positive reinterpretations of a negative story by considering more specific questions that help you focus on the values of *compassionate cooperation.*

Questions prompting you to "see *love*" can help you refocus on *perfection instead of error.*

Questions Prompting You to "See *Love*"

- *Am I seeing perfection or error? If I'm seeing error, what feelings do I need to confront and understand so I can release them?*

- *Are my negative emotional reactions serving me or interfering with my ability to connect?*

- *What feelings am I acting out, and what is my real emotional need?*

- *Am I looking at a present relationship circumstance or situation with a relationship partner through my past?*

Just bringing questions like these to mind when you are experiencing resistance can help you redirect an oppositional force of mind. When you actively choose to see love, you refuse to see errors and assign blame. By stopping yourself from pointing out the faults of others, you step back from trying to control others. As you do this, you will begin to experience *peace:*

> Peace is an attribute in you. You cannot find it outside ... Mental health is inner peace. It enables you to remain unshaken by lack of love from without, and capable, through your own miracles of correcting the external.[42]

---

42 Thompson, ed., *A Course in Miracles.*

Questions prompting you to "see *peace* and *forgiveness*" allow you to release from the past hurts, stress, and suffering. Peace results from being able to let go of hurts. You create peace when you refuse to interpret a story with oppositional force. To forgive is to choose to let go. It is not related to proving your self right. By learning to see forgiveness as a way to release from the past, you can learn to let go of the negative perceptions that cause you pain and suffering. Instead of refusing to forgive a relationship partner because you feel justified in punishing, rejecting, or blaming a person, you can choose to forgive: *"I forgive you because I choose to let go. I forgive you because it is how I release myself and create peace."*

Forgiveness requires you to see others as fallible and imperfect humans just like yourself. When you are able to allow others to make errors, you become more tolerant of yourself when you make mistakes. When you choose to let go, you release yourself.

Questions Prompting You to "See *Peace* and *Forgiveness*"

- *Is holding on to past hurts helping me or hurting me?*

- *What do I need to let go of in order to forgive?*

- *Is it more important for me be right or to feel connected and satisfied in my relationship?*

Questions prompting you to "see *gratitude*" can help you forgive yourself and others.

Questions Prompting You to "See *Gratitude*"

- *Can I create thought and expression to show gratitude in a way I have refused to do in the past?*

- *Can I release my judgment and see this person as vulnerable and imperfect like myself?*

Actively imagining a list of reasons for being grateful to someone who frustrates you can help you refocus from negative attention to positive attention. In creating a "gratitude list" when you feel resistance to a relationship partner or situation, you can help yourself move out of the role of victim and recognize abundance instead of scarcity.

Questions prompting you to "see *service*" can help you move away from an egocentric *I-perspective* so you can rebalance a relationship dynamic. By shifting away from attitudes of entitlement, you correct for lack of power-sharing and positive reciprocity in a relationship dynamic.

Questions Prompting You to "See *Service*"

- *How can I consider others as well as myself in this relationship situation?*

- *How can I extend kindnesses in this relationship situation?*

- *Am I actively seeking to understand the needs and interests of a relationship partner?*

The examples below illustrate how the questions prompting the positive and unifying values of compassionate cooperation can be used to support reframing.

In this example, Beth is newly wed and feels resentment toward her parents because they like to show up at her home unexpectedly on Saturday afternoons. Her resentment distracts her from appreciating the help they give her when they are there. She spends a lot of time wallowing in her own negative imaginings about their future unannounced visits when she's not with them, becoming increasingly resentful about events that haven't even yet occurred. Most of her imaginings are something like the following:

> I can't stand it when they show up without calling! It's so annoying. Why don't they call in advance? They need to have everything their way!

Beth's resentment begins to seep into other parts of her relationship with her parents. She tries to be polite when they come over, but she can actually feel her body tense in their presence from her angst over the situation. All she can think about is how she wants them to go home so she can have a free Saturday with her new husband. Nevertheless, she tries to interact "normally" with her parents, which cause her to invite an inauthentically positive relationship experience with them. Beth's parents aren't sure what's going on, although they intuitively understand that their dynamic with Beth is "off."

Beth doesn't like wallowing in her resentment, but she doesn't know what to do about it. She fails to recognize how she can use reframing as the *bridge* between her own needs and interests and those of her parents. If she had considered the general guidance for reframing, she might have been able to recognize that the issue underlying her resentment is that she wants to have Saturday all to herself with her husband. But the negative attention she gives her interpretation of her parents' unexpected visits distracts her from attending to her real need. Once she recognizes it, she can begin the process of perceptual reinterpretation, aiming for inclusive seeing where she creatively imagines herself as her parents and considers what their needs and interests might be.

She might imagine that her parents are anxious to share time with her and her new husband and realize that she also wants them all to spend time together, but not on Saturday. Coming to this realization, she can embrace the opportunity to reshape her story in a way that balances her needs and interests with those of her parents.

Beth can use the question prompts to help her create her story to reflect *love, peace, forgiveness, gratitude,* and *service.* By seeing *love,* she might recognize that her parents are trying to create a relationship with her and her new husband, not trying to prevent her from having a free afternoon. By seeing *peace* and *forgiveness,* she might understand that she can choose to release her resentment and give up blaming her parents for her own feelings. Instead, she can take responsibility her underlying need, which is to have Saturday afternoons alone with her husband. By seeing *gratitude,* she might imagine how her parents go out of their way to spend time with her and how they always make her a priority in their life. If she guides herself to name specific kindnesses they show to her, positive qualities they have, or how they've supported her in the past, she can help herself move more fully away from egocentric seeing to inclusive seeing. By seeing *service,* Beth might help herself realize that she self-limits by seeing only resentment in the situation. Focusing on *service,* she might come to see all the many options in the situation that would allow inclusive seeing. She might come to see that she could arrange to see her parents later in the day, or on a different day, her home, at her parents', in a park, or at a restaurant. Through inclusive seeing and an orientation toward service instead of entitlement, Beth would be able to understand that she can have Saturday afternoons alone with her husband *and* find time for her parents.

But what does Beth say to her parents?

Beth has always had trouble negotiating when she feels resistance. Her tendency is to become passive-aggressive when her brain postures her for opposition. She avoids confrontation but tends to harbor resentment. It's not uncommon for her to end up doing things she doesn't to do because she has trouble saying "no." Beth neglects to see that she can get her own needs met without rejecting others or hurting their feelings.

Learning how to re-script the negative story she tells she tells herself about her parents can be a helpful preparatory step for Beth when she is striving to redirect negative and polarizing thoughts, recollections, and imaginings concerning her parents. While she can try to be polite and appropriate in her interaction with them, she will project her oppositional force of mind into her interaction with them. They will always understand that something is going on, even if they don't understand exactly what it is. By re-scripting the thoughts, recollections, and imaginings she has on the issue with her parents, Beth can help herself reframe the story she tells her self, which will allow her to restore a balanced relationship dynamic with her parents.

Using positive emotional symbols to reinterpret her story, such as love, peace, forgiveness, gratitude, and service to guide her, Beth can be creative in her reinterpretation. As long as her revised story symbolizes the positive and unifying values of positive perception that generate the force of mind that is compassionate cooperation, Beth can be endlessly creative:

> (1) Mom and Dad, I am so grateful that you and dad take the time to come and visit. (2) It's important to me that we continue spending time together as a family. I wouldn't want it any other way. (3) But Jeff and I really want to have Saturday afternoons together alone. (4) I hope you understand. (5) I'm sure you remember how it was to be newlywed! (6) We can come over to your place on Sunday morning after we go to the gym if that works for you. Or you could visit on Thursday evening. (7) Would one of those ideas work for you?

> Beth might begin by expressing her gratitude to her parents (1) and giving positive attention (2) to the fact that family is important to her before she identifies her real need (3), the need that triggers her brain to generate the attitudes and emotions of opposition. She might mitigate and create linkages with her parents (4 and 5). Then, (6) she might offer a solution that meets her needs as well her parents' needs, asking her parents if any of her proposed ideas work for them (7).

By using inclusive "seeing" to step away from the self-centered and negative values symbolized by her original story, Beth can describe and ask for what she needs without blaming her parents. She can use words in her script to create linkages between her and her parents that invite a positive and unifying *me-and-you* dynamic. Because inclusive "seeing" affects balance in a relationship dynamic, it will allow her to posture herself toward power-sharing and positive reciprocity, and release from feeling entitled to have things her way without considering her parents.

By re-scripting the story you tell yourself, so it aligns with the positive and unifying emotional values of positive perception, such as love, peace, forgiveness, gratitude, and service, you help your brain create habits to generate the attitudes and emotions of compassionate cooperation as soon as your brain postures you for opposition. By carefully watching the flow of thoughts, recollections, and imaginings in your interaction with your self, and being honest with your self, you can take steps to remove the veil of negative perception that limits "seeing" and open yourself up to the infinite possibilities of positive perception.

Consider another situation where Misha is having coffee with her friend Rayna at a local café when an acquaintance of Rayna's unexpectedly joins them. As soon as Rayna invites the acquaintance to join them, Misha feels her self react and notices her thoughts:

I'm going to scream if I have to sit here and listen to the two of them talk! Her voice is so annoying! She just rambles on about nonsense!

While Misha's negative reaction may seem like no "big deal," if she allows her brain to continue generating negative stories, she will strengthen her brain's negative response patterns and predispose her self to more negative thinking.

Misha's script symbolizes negative and polarizing emotional values associated with the PIT mind-set. She expresses entitlement by thinking, *Why should I have to sit here and listen to the two of them talk,* as well as resentment, anger, and criticism with the thought, *Her voice is so annoying! She just rambles on about nonsense!* She also implies her fear of losing time alone with Rayna. Given the social context, it's unlikely that Misha will share her negative script in with Rayna and her acquaintance. Nevertheless, it will affect her thoughts, recollections, and imaginings about the situation and the people involved whenever she brings them into her awareness.

Misha can't help it if her brain reacted to a threat stimulus, but she can step in and actively retell her negative story as soon as she recognizes it. By taking an honest look at her self, Misha may realize that her real need is that she wants to spend time alone with her friend, and she feels threatened and deprived to have to share her friend's attention. She might also realize that the voice of the uninvited guest triggers a past negative memory that for her that causes her brain to position in opposition. Whatever causes her brain to generate the force of opposition, by bringing it into awareness and giving it conscious attention, Misha can begin the process of reframing, actively redirecting opposition as compassionate cooperation, the positive and unifying force of mind that produces the balanced *me-and-you* dynamic that causes connection.

This is how Misha might re-script her narrative:

> (1) I'm going to scream if I have to sit here and listen to the two of them talk! (2) Okay, here I go again, being impatient. (3) I can spare a few extra minutes. Look how happy she is to see her friend. She seems like a very nice person. I'm going to try to make her feel welcome to sit with us …

After (1) recognizing her initial negative reaction, Misha can (2) introspect to recognize what she's doing and describe it to herself. Then, she can (3) reframe using inclusive "seeing" and orienting her script to symbolize *service.*

Consider another situation, and how you can prompt reframing to redirect the force of mind that is opposition as compassionate cooperation when your brain positions you to push others away. In this situation, Eve is resentful and critical of a friend who is responsible for her seating assignment at the her daughter's wedding, attitudes and emotions that posture her in a *me-against-you* dynamic toward her friend, as the story she tells herself suggests:

> I can't believe she sat us here! There is absolutely no one at this table I want to talk to. We're so far from the head table that's it's not even funny! My night is ruined! This is going to be so boring! What was she thinking? I can't believe this! I would never do that to her!

Whether or not Eve shares her negative story with her friend, her husband, or anyone else, the negative and polarizing force of mind she generates causes her to see her friend from a self-centered perspective. If Eve is sufficiently invested in her negative perception, she will use her negative attitudes and emotions toward her friend in this situation as the basis for creating and justifying other negative feelings about her that will cause her to feel distant from her friend. She will also predispose herself to extending similar negative thinking to situations and events with others, contaminating her thoughts, recollections, and imaginings with the negative emotional response patterns she reinforces through her negative story.

The story Eve she herself about her friend and the situation is negatively biased and reflects the perceptual values of the PIT mind-set. When she tells herself, *There is absolutely no one at this table I want to talk to,* she limits herself to negative experience before she gives herself the chance to enjoy herself. Maybe her fear that no one will want to talk to her causes her to react as she does, or maybe she feels too intimidated to engage in conversation with people she doesn't know. She allows resentment, anger, and criticism to shape meaning when she says, *We're so far from the head table that's it's not even funny! What was she thinking.* The thought *I can't believe this! I would never do that to her!* points to her criticism of her friend. Her entire story reflects entitlement and suggests how she feels more deserving than others to be close to the head table.

Consider how Eve might choose to re-script her story so she can revalue her friend and the situation through the positive emotional values generating compassionate cooperation and a balanced relationship dynamic, such as love, peace, forgiveness, gratitude, and service:

> (1) This is not really where I want to be seated. (2) I always feel a little intimidated sitting at a table where I don't know anyone. (3) I'm surprised we're so far from the head table, but I'm sure it wasn't easy for her to figure out the seating plan. I'm sure she did the best she could. (4) There will be plenty of time to walk around and visit with everyone after dinner. (5) I'm grateful not to be sitting next to the band or the speakers that are right next to the head table. We would be deaf by the end of the night!

After (1) acknowledging her feelings, she can (2) confront her underlying issue, her fear of sitting with people she doesn't know. By (3) shifting away from an egocentric *I-perspective* to inclusive "seeing," she can begin to see the situation through her friend's eyes. This can help her (4) imagine options to meet her own underlying need, and to be open to finding reasons to (5) be grateful for where her friend has seated her.

You may routinely allow thoughts, recollections, and imaginings generating the force of opposition to persist in your mind and extend across relationship experiences without realizing it. This happens easily in situations like the one just described and also in situations with strangers. For example, if you've ever stood in line to pay for a purchase while person in line in front of you slows down your turn, you may recognize a familiar negative story that you allow to dominate your thoughts while you're waiting in line:

> Why does she have to do all of this *now*? Can't she see there's a line? Is she ever going to finish? What the …?

The next time you find yourself in a similar situation, try reframing your negative script as you stand in line waiting for your turn. Consider how the script above might be reinterpreted to support the positive emotional values of compassionate cooperation:

> (1) Why does she have to do all of this now. (2) I can see I'm having a hard time being patient again. (3) She's not out to get me. There is no other place for her to do her transactions. (4) I've been in her shoes. It doesn't feel good to know you're holding up a line! (5) I choose to let go of this. (6) Let me think about gratitude. At least I am healthy enough to stand here waiting …

As soon as you (1) recognize your brain has positioned you in opposition, you can (2) work to explain your negative reaction to your self, which can (3, 4 and 5) help you move toward inclusive seeing. By (6) bringing gratitude to mind, you can more fully enable yourself to see in a way that gives positive attention to another person. Even when you generate the force of mind that is opposition with strangers, you can practice reframing and work on rewiring your brain to serve you more productively.

Reframing predisposes you to collaborative problem-solving and decision-making with a relationship partner. You don't have to give up your personal views, beliefs, values, desires, or expectations, but you do need to give up trying to control how others think and behave. By learning how reinterpret a negative story so it reflects positive perception, you learn how to embrace the uniqueness of others and take responsibility for your self, your relationships, and your life.

The more you practice reframing with every person in your life, the more it becomes a habit because your every thought, recollection, and imagining strengthens or redirects your brain's neurological patterns, which cause you to experience people and life as you do.

Disentangling from Patterns of Attack-and-Defense in Interactions with Others

You are likely to be on "auto-pilot" when it comes to shaping your interactions with the people in your life from whom you expect the most, commonly a spouse or domestic partner. When this happens, you produce authentically negative relationship experiences, overt struggles that reflect the negative and polarizing emotional values of an oppositional force of mind.

Overt struggles in interaction with others invite a predicable pattern of *attack-and-defense*[43] that can easily spiral into a back-and-forth of attacks, defenses, counterattacks, and counter-defenses, where you and a relationship partner each try to prove yourself "right" and the other "wrong" in an unwinnable struggle.[44]

Pattern of Overt and Direct Struggle		
Partner 1	Attack	→
Partner 2	Defense/Attack	→
Partner 1	Defense/Attack	→ ...

Consider an example.[45] Pat is explaining to her husband Gordon that their young daughter is tired because she didn't have a nap at school earlier in the day. Gordon invites her to engage openly in an oppositional relationship dynamic when he indirectly criticizes and blames his wife, symbolizing his "attack," a reflexive reaction produced by his brain in response to the perception of a threat or offense. His wife comes back at him with her own counterattack, a defensive

---

43 D'Amico-Reisner, *An Ethnolinguistic Study of Disapproval Exchanges*, 38.

44 D'Amico-Reisner, *Power and Solidarity in Disapproval Exchanges between Intimates: A Gender Issue?* 1993a: Presented at the International Association of Applied Linguistics (AILA, Amsterdam, 1993) and, at the American Association for Applied Linguistics (AAAL, Altanta, 1993).

45 D'Amico-Reisner, *An Ethnolinguistic Study of Disapproval Exchanges*, 38.

justification underscoring that "*it didn't happen before.*" When her husband tries to back down by withdrawing, she aggressively reasserts her defense as a counterattack, pointing out that it hadn't happened before ("*Well, it didn't*") and admonishing him for his sarcasm ("*Don't be sarcastic*"):

> **Husband:** So, is that gonna happen all the time? [Attack]
> **Wife:** Did it happen before at school? [Attack]
> **Husband:** I don't know. [Defense]
> **Wife:** Well, it didn't. Don't be sarcastic. [Attack]

You probably can't imagine having a similar interaction directly with a friend. This is because you "see" your rights and obligations differently with different types of relationship partners. You generally don't feel entitled to control a friend to the same extent that you do a spouse or domestic partner. This explains why just about anything a spouse does or does do can trigger your brain to react and position you for attack-and-defense. Whether your wife didn't put your child down for a nap, your husband left the living room lights on, or you're your partner forgot to run an errand, your brain perceives and responds to a threat stimulus in the same automatic and negative way, posturing you in opposition and disrupting the balance of a relationship dynamic.

In a dynamic created by marital partners, various aspects of *small self* commonly engage to defend their respective views, beliefs, values, and expectations. When struggle is overtly and directly shaped through their interaction with each other, a battle of the small selves can intensify and extend a negative relationship dynamic. It might be a battle between one partner's *control freak* self and the other's *people pleaser* self, or between one person's *needy* self and the other's *enabler* self. Whatever aspects of *small self* step forward to do battle, it will always play out in a predictable pattern of attack-and-defense, reflecting the negative and polarizing force of opposition that can only inhibit connection and cause separation.

Using an example given earlier, notice how spouses shape a negative and polarizing dynamic together through a subtle but clearly understood pattern of attack-and-defense:

> **Jeff:** [Referring to the couch] That thing is filthy. [Attack]
> **Elizabeth:** I know. I tried to clean it, but it just won't come clean. [Defense]
> **Jeff:** You didn't use the right stuff. [Attack]
> **Elizabeth:** Why are you criticizing me as soon as you get home from work. [Attack]
> **Jeff:** I'm not criticizing you. [Defense]
> **Elizabeth:** You are, and you don't even realize it. [Attack]
> **Jeff:** Gets up from the couch and walks out the room in a huff [Attack]

Both Jeff and Elizabeth want the couch clean, and they both want a nice evening with one another. Yet they allow themselves to act out their negative feelings, jointly evolving a negative and polarizing *me-against-you* dynamic that will influence their respective thoughts, recollections, and imaginings about one another in their respective worlds of consciousness. By jointly shaping opposition in their interaction together and entangling themselves in a pattern of attack-and-defense, they allow themselves to sustain an imbalanced relationship dynamic that inhibits power-sharing and positive reciprocity. If the pattern is familiar enough, it will cause them to root more deeply in their respective positions and sustain a lack of power-sharing and positive reciprocity.

What exactly happened? Jeff's brain reacted to the perception of an offense, triggered when he noticed the couch. Although his brain was programmed to produce the negative script, perceptual inattention causes him to continue "on automatic" after he realizes what he's doing. He shares his negative story with his Elizabeth, indirectly but overtly criticizing her for not cleaning the couch when he says, *"That thing is filthy."*

At first, his wife rejects his invitation to create imbalance in their dynamic (*"I know. I tried to clean it, but it just won't come clean"*). We know this because she responds by agreeing with him and acknowledges how what he says is true. Her attempts represent her effort to maintain balance as Jeff tempts her to lose her emotional footing. But when he counters with a *direct* criticism (*"You didn't ..."*), she reacts with her own defensive criticism (*"Why are you ...?"*). Jeff becomes defensive and denies what is really true for him, that the dirty couch bothers him, which causes Elizabeth to emphasize her criticism. The interaction ends with Jeff leaving the room "in a huff," a passive-aggressive but antagonistic move that clearly announces his disconnection from Elizabeth at that moment.

Over time, the couple may extend their negative thoughts, recollections, and imaginings from this single relationship situation to how they more generally "see" each other. Elizabeth may come to feel Jeff *always* criticizes her while Jeff may feel Elizabeth *never listens*. If they don't learn how to rebalance the negative and polarizing dynamic they evolve jointly, and if they are each sufficiently invested perceiving themselves to be "right" and one another "wrong," their negative perceptions of one another will cause them to produce the same familiar negative melody every time they engage in overt struggle with each other. His *always critical* self and her *never listens* self will reliably and easily come into play to fight their emotional battles with one another, entangling them in a familiar pattern of attack-and-defense. They may even come to see their entire relationship only as this familiar melody, limiting their experiences of one another to their respective negative perceptions.

At any point in their interaction together, either of them can choose to reframe the story they tell themselves, enabling them to interrupt and revalue the emotional struggle between her *always critical* self and his *never listens* self. To do that, one of them needs to refuse to be pulled into the negative and polarizing dynamic and revise how they "see."

In response to Jeff's initial criticism (*"That thing is filthy," "You didn't use the right stuff"*), Elizabeth can stop herself from accepting her husband's invitation to engage in a familiar and negative pattern that they "know" from past experience will not serve the relationship. If she does this, she can avoid encouraging the negative attack-and-defense spiral from gaining negative momentum. She might consider her husband's perspective. If she chooses to see that he is tired and hungry after a long day at work, she can suggest, *"Let's talk about this later, after we've had dinner and you've had a chance to relax."* Instead, she allows herself to react negatively without thinking. Maybe she doesn't feel that she is doing enough to keep the house clean. Or maybe she is just looking for an excuse to argue. Whatever the reasons for perceptual inattention, she can willfully choose to "see differently," in a way that supports a *me-and-you* relationship dynamic with her husband and will allow them to have a nice evening together. Even though she isn't the one who invited the *me-against-you* dynamic that put their struggle and entanglement into motion, she can be the one to choose to invite her husband to rebalance it.

Jeff can also invite Elizabeth to rebalance the dynamic he sets in motion. Once he recognizes that his brain has postured him for opposition, as soon as he hears himself say, *"That thing is filthy,"* or at any point in their interaction, he can reframe the story he tells himself to invite emotional linkages with his wife and align his interpretation of the situation with love, peace, forgiveness, gratitude, service or other positive and unifying emotional values generating the force of mind that is compassionate cooperation. Where Jeff to do this, he might have redirected opposition as compassionate cooperation in the following way:

> **Jeff**: [Referring to the ottoman] That thing is filthy. [Attack]
> **Elizabeth:** I know. I tried to clean it, but it just won't come clean. [Defense]
> **Jeff**: <u>I appreciate that you tried to clean it. But it really bothers me to see it looking dirty. I know it's not your fault. Maybe we can find a better product, one that'll do a better job. What do you think?</u> [Negative feelings revalued to invite linkages]
> **Wife:** Ok, sounds good. We can do it this weekend. [Agreement reflecting genuinely positive feelings]

The underlined text shows how Jeff uses his negative feelings to maintain balance in the dynamic he shapes with Elizabeth. By recognizing and expressing *gratitude* to his wife for her efforts (*"I appreciate that you tried to clean it"*) and by proposing a solution that considers inclusive needs and attends to power-sharing (*"Maybe we can find a better product, one that'll do a better job. What do you think?"*), he invites Elizabeth to transform their *always critical-never listens* power struggle and redirect their relationship experience. He doesn't have to give up his views about the couch, only talk about them differently in his interaction with himself as well as with his wife.

Reframing allows you to take responsibility for you *self*, who "you" are in any given instant, and your world of perception:

> By taking the responsibility for the consequences of his own perceptions, the observer can transcend the role of victim to an understanding that 'nothing out there has power over you'. It isn't life's events, but how one reacts to them and the attitude that one has about them, that determines whether such events have a positive or negative effect on one's life, whether they're experienced as opportunity or as stress.[46]

The exchange below is another example of how married partners tend to produce overt and direct struggles in their interactions with one another, and how they jointly and overtly shape an imbalanced *me-against-you* relationship dynamic, evidenced by the attack-and-defense pattern symbolizing a lack of shared power and positive reciprocity. In the example below, Mara's *control freak* self and her husband's *people pleaser* self engage in a familiar struggle they both recognize:

> **Mara:** Where were you with the television on. [Attack]
> **Richard:** Outside. [Defense]
> **Mara:** You know I don't have the key. [Attack]
> **Richard:** I didn't think you'd be here. [Defense]
> **Mara:** I've been waiting here for fifteen minutes. [Attack]
> **Richard:** I didn't think you'd be back so soon. [Defense]
> **Mara:** I said, "I'll be right back." I mean, do you know how frustrating that is? You said you'd be here. [Attack]
> **Richard:** So-rry. I didn't do it intentionally. [Defense (Apology)]

When a *control freak* and a *people pleaser* struggle, *control freak* typically takes an attacking role and *people pleaser* typically takes a defensive role. In the example, Richard's *people pleaser* final defense is an apology, which closes the conversation, but this doesn't necessarily mean that

---

46   Hawkins, *Power vs. Force*, 72.

he is genuinely sorry. In fact, when this exchange was overheard, the intonation of Richard's words communicated his resentment toward Mara, a response to her verbal attack. This suggests how you use language without thinking to convey emotional meaning beyond the symbols of words. You can say "sorry" and mean it, or you can not mean it, because words can camouflage or explicitly convey the attitudes and emotions that shape your relationship experiences. While camouflaging may preserve outward appearances and help avoid overt conflict, it neither corrects an imbalanced relationship dynamic nor means that people don't "read" the force of mind that is opposition.

Whatever triggers *people pleaser* to engage, and however it plays out, *people pleaser* is likely to use indirect and passive-aggressive strategies to bait *control freak* to react so he can play his familiar role of acquiescing. *Control freak,* on the other hand, is likely to use direct and aggressive strategies, which will cause *people pleaser* to defend, encouraging a counterattack from *control freak.* Together, they evolve a negative and polarizing dynamic that can spiral out of control as they push one another further away. Even if they maintain the appearance of polite interaction, they will recognize the familiar melody of their dynamic soon as one of them invites the other to engage. At any moment, either of them can reframe their story to redirect the force of mind that is opposition, which will affect the dynamic they evolve together and their joint experience of one another and their individual selves.

Consider another example where Sally's *needy* self engages with her domestic partner's *enabler* self in the attack-and-defense pattern shaping their overtly negative and polarizing relationship dynamic:

> **Sally:** You never pay attention to me. You're always doing work. [Attack]
>
> **Cooper:** What you mean. I *do* pay attention to you. [Defense]
>
> **Sally:** No, you don't. You're always doing work. [Attack]
>
> **Cooper:** I'm *not*. I'm right here. [Defense]
>
> **Sally:** Well, it doesn't feel like it. I'm really getting tired of this. You put everything else first, above me. [Attack]
>
> **Cooper:** Tired of what? What are you talking about, "I put everything above you"? I don't get it. I don't know what you want me to do. [Defense]
>
> **Sally:** (Walks out of the room and slams the door) [Attack]

Instead of being able to get what she needs from her partner, his attention, Sally's *needy* self ends up pushing Cooper away and disrupting their connection. Once she invites Cooper to extend the struggle she opens with her criticism, a verbal attack where she accuses him, "*You never pay attention to me. You're always doing work,"* and he responds defensively, their game is on. Unless one of them chooses to reframe their story, they will continue to shape a negative and polarizing *me-against-you* dynamic, where each is invested in his or her respective egocentric perspective, which can only produce separation, whether or not they engage openly with one another in struggle. In this situation, Sally wants attention and Cooper wants a pleasant and relaxing evening with Sally, but neither of them takes active steps to get what they need.

Overt, covert, indirect, or direct, any polarizing relationship *me-against-you* dynamic you invite or support negatively affects how you see a relationship partner in a present moment and will influence your thoughts, recollections, and imaginings about the person. When you allow the aspects of *small self* to engage as your brain directs you to, you avoid taking responsibility for your needs and interests in a way that preserves connection with others. Even if you keep your *small self* stories to your self, and you do your best give the appearance of a balanced relationship dynamic in your interaction with others, you will still inhibit connection because inauthentically positive relationship experiences can only support separation.

Redirecting Negative Alignments

The exchange below between two friends[47] shows how educated American women typically pull others into negative and polarizing alignments, extending a negative relationship dynamic beyond a single relationship and encouraging others to extend oppositional alignments against an absent person-object:

> **Amy:** We went over to Steve's mother's for dinner last Saturday night. The last time I was there for dinner we discussed how much I hate, absolutely hate, pot roast. So, what does she make for dinner? *Pot roast.* Ugh! And it was like shoe leather. I told her I don't like the meat because it falls apart. Well, this meat couldn't be ripped apart. Then she asks if I've had my thyroid checked.
> **Friend:** Oh, Amy.
> **Amy:** And the worst is that he's so close to her.
> **Friend:** How can anyone be like that?

In the example, Amy aligns her friend against Steve's mother, using her negative feelings about Steve's mother to get her friend to connect with her by making Steve's mother "wrong." At

---

47   D'Amico-Reisner, *An Ethnolinguistic Study of Disapproval Exchanges*, 122.

the expense of Steve's mother, Amy invites her friend to support her own negative biases. Amy's criticism about Steve's mother reflects her own egocentric "seeing" about Steve's mother. While Amy postures herself with her friend in a *me-and-you* orientation, she does so by using the *me-against-you* dynamic she creates with Steve's mother, and she encourages her friend to join in her negative alignment against Steve's mother.

Amy tells her friend that she told Steve's mother, *"I don't like the meat because it falls apart,"* then expresses criticism that *"this meat couldn't be ripped apart."* Amy's own words suggest that she would have found fault in however Steve's mother prepared the meat (*"like shoe leather"* or *"falls apart"*), or in whatever else Steve's mother might have decided to prepare for dinner instead of the meat. The issue for Amy isn't the meat. The comment *"And the worst is that he's so close to her"* suggests that Amy's real emotional issue is that she fears and resents the close relationship Steve and his mother share. It makes her angry because she feels entitled to have Steve to herself.

As Amy shares her negative story about Steve's mother with her friend, she simultaneously distances herself from Steve's mother, encouraging her friend to do the same. The friend aligns herself with Amy when she says, *"Oh, Amy,"* which encourages Amy to go on with her negative story about Steve's mother. While the friend may be unaware of her own contribution to strengthening Amy's opposition toward Steve's mother, her words, *"How can anyone be like that?"* are a criticism of Steve's mother that encourages Amy to cling more stubbornly to her unproductive and polarizing perceptions about Steve's mother.

Even though the friend may never have met Steve's mother, she buys into Amy's polarizing dynamic and makes it likely that Amy will perpetuate her negative perceptions about Steve's mother in future interactions with her. Instead of helping Amy reframe the negative story that prevents her from generating the force of compassionate cooperation and a unifying dynamic with Steve's mother, the friend encourages Amy to disconnect from Steve's mother. As a result, it is likely that Amy will continue to share the negative stories she tells herself about Steve's mother with her friend in future discussions, since she expects her friend to agree with her and support the negative alignment she perpetuates.

Even if Amy has no further interaction with Steve's mother, the negative stories she shares with her friend will reinforce and deepen her negative perception of Steve's mother. The more Amy and her friend talk about Steve's mother together while maintaining their negative alignment against her, the more deeply opposition will root and extend. While Amy's friend may think she is being a true friend by supporting Amy, she plays a critical role in encouraging Amy's oppositional relationship dynamic with Steve's mother and in strengthening Amy's habit of negative perception. The friend also strengthens her own predisposition to negativity as she helps shape the negative narrative about Steve's mother with Amy.

At any point in the exchange, either Amy or the friend could have chosen to redirect the force of opposition they jointly evolve about Steve's mother that encourages Amy to keep Steve's mother at an emotional distance. Importantly, they could have done this without jeopardizing their own connection. Consider how differently their conversation might have looked if Amy had taken an active role in revaluing her perceptions about Steve's mother once she realized she was generating the force of opposition that interrupts her potential for connection with Steve's mother:

> **Amy:** <u>We went over to Steve's mother's for dinner last Saturday night. The last time I was there for dinner we discussed how much I hate, absolutely hate, pot roast. So, what does she make for dinner? *Pot roast.* Ugh!</u> [Automatic reaction to the trigger of discord] It's definitely not my favorite, but I realize that she was doing her best.
>
> **Friend**: That's a really good way to look at it.
>
> **Amy:** Besides, it really wasn't about the food. It was about Steve getting to see his mother. I have to really work at not being upset by how close they are. It's really easy for me to feel jealous, because he thinks he's mother is such a great cook.
>
> **Friend:** Yeah, I know what you mean.

The underlined text points to Amy's initial automatic negative reaction. As soon as she recognized that she was postured in opposition, she might have clarified her feelings by asking herself, *"What's my real emotional issue?"* Had she been honest, she might have realized that her own irrational fears were causing her to react negatively toward Steve's mother, fears such as the fear of losing Steve to his mother or having Steve prefer his mother's cooking to hers. By recognizing the real issue, she would no longer need to continue spinning negative stories. By choosing to talk rationally about her feelings, she would be taking steps to connect with Steve's mother as well as with her friend.

Amy might have created alternative interpretations of the situation with Steve's mother, reframing her negative and polarizing narrative as a positive and unifying one. To transform her feelings of fear, anger, resentment, criticism, and entitlement into those of love, peace, gratitude, forgiveness, and service, Amy might have started by asking herself, *"What's my real issue?"* By confronting her feelings and trying to understand her real need, she might have been able to understand her negative biases. If she refocused her mind to hold herself accountable for supporting connection, she might have been able to realize that there is sufficient love to go around, and that it is unproductive and harmful to allow her negative perceptions about Steve's mother to persist.

Amy might also have realized that she was interfering with her own peace of mind by clinging to her biased perception of Steve's mother. She might have been able to realize how unfair and hurtful she was being by creating a negative picture of Steve's mother, and by encouraging her friend to align with her polarizing feelings about Steve's mother. Mostly, she might have come to see how she was causing herself pain by perpetuating a negative story about Steve's mother in self-talk. She might also have recognized that she alone could choose to generate the emotional values inviting compassionate cooperation that would cause her to feel connected to Steve's mother.

Amy might also have forgiven Steve's mother for ruining the meat, realizing she was doing her best, just as we all do. By choosing to see Steve's mother from a more inclusive perspective, rather than from the perspective of her own egocentric seeing, Amy might have been able to see her own humanness in Steve's mother. She might have tried to remember a time when she had wanted to prepare a special meal and it didn't come out exactly as she had hoped. She might also have thought about how the food was not as important as the opportunity to connect and feel satisfied with people, and how hard it must be for Steve's mother to have so little time with him after devoting a lifetime to raising him.

Amy might have shifted her thoughts to appreciating Steve's mother for preparing dinner, setting the table, and having them over for dinner. She might also have appreciated that Steve's mother works full time and that it took a lot of effort to create dinner, serve it, and clean up afterwards. She might also have thought about how she could help Steve's mother the next time they were invited over for dinner. Maybe she could prepare a dish and bring it along, or offer to come over early to help his mother set the table and do some of the pre-dinner clean up. The most important way that Amy could be of service, however, would be to see Steve's mother without error and reframe the negative and unproductive feelings inhibiting her from creating connection with Steve's mother.

At any point in their conversation, Amy's friend could have helped Amy "see" Steve's mother differently, in a way that encouraged Amy to position for connection with Steve's mother. By modeling compassionate cooperation, Amy's friend could have helped redirect Amy's negative and polarizing talk about Steve's mother. In so doing, she could have helped Amy heal her negative perceptions about Steve's mother, which position her to invite connection.

CHAPTER 4

Symbols, Strategies, and Techniques:
Tools for Shaping Compassionate Cooperation

True compassion is not just an emotional response, but a firm commitment founded on reason ... A truly compassionate attitude towards others does not change even if they behave negatively ... Whether people are beautiful and friendly or unattractive and disruptive, ultimately they are human beings, just like oneself ... When you recognize that all beings are equal in both their desire for happiness and their right to obtain it, you automatically feel empathy and closeness for them. Through accustoming your mind to this sense of universal altruism, you develop a feeling of responsibility for others.[48] —The Dalai Lama

The symbols, strategies, and techniques described in this chapter support the reframing process described in chapter 3. Using these tools can help you take an active participant-observer role in your interaction with your self and with others. They provide support for redirecting the force of mind that is opposition as compassionate cooperation and creating the authentically positive relationship experiences with others. Even with the most challenging relationship partners, you can take steps to remove the obstacles to connection, redirect the negative attention you give your thoughts, recollections, and imaginings, and rebalance a relationship dynamic to invite and support connection.

Language and Other Symbols — *The Notes of Your Song*

Every thought, recollection, or imagining you create and allow to persist in consciousness affects the quality, authenticity, and outcomes of your personal relationships. Because your brain is in

---

48   His Holiness, The Dalai Lama, "On Compassion," http://www.dalailama.com/messages/compassion.

a constant process of interaction with internal and external stimuli, it is continuously inferring, extending, deepening, and reshaping meaning. Your brain extends meaning to images, sounds, and other stimuli, which is why you shape how you see a person or relationship situation in your consciousness, using many different kinds of symbols.

Language elements are not the only kind of symbols you use to shape perception, but they are the ones focused on here. Because you are socialized into using language in ways that other members of your "in group" understand, you are adept at using language elements to symbolize meaning in complex ways. This explains why you can learn the grammar and vocabulary of a foreign language and lack an understanding of the complicated social rules that govern its symbolic use. It also explains why you can improve how you communicate with a relationship partner without improving your relationship.

You routinely draw on linguistic elements to shape your thoughts, recollections, and imaginings. The symbols you choose to shape the attention you give to a relationship partner or situation determine what you think, how you feel, and what you remember about people, relationships, and life in general. Without much awareness, you use language elements in your interaction with your self and others to create your illusions of people and relationship situations.

The language symbols you draw to shape how you see people and life, include sentence patterns (syntax), word choices, intonation, body posturing, and gesturing.[49] By learning more about how you use these language elements to generate the force of mind that is opposition or compassionate cooperation, you can learn how to make more active choices to redirect opposition and the negative and polarizing relationship dynamic associated with it.

Sentence Patterns

Have you ever wondered why there are so many ways to express the same idea? In the constantly evolving symbolic system that is language, a dynamic process of inferred and implied meaning, these different grammar patterns enable you to shape emotional meaning in subtle and not so subtle ways, to emphasize, prioritize, make things count, and ignore.

When it comes to shaping negative perception and authentically negative relationship experiences, grammar patterns play an important role. Some patterns overtly and directly symbolize opposition, tending to cause predictable struggles of attack-and-defense in social interaction, while others covertly or indirectly symbolize opposition. The more covert or indirect a symbolic value, the less likely it will cause overt conflict. But since all negative attitudes and

---

49   Linguistic, paralinguistic, and nonlinguistic elements are referred to as *language elements*.

emotions generate the force of mind that is opposition, whether overt and direct or covert or indirect, they polarize and interfere with connection, however social interaction with others plays out.

One grammar pattern that overtly and directly symbolizes the force of mind that is opposition and postures you for struggle in interaction with others is the *rhetorical question,* an arrangement of words with falling intonation at the end that resembles a question form but implies the answer to the question in the question itself.

Rhetorical Questions

- *What are you crazy?*

- *How the hell am I supposed to know?*

- *What the fuck were you thinking?*

- *Now, what am I supposed to do?*

The symbolic value of the *rhetorical question* is strongly and clearly oppositional. It leaves no room for alternative interpretations, explicitly symbolizing the *me-against-you* relationship dynamic produced by a negative and polarizing force of mind.

The *rhetorical question* strongly symbolizes opposition on its own, but word choices with inherently negative symbolic value, such as *crazy, hell,* and *fuck,* intensify negative and polarizing value even more. In your interaction with your self, when you shape perception using a *rhetorical question,* you box yourself into negative "seeing" and invite a *me-against-you* relationship dynamic with the person or people who are the object of your thoughts, recollections, and imaginings. In your interaction with others, you make your intention to polarize and separate from a relationship partner clear. You also invite overt struggle.

Consider an example where Jason's wife has just triggered his brain to react negatively when she points out that *"the dishes in the dishwasher are clean,"* implying that he should have emptied the dishwasher. Jason thinks, *"Why do have to do this now? Can't you see I'm working? The last thing I'm thinking about is the dishes."* While his private thought generates the force of mind that is opposition and may cause him to see his wife as a "nag" or through the veil of other negative perceptions, it probably won't provoke overt struggle with his wife unless she criticizes him for ignoring what she's said (or other situational symbols may cause them to engage openly in conflict). However, if Jason is on "auto-pilot" and speaks his thought to his wife in interaction with her, it is likely to cause a predictable pattern of attack-and-defense between them. Even if it doesn't, it will affect the way Jason's wife sees him, because it clearly displays an imbalance of power-sharing that favors Jason.

A *rhetorical question* symbolizes clear power-taking in a relationship dynamic, whether you keep a thought to yourself or share it in interaction with others. It has great potential to disturb the balance of *compassionate cooperation,* the positive and unifying force of mind reflected in a balanced dynamic. As a result, it has great potential to interfere with connection. On the other hand, if you are trying to provoke a relationship partner to engage in struggle, or you want to push a relationship partner away, shaping meaning with a *rhetorical question* will do it.

A second type of grammar pattern that symbolizes opposition is the *directive,* an order to do something or stop doing something.

Directives

- *Move that shit!*
- *Get the fuck off the road!*
- *Don't do that!*
- *Just do it!*

When you use a *directive* to shape your thoughts, recollections, or imaginings about others, you overtly and directly take your power in a relationship dynamic, causing an imbalance in the dynamic. Ordering a person to do something or avoid doing something reflects entitlement, your perception that you have the right to exert control over another person. While you might use a *directive* to warn someone of danger (*Get away from the stove!*), you would intend a different symbolic meaning because of the different context. When your brain postures you for opposition and you draw on a *directive* to symbolize it, you overtly and directly convey a negative and polarizing force of mind when you interact with a relationship partner.

As with a *rhetorical question,* opposition symbolized by a *directive* clearly invites a *me-against-you* relationship dynamic and encourages struggle, because it clearly and undeniably conveys an oppositional force of mind. If you want to start an argument with your spouse or domestic partner, these two sentence patterns are likely to do it, because they invite a defensive reaction or counterattack. Because they are so disruptive to power-sharing in a relationship dynamic, they tend to lead to overt struggles. Even when they don't, they intensify opposition and separation, because they are symbolically polarizing.

Lack of power-sharing invites a lack of positive reciprocity in a relationship dynamic, where you feel more entitled and deserving than a relationship partner. This tends to cause you to withhold the kindnesses and linkages that cause balance in a relationship dynamic. Even if you keep a thought private, if you shape it with symbolically polarizing value, you generate the force of mind that is opposition. If Allan is annoyed when his husband asks him to water the plants and thinks, *Do it yourself*, this thought, if allowed to persist, draws on its symbolic value of entitlement to reinforce a lack of power-sharing and positive reciprocity in the evolving dynamic between them. The symbolic value of your every single thought, however insignificant it may seem, determines where your relationship "is" at any instant as well as who "you" are.

The oppositional value of a *wh-question* or a *comment* symbol tends to be more ambiguous and deniable, which is why these patterns are less likely to cause overt struggle in interaction with others than a *rhetorical question* or *directive*. There is no guarantee that shaping negative thoughts, recollections, and imaginings with a *wh-question* or *comment* will generate a polarizing force of mind, or that these symbols won't lead to overt struggle, but when you use these forms in interaction with others to convey opposition, they are less likely to provoke overt struggle.

Wh-questions begin with the words *who, what, where, when, or why*. When this sentence pattern symbolizes opposition, it is shaped by "falling intonation" at the end of the sentence pattern, a shift in pitch and frequency that distinguishes it from a "genuine information-seeking question"[50].

Wh-Questions

- *Why did you move my books?*
- *Who made the mess in the kitchen?*
- *What are you doing with my keys?*
- *Where are my shoes?*

---

50 Thanks to a small grant I received from the Haskins Lab, an affiliate of Yale University that conducts research on spoken and written language, I was able to feed natural speech samples into a VAX computer and quantify differences in pitch and frequency between *wh-questions* intended to convey disapproval and those intended as genuine information-seeking questions, confirming that intonation alone can be a distinguishing feature of expressions of disapproval. The results of this work are summarized in D'Amico-Reisner, 1985.

Compare a *wh-question* exchange where the question is intended as a genuine information-seeking question with one symbolizing opposition:

Genuine Question → Genuine Response
    John: What are you doing this afternoon?
    Alex: I'm going to stay home and read.

Opposition → Defense (Justification)
    Bill: Who made the mess in the kitchen?
    Derrick: I'm going to clean it up.

A *wh-question* symbolizing the force of mind that is opposition points directly to what you feel a relationship partner did or said "wrong." Yet, it allows you to do so without owning up to your own negative biases or what's driving them. While the ambiguity of the grammar pattern, the fact that it "appears" to be a genuine question, allows you to claim, *"That's not what I meant"* when a relationship partner confronts your opposition. Of course, since intonation typically clarifies the symbolic value of the grammar, your denial of your intended meaning tends to advance the attack-and-defense pattern of struggle with a relationship partner.

Typically, when you shape opposition in your interaction with a relationship partner using a *wh-question* that begins with *"Why,"* you invite a defensive response, often symbolized by justification or apology. Consider an example given earlier and how the *wh-question* symbolizes opposition and provokes a defensive response, an apology: *"Sorry. I thought you could just go for an hour."*

> **Mark:** <u>Why did you tell your brother I'd help him on Saturday</u>? I told you I don't want to go over there this week. [Attack]
> **Erica:** Sorry. I thought you could just go for an hour. [Defense]
> **Mark:** No, I can't. It's my one free afternoon over there, and I don't want to spend it there. [Attack]
> **Erica:** Sorr-y. You don't have to get all mad about it. [Defense]

Although opposition symbolized by a *wh-question* form clearly disrupts the balance of power-sharing and reciprocity in a relationship dynamic, evidenced by the attack-and-defense pattern that always indicates an imbalanced dynamic, its resemblance to genuine information-seeking questions makes it *seem* more polite than opposition symbolized by the unambiguous symbol a *rh-question* or *directive*. After all, *"that's not what I meant"* is a possible response option to a *wh-question* symbolizing opposition, however disingenuous it is.

The most ambiguous grammar pattern symbolizing opposition is the *comment,* because it is the most deniable. *"I'm just saying …"*

Comments
• There's no more coffee.
• The trash needs to be taken out.
• That [thing] is filthy.
• There are no more paper towels.

Comments symbolizing opposition are typically the least coercive because they reflect "normal" statement form, subject-verb-object, and lack the shifts from this baseline that produce emphasis or prioritize information in a way that strongly disrupts the balance of power-sharing and reciprocity in a relationship dynamic. This doesn't mean they can't be strong symbols of opposition, only that they don't provoke overt struggle in interaction with a relationship partner. Because of their highly ambiguous nature, *comments* are most likely to make interaction seem polite and preserve "face" while they may hide an intensely oppositional force of mind. This happens frequently in workplace situations and other hierarchy networks, resulting in inauthentically positive relationship experiences where there is a mismatch between a negative force of mind and inauthentically positive interaction.

Comments symbolizing opposition typically reflect word choices that have polarizing meaning unique to relationship partners, and are accompanied by recognizable shifts in gestures, body language, and intonation from what you recognize as "normal" in your interaction with others. These symbolic shifts convey an oppositional force of mind.

With *comments* symbolizing opposition, criticism is usually clearly conveyed through these symbolic shifts and through word choice. The more ambiguous the word choice, the more space you have for denying your intended message to a relationship partner. One spouse who says to the other, *"There are no more paper towels"* can easily deny your intent to criticize, claiming, *"It was just an observation."* However, *"You should have bought more paper towels,"* or, *"Why the hell didn't you stop at the store to buy paper towels?"* are directly accusatory and more strongly invite overt struggle.

You are most at risk for inviting overt struggle when you are tired, hungry, or irritable. This is when you are most vulnerable to perceptual inattention with the people you feel most comfortable with, typically a spouse or domestic partner. At these times, it's easy to allow your brain to take over, responding automatically and negatively to perceived threats as it postures you for opposition and evolving the *me-against-you* dynamic that inhibits connection and causes separation. When this happens, even when you use *comments,* the most ambiguous sentence pattern symbol you can use to convey an oppositional force of mind, you will likely disambiguate your meaning by drawing on other negatively symbolic features, such as intonation and body posture.

On the other hand, some sentence patterns are symbolically positive and unifying because they draw others in and reflect inclusive seeing. *Genuine questions* are an example, especially in situations where you need to problem-solve issues with a relationship partner. Reconsider an example given earlier where Beth reframes an oppositional force of mind and re-scripts the negative story she tells herself about her parents:

Mom and Dad, I am so grateful that you and dad take the time to come and visit. It's important to me that we continue spending time together as a family. I wouldn't want it any other way. However, Jeff and I really want to have Saturday afternoons together alone. I hope you understand. I'm sure you remember how it was to be newlywed! We can come over to your place on Sunday morning after we go to the gym if that works for you. Or you could visit on Thursday evening. <u>Would one of those ideas work for you?</u>

Using genuine questions to reflect inclusive needs and interests symbolize an attempt to evolve a relationship dynamic cooperatively. They are critically important in your interaction with others when you are striving to sustain a balanced relationship dynamic because they symbolize power-sharing and positive reciprocity between you and a relationship partner.

Word Choices

You intensify a language symbol of opposition when you use word choices that convey or enhance negatively meaning.

Some words, like *fuck, shit,* and *hell,* are inherently negative symbols. Although you can use them playfully or humorously, they have negative value and generally enhance the intensity of polarization. If your husband moved your coat from the chair in spite of your protests and you said, *"What the fuck are you doing?"* he'd probably perceive your words as a stronger and more polarizing symbol of your oppositional force of mind than if you said, *"What are you doing?"*

Negative Words Strengthen Opposition

- *What <u>the fuck</u> are you doing?*

- *How <u>the hell</u> did you do that?*

- *Why <u>the hell</u> did you tell him I'd be there?*

Words do not have to be inherently negative symbols to become negative symbols to the relationship partners who come to perceive their negative meaning. In family systems, any words can become negative symbols representing familiar conflict themes across time and physical space. Consider, for instance, a situation where David struggled continuously with his teenage daughter Sarah because she didn't want to practice the violin and he wanted to control the amount of time she practiced. In their family system, the word *violin* became negatively "loaded." Just the thought of the word caused the anticipation of struggle. Even years later, the word carried remnants of oppositional force from the recollections of past struggles even though the issue no longer triggers opposition between David and his daughter.

Just as you can choose words that strengthen the polarizing force of opposition, you can choose words with positive and unifying symbolic value to mitigate an oppositional force of mind as you work to create linkages with others.

Mitigating phrases are an important tool for lessening the force of opposition and creating a balanced power and reciprocity dynamic in a relationship. They allow you to "own" an opinion or view without trying to force a relationship partner to have to have the same opinion or view. Examples include *"I think that," "In my view,"* and *"In my opinion."* Consider an interaction between an adult daughter, Susan, and her mother, Elaine. If Susan rejects her mother's view with a criticism like *"That's absurd,"* it is more polarizing than if she says, *"<u>I think that's</u> absurd."*

Terms of endearment are also examples of mitigators. You can use words such as *sweetie, darling, honey, love,* and *babe* to address a spouse, domestic partner, or child if you use them normally in interaction with these partners that do not reflect an oppositional force of mind. If so, they will help you invite a balance of power and reciprocity between you as you work to clarify your feelings and express your needs rationally:

Parent to Child: <u>Sweetie</u>, I am feeling really frustrated right now. I need your help or I'm really gonna lose it. I need you to turn off the TV and take out your homework, okay?

Spouse to Spouse: <u>Honey</u>, I'm started to feel irritated. I'm really hungry. If I don't stop and get something to eat, I'm going to be grumpy. Can you stop for pizza at the next place you see?

In the examples, these words mitigate opposition and invite a balanced relationship dynamic, as do the genuine questions, *"I need you to turn off the TV and take out your homework, okay?"* and *"Can you stop for pizza at the next place you see?"* that symbolize inclusive seeing.

You can use any words to rebalance a relationship dynamic and redirect opposition but they have to reflect positive perception and the genuinely positive and unifying force of mind it generates that is *compassionate cooperation.*

Intonation

Shifts in intonation, pitch and frequency, deviations from a recognized "normal" reflecting a balanced relationship dynamic, symbolize the force of mind that is opposition and can provoke patterns of attack-and-defense in interaction with others. In the example below, Francesca and Bo are domestic partners. Francesca accuses Bo of taking her keys, creating polarization in their relationship dynamic symbolized by the falling intonation of a *wh-question, "What did you do with my keys?"*

> **Francesca:** What did you do with my keys? [Attack]
> **Bo:** Why don't you check your bag before you start accusing me? [Attack]
> **Francesca:** I'm not accusing you! I just asked ... [Defense]

While Francesca's language clearly symbolizes opposition, she is able to deny her intention (*"I'm not accusing you! I just asked ..."*) because the sentence pattern she uses sometimes serves other functions. Of course, since her intonation is a negative symbol in itself, she's not fooling anyone but herself by not owning up to her accusation. Bo's counterattack shows that he has understood Francesca's accusation, *"Why don't you check your bag before you start accusing me?"* Like Francesca, Bo uses a *wh-question*, drawing the negatively symbolic value of his intonation to show he's taken the bait of Francesca's opposition and positioned himself defensively, at the ready for a struggle.

Wh-question patterns with falling intonation are clear symbols of an oppositional force of mind. Native speakers of American English can easily recognize the symbolic value of a message from intonation alone. Compare the example just given with the following exchange, where a different, typically more rising intonation at the end of the sentence, communicates a genuine question: "*What are you doing Saturday night?*"

> **Eve:** What are you doing Saturday night?
> **Gary:** Not sure. Why?
> **Eve:** I was thinking of catching a movie. Wanna come?
> **Gary:** Maybe.

In the example, Gary clearly understands that the question is genuine[51] and responds accordingly by giving an answer to Eve's question, "*Not sure. Why?*"

Intonation is an important symbol of negative perception and plays an enormously important role in how you communicate and interpret opposition in your interaction with others. It is often an indicator of resentment. By learning to recognize how it affects the way you communicate a negative and polarizing force of mind, you can become more aware of using this symbol in ways that maintain and restore balance in a relationship dynamic.

Body Posturing, Facial Expression, and Gesturing

Subtle shifts in body posturing, facial expression, and gesturing are negatively symbolic when they reflect deviations from "normal," the values associated with a balanced relationship dynamic. These recognizable deviations symbolize an oppositional force of mind and convey fear, anger, resentment, criticism, and entitlement, and other emotions of negative perception. Often, these negative symbols are the giveaway in an inauthentically positive relationship experience, where you attempt to hide your negative feelings in interaction with others. While you probably won't be called on to own up to your negative feelings if those shifts are subtle and indirect, there's little doubt you'll be messaging your attitudes and emotions of opposition.

Reconsider a situation introduced earlier where Dee agrees to have dinner at her mother-in-law's with her husband Jay although she doesn't want to go, having convinced her self that her mother-in-law is controlling. The exchange shows how you can communicate an oppositional force of mind in a way that allows you to avoid overt confrontation with a relationship partner. In the example, Dee reluctantly agrees to go to dinner, a situation that always causes an argument

---

51   More specifically, he understands the question as an invitation to negotiate a social commitment. See Nessa Wolfson, Lisa Huber, and Lynne D'Amico-Reisner, *How to Arrange for Social Commitments in American English: The Invitation,* In Nessa Wolfson and Elliot Judd, eds., *Sociolinguistics and Language Acquisition* (Rowley, MA: Newbury House, 1983).

between her and Jay before they go. Once they are there, Dee is sufficiently polite to avoid confrontation at dinner. But everyone there will likely understand that she's got an issue, even if they aren't sure what it is:

> **Mother-in-Law:** [Begins to serve Dee a piece of fish]
>
> **Dee:** No, no, that's okay [Raises the palm of her hand to signal stop as she looks at the plate of fish with mild disgust]. I'm good.
>
> **Mother-in-Law:** I thought you liked fish.
>
> **Dee:** No, it's okay. I'm good. [Picks at the vegetables on her plate, avoiding eye contact for the rest of the meal and staying quiet.]

Dee's subtle but negatively symbolic body posturing, facial expression, and gesturing communicate her *me-against-you* force of mind. Chances are that when Dee and Jay leave dinner, Jay will confront her opposition. If he does, it will likely spark an overt verbal struggle between them, since it's a negative theme in their relationship. It might even cause a struggle between them that spirals out of control and interrupts connection to one another for hours or days. If it continues to be an issue that deepens and extends across their relationship, gaining momentum from other negative themes that imbalance the relationship dynamic they create together, it might even contribute to the demise of their relationship.

Non-verbal expressions can be powerful symbols of negative perception it and a passive-aggressive invitation to engage in overt conflict. Any deviation from a recognized "normal" associated with positive perception will convey an oppositional force of mind and can invite struggle.

Non-Verbal Symbols of Opposition

- Walking out of a room in a huff
- Smirking
- Scowling
- Sighing loudly
- Clicking the tongue

Non-Verbal Symbols of Opposition
• Rolling the eyes
• Crossing the arms in front of the chest
• Turning the body away from a person who is talking
• Slamming the door
• Averting the eyes during conversation
• Pursing the lips
• Dismissing wave of a hand
• Pointing and shaking the index finger

Context determines the meaning of non-verbal symbols. You can cross your arms in front of your chest because you are cold or because your negative force of mind is so intense that it causes you to project the separation you generate in consciousness. As you bring more attention to your non-verbal habits, you can become more aware of how non-verbal symbols can interfere with your relationship goals so you can adjust them to help you redirect opposition and the polarizing *me-against-you* dynamic it causes. Even without words, you have a moment-by-moment opportunity to rebalance a relationship dynamic to demonstrate the values of positive perception that cause compassionate cooperation.

Strategies and Techniques – *Creating the "Song of Heart"*

You can use the strategies and techniques described below to help you revalue negative perception and redirect the force of mind that is opposition as compassionate cooperation. As you work to reframe thoughts, recollections, and imaginings characterized by negative emotional values such as fear, anger, resentment, criticism, and entitlement into those characterized by love, peace, gratitude, forgiveness, and service, these tools can help you rebalance a negative relationship dynamic by restoring power-sharing and positive reciprocity, indicative of *me-and-you* "seeing."

Engage in Compassionate Listening

Compassionate listening is active and empathic listening. It is a way for you to work on understanding the needs and interests of others so you can strive to take them into account as you problem-solve and negotiate together. By genuinely listening to a relationship partner, you can work together to uncover the underlying need causing an oppositional force of mind. Every human wants to be heard. Compassionate listening allows you to give a relationship partner a voice.

Two Steps to *Compassionate Listening*

1   Acknowledge a relationship partner's feelings, and the emotional need driving an oppositional reaction.

2   Ask for, or propose, a solution for the good of the relationship that addresses the other person's real need.

Resist allowing yourself to get caught up in a relationship partner's negative reaction. This isn't easy, because a negative reaction typically provokes a negative response. This is where it's useful to remind yourself how the brain causes automatic negative and irrational responses. Instead of allowing yourself to support a negative dynamic, stay focused on the process of compassionate listening. Remind yourself that a dramatic performance masks the real need behind the negative reaction that is the source of opposition. Try to understand the real need underlying a partner's words, what is driving the emotional reaction. Avoid judging, criticizing, rejecting, defending, and attacking, because it will encourage deeper resistance and perpetuate *me-against-you* posturing, increasing the chances of overt struggle. Put yourself in a relationship partner's shoes and genuinely try to understand what the real need is. Oftentimes, it has nothing to do with the words a person is speaking.

Listen without judgment. Avoid seeing the other person's feelings as silly, crazy, unfounded, ridiculous, or invalid. Just listen and try to make your partner feel safe in confronting the egocentric expressions of "small self." Avoid interrupting when a relationship partner is talking. Once she is finished, reflect back on what you have heard. "*I hear that you are* [upset/frustrated/annoyed]." While these words may seem trite, they validate a person's feelings and help rebalance a relationship dynamic.

Avoid entangling yourself in a relationship partner's emotions and strive to keep thought and expression aligned with the positive values of compassionate cooperation such as love, peace, gratitude, forgiveness, and service. Work to suggest a solution for the good of the relationship that genuinely satisfies a relationship partner's needs. Ask for what you need and help a relationship partner do the same. *"What do you need? How can I help?"* and *"Let me tell you what I need so you can help me"* prompt rational talk about the real emotional needs driving oppositional reactions.

Compassionate listening is a way for you to disengage from the pattern of attack-and-defense that defines overt struggle. At any moment, in situations where relationship type and circumstance allow, you can use compassionate listening to move away from the egocentric seeing that causes you to defend your positions, views, values, and expectations with singleness of purpose. By learning that you do not need to prove yourself right and others wrong, you can step away from the emotional struggle.

Consider the following example. Rob has just come home from work and is hungry, tired, and irritable. He sees that his domestic partner Vicki has not emptied the dishwasher, which causes his brain to react automatically with resentment. Before he can stop himself, he communicates the negative script that flows into his mind, pointing out what Vicki has done wrong:

Rob: Why didn't you empty the dishwasher? [Attack]

Rob's oppositional force of mind causes him to invite Vicki to the *me-against-you* relationship dynamic he proposes. Consider what might happen if Vicki has also had a bad day and she allows herself to buy into the negative and polarizing dynamic Rob initiates. She might respond,

Vicki: Why didn't I empty the dishwasher? Why didn't YOU empty the dishwasher? [Attack] I do more work around here … [Defense] When was the last time you went to the grocery store? [Attack]

It's easy to imagine how a seemingly insignificant matter such as emptying the dishwasher can generate an oppositional force of mind that causes momentary separation or even spiral you so far away from a partner that it ruins your entire evening or day together. It can also dramatically and negatively bias your thoughts, recollections, and imaginings about a person, which strengthens a negative dynamic and causes negative patterns to root. With a spouse or domestic partner, these patterns shape familiar "songs and dances" in a relationship, reflecting conflict themes that are often stacked and merged[52] in a futile struggle that can only lead to separation.

---

52   Lynne D'Amico-Reisner, "That Same Old Song and Dance: Repetition as a Critical Discourse Feature in Disapproval Exchanges between Intimates." 1993b. Presented at the American Association for Applied Linguistics (AAAL, Atlanta, GA: 1993) and the International Association of Applied Linguistics (AILA, Amsterdam: 1993).

Compassionate listening can help you avoid entanglement in a negative relationship dynamic. If Vicki had chosen to engage in compassionate listening instead of buying into Rob's *me-against-you* dynamic, she could have helped rebalance their dynamic. Instead, she allows a familiar struggle to emerge between Rob's *controller* self and her *never good enough* self. If Vicki were to engage compassionate listening to help redirect opposition, their conversation might have looked something like this:

> **Rob:** Why didn't you empty the dishwasher. [Attack]
> **Vicki:** <u>I hear that you are upset because</u> I didn't empty the dishwasher. [Acknowledgement] <u>What do you need? How can I help?</u> [Cooperative Posturing] I didn't realize it was so important to you or I would have done it. [Cooperative Posturing] Why don't you go take a shower and change, and I'll do it now, and then we can have a nice dinner together. [Solution]

Choosing to engage in compassionate listening is a commitment to redirect a negative and polarizing relationship dynamic because it shifts your awareness from "me" to "we" and prioritizes inclusive seeing.

Clarify *True-For-Me* Statements (Avoid *Accusatory You Statements*)

Accusatory you statements assign blame to a relationship partner and symbolize criticism. Some are overgeneralizations of behavior that with begin with the words, *You never …* or *You always …*

You always … You never …
• <u>*You always*</u> *expect me to pay the bills.*
• <u>*You always*</u> *say you're going to help, but you never do.*
• <u>*You never*</u> *make time for me.*
• <u>*You never*</u> *pick up your clothes.*

Accusatory you statements invite separation by baiting a relationship partner. They reflect egocentric seeing and a commitment to polarizing, encouraging responses that justify, defend, and enhance the risk of overt argument:

Wife: <u>You always</u> expect me to pay the bills. [Accusation]

Husband: That's not true [Defense]. <u>You never</u> ask me to pay the bills. <u>You always</u> ... [Counter-Accusation]

Other types of *accusatory you statements* imply blame, pointing out that a relationship partner has done something *wrong* or failed to do something *right,* communicated by the phrases, *You should ... You shouldn't ... You should have ... You shouldn't have ... You did something ... You didn't do something ... You could've ...*

You should, shouldn't, did, didn't, could've, should have, shouldn't have ...

- *<u>You should</u> watch her, dear.*

- *<u>You shouldn't</u> fold those like that.*

- *<u>You [did something,</u> e.g. took my car keys].*

- *<u>You didn't</u> empty the dishwasher.*

- *<u>You could've</u> stopped at the store.*

- *<u>You should have</u> stopped to get milk.*

- *<u>You shouldn't have</u> put my sweater in the dryer.*

Accusatory you statements are judgments that reflect biased seeing and your attempt to control how others think, speak, act, and look. They point the finger of blame at a relationship partner and represent a refusal to accept personal responsibility for the real need causing negative perception.

By becoming more aware of your interaction with your self, you have the opportunity to take responsibility for the real emotional needs causing your *accusatory you statements.* By learning how to talk about your real needs using *true-for-me statements,* you can take responsibility for negative feelings and move beyond them to innovate collaborative solutions that serve the good of a relationship.

True-for-me statements are a strategy for confronting and talking about the underlying needs causing your negative perceptions. When you learn to introspect and confront your own needs and interests without placing blame on others, you begin to take responsibility for your feelings so you can use them productively to create connection. It is human to have negative feelings, but it is destructive to others and you when you blame others for causing your own oppositional force of mind.

True-for-me statements serve compassionate cooperation because they provide a means for using negative feelings productively, without pushing others away or denying them. They are a way for you to transform *accusatory you statements* into *true-for-me statements,* which enables you to shift your focus from blaming others to taking responsibility for your own needs and interests.

True-for-Me Statements

- *I feel … It would really help me if you could …*
- *I react negatively when … It would really help me if you could …*
- *I realize my feelings are irrational when … Let me tell you what would help me …*

Compare each of the following *accusatory you statements* to see how they can be transformed into *true-for-me statements:*

Example 1
Accusatory You Statement
<u>You never</u> tell me I look nice.
True-for-Me Statement
<u>I feel</u> that you don't like the way I look when you don't tell me I look nice. <u>It would really help me if you could</u> tell me I look nice every day because it would make me feel loved.

Example 2
Accusatory You Statement
<u>You always</u> read the mail before you even say hello to me.
True-for-Me Statement
<u>I feel</u> that I don't matter to you when you come home from work and immediately read the mail. <u>It would really help me if you could</u> read the mail after we've had a chance to sit with each other and connect.

Example 3
Accusatory You Statement: <u>You always</u> try to control things.

True-for-Me Statement: <u>I react negatively when</u> I feel that anyone is trying to control me. It kicks up the feelings I used to have growing up when my father didn't give me any voice. <u>It would really help me if</u> you could just tell me how you feel instead of trying to direct me. <u>I realize my feelings are irrational when</u> that happens, and I don't want to react that way, but I can't help it.

True-for-me statements can take any form, as long as they represent an *honest and rational* expression of your feelings:

- I want to find a way to help you without being angry about it.
- I want to work on being more loving to your mother even though she irritates me.
- I want you to have time to talk to your brother, but I don't want us to spend every Saturday with him.

By clarifying your feelings and learning how to talk about them rationally using *true-for-me statements*, you can come to understand your self better. When you take responsibility for your own feelings without blaming others and look for solutions to help others meet your needs, you create and strengthen the emotional linkages supporting connection.

Use Language that Connects

In your interaction with your self and others, use *language that connects* you to a relationship partner, language that "bridges" opposition and create linkages between your individual uniqueness and that of a relationship partner. When your views, positions, values, positions, expectations, and representations differ from those of others, you can disagree with them without rejecting them, making them wrong, or supporting evolving an imbalanced relationship dynamic. When you strive to connect with a relationship partner, you work at generating a force of mind that is kind, empathetic, and tolerant of other ways of thinking and being in the world, even when they are dramatically different from your own. You remind yourself that all perception is subjective, biased, and highly unreliable.

Language that connects is an important tool for reframing opposition as compassionate cooperation, especially when you interact with partners whose religious, political, or other views threaten your sense of self. It is normal to feel defensive when you feel your core values are being threatened. However, by challenging yourself to *separate your reactions to people's values from people themselves*, you advance your capacity to engage in collaborative decision-making and problem-solving. *Language that connects* gives you a way to create linkages with others that support a *me-and-you* relationship dynamic even though you may not share the same views, positions, values, or expectations.

In the same way that "you" are not your opinions and views, others are not theirs. You can hold different views, positions, values, expectations, and representations from others without having to punish them or reject them. If your father-in-law's ultra conservative views on women have caused you to see him as an idiot you'd rather not talk to, challenge yourself to connect with him as a fallible human just like yourself. You don't have to change your own views, positions, values, and expectations. However, you do need to find a way to bridge your differences when you talk together on charged topics if you want to create a genuinely satisfying relationship together. Be innovative. If you know a topic will trigger a person to generate the force of opposition, find other topics to talk about where you can more easily find common ground. If you know your father-in-law likes to talk about cars, for example, engage him on the topic and welcome his views. You have to actively generate the force of mind that is compassionate cooperation, precisely when a partner invites you overtly or covertly into struggle.

Language that connects requires inclusive seeing and the willingness to consider others. It is shaped by language that symbolizes acknowledgement, collaboration, cooperative problem-solving, and positive venting. By engaging these types of language together, you can intensify the force of compassionate cooperation and the positive and unifying relationship dynamic it supports.

Acknowledgement and Collaboration

Acknowledgement validates a relationship partner and suggests the intention of inclusive seeing. It provides a way for you to avoid making others wrong while maintaining your own feelings. It also invites collaboration as you work on shifting away from values symbolizing an oppositional force of mind to those reflecting compassionate cooperation.

Acknowledgments

- *You have a point ...*
- *I can see where you're coming from ...*
- *I agree with your point about ...*

Acknowledgments
• *I understand what you're saying ...*
• *You make a good argument ...*
• *I can see where you're coming from ...*
• *I hear what you're saying ...*

Using language that symbolizes collaboration advances your recognition of a partner's point but takes the next step in actively unifying divergent views or positions by creating common ground. If your opposition centers on disagreement over a behavior that requires problem-solving, you can explicitly invite a relationship partner to collaborate with you: *"Let's figure out what to do." "Can we give some thought to how we can work this out so we both get our needs met?"* With spouses and domestic partners, the suggestion to collaborate is often implied in a conversation itself.

Let's look at two different examples. In the first, Jay's brain reacts automatically to the threat trigger of unexpected guests, causing him to generate attitudes and emotions posturing him in a *me-against-you orientation* toward his Dana, his wife:

Jay: Why did you invite them over on a work night? You know I hate that. [Attack]

Dana: I didn't think it would be a problem. [Defense]

Jay: Well, it *is* a problem. I don't want anybody here when I get home from work. How many times do I have to tell you? It's not okay. [Attack]

Dana: You're being ridiculous. Anyway, I don't know what you expect me to do about it now that they're here. [Attack]

Jay: I expect you to get rid of them. [Attack]

Dana: I'm not going to get rid of them. YOU get rid of them if you want them to leave. I don't know what the big deal is. [Defense]

Jay: (Marches into the bathroom and firmly closes the door) [Attack]

Dana takes the bait of opposition, *"Why did you invite them over on a work night?"* and engages in a familiar struggle with Jay when she responds, *"You're being ridiculous."* By diminishing Jay's feelings and refusing any responsibility in the situation, Dana entangles herself in a predictable pattern of attack-and-defense with her husband. Dana reacts to Jay's criticism and not to his real need, which is not to have visitors in the house when he gets home from work. Her dismissal of his feelings, *"You're being ridiculous,"* reflects egocentric seeing that causes her to overlook the opportunity she has to rebalance the dynamic between them that Jay has disrupted with his accusation. Even though Jay's accusation, *"Why did you ..."* causes their overt struggle, if Dana can shift her *I-perspective* to more inclusive seeing, she might ask herself why she didn't include Jay in decision-making before she invited people over on a work night.

By using acknowledgement and collaboration to create linkages with her husband, in spite of their different perspectives, Dana could have bridged opposition as she worked to rebalance their relationship dynamic. If she had, she would have been able to disentangle from the pattern of attack-and-defense that advances their struggle. By acknowledging that she hears Jay, Dana might say, *"Okay, I hear what you're saying ..."* and explicitly suggest to Jay that they collaborate: *"Let's figure out what to do."*

> **Jay:** Why did you invite them over on a work night? You know I hate that.
> **Dana:** I didn't think it would be a problem.
> **Jay:** Well, it *is* a problem. I don't want anybody here when I get home from work. How many times do I have to tell you? This is not okay.
> **Dana:** Okay, I hear what you're saying, [Acknowledgment] that having people here right now is a problem for you. Let's figure out what to do. [Collaboration]

The second example is an exchange between Jill and her father-in-law, Doug. When Jill first met her father-in-law, she admired his intelligence and success and was proud to be associated with him. Before long, she started to resent him and find him difficult. Jill's father-in-law always seemed to talk about topics that made her angry, and she always felt as if she has to defend herself. Jill and Doug have allowed their different political and social values to cause friction between them. Jill sees her father-in-law as old fashioned and his views (as well as him) as idiotic, while he sees her as argumentative, disrespectful, and controlling. Here's an example of their interaction together and the negative and polarizing dynamic they typically evolve together:

> **Doug:** If there weren't so many women taking jobs away from men, the economy would be in better shape. [Assertion]
> **Jill:** How can you say that? It's not women who are causing the problem. [Attack/Defense]
> **Doug:** Well, they're definitely making it harder for men to find work. Fewer jobs. Men can't find work. [Defense]
> **Jill:** That's absurd. [Attack]

Doug's assertion *"If there weren't so many women taking jobs away from men, the economy would be in better shape"* triggers Jill's brain to perceive it as a threat stimulus, and she prepares for her own defensive attack: *"How can you say that. It's not women who are causing the problem."* When Doug defends his position with *"Well, they're definitely making it harder for men to find work. Fewer jobs. Men can't find work,"* Jill rejects what he says firmly with an attack that highlights the *me-against-you* dynamic they shape: *"That's absurd."* Jill is more interested in proving her position that women aren't causing the job problem for men than in connecting with her father-in-law, a fact that is obvious from the way she tries to prove him wrong. Although her views provoke him, he doesn't try to make her wrong by power-grabbing in the interaction the way Jill does, evidenced by the grammar pattern she uses to shape her talk. She unambiguously communicates her oppositional force of mind when she expresses herself using a *rhetorical question*: *"How can you say that."* Later, when she uses a *comment* to make her criticism clear, *"That's absurd,"* it's obvious that she has she has confused Doug's views with Doug's person and has no desire to create bridges between them. While Doug may have very different opinions than Jill, he uses the most ambiguous sentence pattern, the *comment,* to express his views. And unlike Jill's comment, *"That's absurd,"* which is a criticism of Doug's for having the views he has, Doug's comments are opinions that are not an attack on Jill.

Both Doug and Jill neglect to shape their relationship dynamic to sustain connection between them. They allow their different views to cause separation between them. They miss the opportunity to create stay connected, regardless of their different views and opinions. If Jill were to change her approach, using acknowledgement and implied collaboration, the conversation might have looked like this:

> **Doug:** If there weren't so many women taking jobs away from men, the economy would be in better shape.
> **Jill:** <u>You have a point</u> [Acknowledgement]. There aren't enough jobs to go around, and <u>the fact that women work means there is more competition for the jobs that are available</u>. [Collaboration]

Jill mistakenly assumes that she needs to control father-in-law's views and get him to change them in order to connect with him. She fails to see her own grip on having to prove herself right, which causes her *me-against-you* posturing in the original conversation. However, Jill create and sustain connection with Doug *and* keep her own views on the issues by using language that bridges their differences and creates linkages between them, as shown in the re-scripted narrative when she uses acknowledgement, *"You have a point,"* then goes on to invite collaboration, *"The fact that women work means there is more competition for the jobs that are available."*

Doug could also have bridged their opposition and invited linkages between them. If he had, the conversation might have looked like this:

> **Doug:** If there weren't so many women taking jobs away from men, the economy would be in better shape.
>
> **Jill:** How can you say that? It's not women who are causing the problem. [Attack/Defense]
>
> **Doug:** <u>I understand what you're saying. Women aren't causing the problem,</u> [Acknowledgement] but it is harder for men to find work these days because <u>there are fewer available jobs</u>. [Collaboration]

Instead of sticking firmly to his view as he does in the original conversation when he says, *"Well, they're definitely making it harder for men to find work,"* he can loosen his grip on his views by acknowledging to Jill, *"I understand what you're saying. Women aren't causing the problem."* He also invites collaboration by mitigating his views when he says, *"It is harder for men to find work these days because there are fewer available jobs."* By using acknowledgement and collaboration, he invites the values of *compassionate cooperation*, generating a unifying rather than polarizing force of mind that allows him to bridge his own view with Jill's.

Acknowledgment and collaboration are strategies for creating the bridges that cause linkages between people in a relationship dynamic. These strategies can help you as you work to reframe a force of mind that is opposition as compassionate cooperation because they bridge separation, help you from becoming entangled in the *me-against-you* dynamic, and allow you to rebalance power-sharing and reciprocity in a dynamic.

Cooperative Problem-Solving

Cooperative problem-solving is a tool for maintaining an inclusive orientation toward imagining solutions as you strive to redirect the force of mind that is opposition as compassionate cooperation. It requires inclusive seeing and a willingness to create bridges and invite linkages with a relationship partner as you work to understand and address the underlying needs causing polarization.

Consider the example below, where Marge is angry because she has been trying to help her adult son get back on his feet by giving him money. It shows how cooperative problem-solving can be used to make productive use of feelings without harming others. Cooperative problem-solving requires you to explore, confront, and accept responsibility for your own feelings instead of criticizing and blaming a relationship partner.

The script below represents a familiar theme in Marge's interaction with her self about her son:

> He's an ingrate! So irresponsible when it comes to money. He just assumes I'm going to keep paying. I should cut him off! Pisses me off!

Marge's thoughts, recollections, and imaginings about her son center on this theme and negatively color how she sees him. She focuses on her own negative biases, neglecting to consider how her own real underlying need generates the force of her opposition. She blames her son for being irresponsible with the money she gives him, but she doesn't take responsibility for her underlying need. The re-scripted narrative below illustrates how Marge could reframe how she sees things with her son. She could confront her own underlying need in the situation by prompting herself with the question, *"What's the real issue for me?"* and she can imagine a creative solution that embraces inclusive seeing, where she can *both* satisfy her own need and help her son. By asking herself, *"How can I solve this cooperatively?"* she prompt herself to move away from egocentric seeing dominated by a negative expression of her *small self*.

In re-scripting the negative story she tells her self about her son and the situation, Marge prepares for an interaction with her son:

> <u>What's the real issue for me</u>? ... I hate when I give him money and he doesn't use it the way I intend him to. I could stop helping him, but I feel I need to. After all, I'm his mother and he's having a hard time. But I really resent that he's so bad with money! I need to get creative here. <u>How can I solve this cooperatively</u>? How can I make sure the money's used the way I want it to be? I do want to help him out, but I don't want to resent doing it ... I could pay his bills directly. That would feel good. It would also free me from resenting him ...

Based on the re-scripted story she tells her self about her son and the situation, Marge can choose to create an authentically positive relationship experience with her son, where she generates a positive and unifying force of mind and communicates it in her interaction with him. She can own up to her negative feelings and use them productively to guide a cooperative solution that will address her need and help her son:

I want to help you with your bills, but I feel resentful when I give you money to help you with your bills and I have no idea what you've done with it [True-for-Me Statement]. It would really help me if you would give me $300 worth of your bills every month for the next twelve months until you get back on your feet. I'll pay them directly so I know they are paid and that I've helped. I hope that works for you. [Cooperative Problem-Solving]

Identifying the source of you negative feelings without blaming others and learning to express them in *true-for-me statements* allows you to use your feelings productively to get your needs met without pushing others away. In the example just given, Marge wants to help out, but she also wants to make sure the money she gives her son is used for the purpose she intends.

Cooperative problem-solving empowers you to find solutions that meet the inclusive needs and interests of a relationship partner. It requires a willingness to move away from egocentric seeing and open yourself to the limitless possibilities for creating bridges between individual differences and the linkages required for connection. Egocentric seeing causes you to narrow your scope of vision and situational interpretation to an extent that you overlook your own role and contribution to a relationship dynamic. When this happens, the parts of your *small self* that typically come forward to fight your battles cause you to root stubbornly to your narrow views. Cooperative problem-solving encourages you to expand your interpretations of people and situation and to consider how your own thoughts, recollections, and imaginings may be generate the polarizing force of mind that invites a relationship partner to engage as they do.

Consider the following situation. Mary works at a very demanding corporate job and is used to supervising others. She is highly organized, proactive, and detail oriented. At home, Mary does most of the household chores without the help of her husband, Jack, and their two sons. The way she sees the situation is very different from the way her husband and sons see it.

In Mary's view, she resents Jack and their sons for not pulling their weight with home chores and letting the household responsibilities fall on her. She sees her husband and sons as lazy and unwilling to help out. When they do help, she isn't satisfied with the way they do things. Her feeling is *"If I want it done right, I have to do it myself."* Mary feels taken advantage of and has become very resentful over the years about the situation. Her resentment has affected how she feels about the people involved. When they argue over the issues, her husband and the boys align themselves with her husband against her. Most of the time, she's happier at work where than she is at home with her family.

From her husband and sons' perspectives, Mary doesn't give them a chance to help out before she steps in and does things her way. They resent that Mary feels compelled to take care of everything and then complains about how much she does. When they do help out, Mary always finds fault and imperfection in what they do, which causes them to withdraw and not want to do anything to help. Frustrated because they feel Mary has to control everything and everyone around the house, they feel they can never please her. In their view, Mary doesn't trust them to do anything and would rather take care of everything herself even though she criticizes them for not helping.

The topic of household chores, cleaning, and organizing ignites a familiar conflict theme between Mary and her husband, Mary and her sons, and Mary and her husband and sons. They have become entangled in a familiar pattern of attack-and-defense where Mary's sons take their father's side, causing Mary to feel separated and alienated from all of them. The force of opposition they generate in response to the trigger of household chores has deepened and extended its impact across their relationships over time. Even the sound of the vacuum cleaner intensifies the negative and polarizing dynamic that ripples across their respective thoughts, recollections, and imaginings. Unless they can each come to see how they play a contributing part in the negative and polarizing dynamic they jointly evolve, they will continue to stay rooted in their own egocentric seeing and harbor resentment and anger.

With introspection, Mary might see how her pattern of proactively taking care of everything around the house makes it difficult for others to help. She might also discover that her compulsive need to take care of everything and everyone is a reaction to her father's absence when she was growing up, which caused her to depend on the *take charge* and *perfectionist* aspects of her *small self*. If Mary can come to see how her own automatic response patterns are preventing others from stepping up, she might be able to loosen her need to control. By expanding her interpretation of the situation to recognize her own contribution to the negative dynamic they evolve together, Mary can strive to invite rebalancing in the relationship dynamic.

Similarly, Jack would benefit from confronting his own passive-aggressive habits and recognizing how harmful and unproductive the negative alignments he creates with his sons against Mary are. If he did, he might be able to see how he provokes Mary to engage as she does, and how his own behaviors contribute to the authentically negative and inauthentically positive relationship experiences he and Mary jointly create.

Either one of them could reframe the negative story they tell themselves about one another and the situation and use re-scripting to help them prepare to negotiate the topic in their interaction with one another. If Mary decided to share her re-scripted story with Jack, their interaction together might look something like this:

Mary: Can we talk about what's really going on for us about the chores? I feel resentful and angry when I do all the chores around the house and no one is helping, but I can't help myself when I see that things need to be done. I feel compelled to do everything and then I resent it when I do. I don't want to be feeling this way. The fact is that the chores need to be done, and I do them.

Jack: That's true, you do a lot around here. I've tried to be helpful, but you always get things done before I even have a chance to think about them, and when I do help around here, it's always the wrong thing or the wrong way, and you usually do it over again your way. How do you think that makes me feel? How do you expect me to help when you don't like the way I do things? I feel incompetent, like I can't do anything right in your eyes. It makes me not want to try. Yeah, I realize I don't do a lot around here, but you seem to like the control.

Mary: I know I'm controlling. I just can't help myself. I do tend to feel I do things better than anyone else, but it's not rational thought—it's just feelings. I know you would be able to perfectly well take care of everything around the house if I weren't here. I also know everyone does things differently, but it's hard for me to let go. I want to work on being more open to letting you help and not being critical about it. I know it won't be easy for me. Do you have any ideas how we could do that together? Maybe we can decide on a code word that you could say when you feel I start to criticize. That way, I could have a signal to back off. I think it would help me.

Jack: I really like that idea. We could also make a schedule with assignments for chores and see how that works. Maybe we could come up with some guidelines on doing chores, like what's important when you're doing the laundry. Maybe a checklist. We also need some rule, like you can't criticize the person who's assigned a chore. If they haven't done an item on the checklist, that would be valid, but no criticisms allowed!

In cooperative problem-solving, there is a focus on trying to use language that connects and avoiding confrontational grammar patterns and word choices. You can support this approach by asking genuine questions that welcome a relationship partner's input in problem-solving and by practicing compassionate listening. Whatever ideas they come up with, Mary and her husband are working together in the example interaction to preserve balance in their dynamic together. Their interaction reflects their priority to stay connected as they bridge their unique needs and desires around the theme of household chores. By each taking responsibility for what's true for them, without having to blame each other, they can each strive to generate the force of mind that is compassionate cooperation. Whatever their respective positions, they can work together to cooperative problem-solve in a way that evolves a balanced relationship dynamic between them.

Positive Venting

Positive Venting is a tool for reshaping negative alignments that tie people together through negative talk about others in their absence. Typically, one person encourages others to buy into their own negative perceptions about the absent object-person, and the person being "baited" responds by offering support and agreement that intensifies negative perception:

> **Marni:** <u>My brother needs a psychiatrist. He's a nutcase! I can't believe how irresponsible he is with money</u>! [Attack] I sent him a check last month, and now he says he can't pay his bills!
> **Friend:** What a jerk! I'd make him pay me back. [Support and Agreement]

In the example, Marni encourages her friend to support and strengthen the *me-against-you* dynamic she shapes with her brother. Her friend provides the support and agreement she seeks, validating her negative story about her brother. While Marni's criticism of her brother allows her to vent her frustration and also draws her friend closer to her through negative information-sharing, it is harmful to her brother as well as to Marni, her friend, and others who might be told the same negative story about the brother as a result of this interaction. Even though Marni's friend might not know her brother personally, she biases her friend's view of him, which will likely affect how the friend thinks about him in the future or interacts with him if she does meet him. The friend's encouragement gives Marni permission to intensify her own negative feelings about her brother, which will deepen her opposition toward him in the future and increase the likelihood that the negative story Marni and her friend create together in this interaction will come up again in their future interactions together.

You can use *positive venting* to release your frustrations productively and deepen connection with others *without having to criticize or make an absent person-object wrong*. *Positive venting* allows you to explore, confront, and accept responsibility for your own feelings instead of criticizing and blaming an absent relationship partner. Without having to accuse others, you can address your own underlying needs as you strive to create and strengthen *positive alignments* with absent person-objects, modeling behaviors for others that support compassionate cooperation.

Consider below how Marni might have used *positive venting* to retell her story about her brother to her friend. By using *true-for-me statements* and *cooperative problem-solving*, she could have helped herself see her brother in a more productive light:

> **Marni:** I feel angry with my brother because I sent him a check last month, and now he says he can't pay his bills! I resent giving him money and then finding out he didn't use it to pay bills. I'm really trying to help him get back on his feet [True-for-Me Statement]. What should I do? Do you have any ideas?
>
> **Friend:** Why don't you ask him to give you the bills you want to pay. That way, you'll be sure the money gets used the way you want it to be used.

By creating *true-for-me statements*, Marni strives to understand her own frustration without having to blame her brother. Once she confronts and admits her resentment over giving her brother money that she wrongly assumed he would use to pay his bills, she can move to cooperative problem-solving with her friend. Instead of aligning her friend negatively against her brother, Marni can ask for her help in trying to get her own underlying needs met.

Positive venting allows Marni to use her feelings productively to maintain a *you-and-me* orientation toward her brother. This dynamic strengthens her ties to her friend without having to do so at her brother's expense. This creates a balance in the relationship dynamic that is absent in *negative venting*, where Marni and her friend "gang up" on the brother, who isn't even present in the interaction.

Rebalancing power-sharing and reciprocity in an interaction symbolizing *negative venting* when someone else tries to draw you into a negative alignment with them against an absent person-object requires a willingness to move beyond compassionate listening. While compassionate listening will allow you to validate and acknowledge the friend's feelings, you will have to help her *see an alternative interpretation* of her story if you want to support *positive venting*. This is the most challenging part of redirecting negative venting as positive venting because your friend's expectation is that you will intensify her negative dynamic against her brother.

Compare the following two exchanges. The first exchange shows how you might participate in negative venting, aligning yourself with a friend's negative perception of her sister's husband:

> **Friend:** He's such an idiot. I have no idea why my sister married him … He just sits there reading when he comes to my parents' house for dinner on Sundays … He doesn't do anything.
>
> **You:** What a jerk! Your sister must be crazy to stay with him.

The second exchange shows how you might redirect a friend's attempt to draw you into negative venting, acknowledging your friend's feelings but helping her see an alternative interpretation of her negative story instead of supporting it:

> **Friend:** He's such an idiot. I have no idea why my sister married him ... He just sits there reading when he comes to my parents' house for dinner on Sundays ... He doesn't do anything.
>
> **You**: <u>I hear your frustration</u> [Acknowledgement], but he seems to be left out of the loop by your parents and your sister. Actually, <u>I've always found him to be friendly and polite to me the times I've been there at dinner with all of you</u> [Alternative Interpretation].

Similarly, the example below illustrates how it is possible to help others redirect negative venting as positive venting, thereby helping others rebalance a negative and polarizing dynamic they are shaping with an absent person-object. In the example, Adrienne is angry and hurt because her brother isn't coming to her daughter's wedding. Instead of encouraging Adrienne to "write the brother off," Collie chooses to help her friend see an alternative interpretation of her negative story, one that allows Adrienne to understand the situation in a different way:

> **Adrienne:** <u>I'm writing my brother off.</u> He's not coming to the wedding. No explanation, nothing. Can you believe it? I'm not going to forgive him for this! I'm writing him off. I don't want anything to do with him.
>
> **Collie:** You're kidding! What's going on? Why isn't he coming?
>
> **Adrienne:** No, I'm not! I have no idea. He didn't even call!
>
> **Collie:** I'm so sorry. I know how much this means to you. What's going on with him? Have you talked to him lately?
>
> **Adrienne:** Nope. He's totally MIA. Haven't seen him in years. He's married to that nutcase.
>
> **Collie:** So, why are you surprised he's not coming? He never shows up for family events.
>
> **Adrienne:** I know, but I thought he'd come to the wedding. He didn't even call! Can you believe it? I'm writing him off. I don't want anything to do with him.
>
> **Collie:** <u>That's not you. You're a loving person.</u> Who knows what his real story is. He is probably just trying to keep the peace with his wife. Your expectations are

unrealistic. He's never come to family events before—why do you expect him to come to the wedding? I'm not saying I agree with his decision, and I hear your frustration, but don't let his decision not to come make you unloving.

Adrienne: <u>You're right. I am a loving person. I'll try to let it go.</u>

In the exchange, Adrienne comes to see how a different interpretation of her brother can help her be the loving person she wants to be rather than a vindictive and reactive expression of her *small self*. Had Adrienne stayed committed to cutting her brother off, she would be demonstrating *negative reciprocity*, an expression of attack-and-defense: *"You do this negative thing to me, and I do this negative thing to you."* By refusing to engage in negative reciprocity, Adrienne supports *positive reciprocity* in her dynamic with her brother, making positive assumptions that will affect how they jointly shape their relationship dynamic.

Call on *Big You* – Emotional Symbols of Pure Consciousness

Big You is your best self, the part of you that is *pure consciousness*, an expression of self that "sees" without the veil of negative perception that reflects values such as *fear, anger, resentment, criticism,* and *entitlement*. It is the part of you that sees yourself in others, and your connection to humanity. By calling on *Big You* when your brain reacts to a threat stimulus and generates the force of mind that is opposition, you can take active steps to redirect opposition as compassionate cooperation. As you develop the habit of inclusive seeing, you become less responsive to the emotional reactions of *small self* and egocentric relationship problem-solving and decision-making.

Striving to shift to a *Big You* perspective helps you transition away from the *me-against-you* posturing that causes you to want to control and blame others. It helps you release from egocentric seeing where individual needs and wants are central to relationship problem-solving and decision-making so you can reinterpret the negative stories you tell your self about people and relationship situations. The more you move away from egocentric seeing toward inclusive seeing, the more you move toward a fuller expression of *Big You*.

Big You competes for voice with the various aspects of your *small self* in your interaction with your self. Whatever aspects of your *small self* routinely engage when you react to a trigger that causes you to position for opposition, if you can learn to recognize them and call on *Big You*, you will be more able to shift away from egocentric seeing, where it's all about you, to inclusive seeing, where it's about problem-solving and decision-making for collective good.

You can call on *Big You* when you recognize a part of your *small self* is causing you to spin a negative story about a relationship partner or situation in your interaction with your self.

In the example below, Lauren feels frustrated, resentful, and angry with David because he video calls with his brother on the weekend. Lauren's *spoiled only child* routinely engages every time she thinks about the calls. She resents David for wanting to video call with his brother and reacts with anger every time he mentions it or sets up his computer to prepare for a call. During the week, she finds herself distracted by the anticipation of the calls. Even though the calls last only fifteen minutes and take place once every couple of weeks, Lauren spends countless hours every week obsessing over the calls:

> Why does he have to waste our time. I just don't get it. Why can't he just do it on a day when we're not together. This is the last thing I want to do! We only have a limited amount of time together and this is not how I want to spend it!

If Lauren allows her *spoiled only child* to continue distracting her, chances are the video call issue will deepen and strengthen her negative feelings toward David, sustaining an imbalance in the dynamic they evolve together. Whether or not she shares her negative story with David, chances are she'll spark a struggle with him if she communicates her opposition through body language and other non-verbal signals. Lauren's sense of entitlement in the situation and her focus on egocentric interests show her disregard for David's needs and interests, and make Lauren feel powerless to control the situation.

Lauren can call on *Big You,* the part of her self that will enable her to see David and the situation through the eyes of pure consciousness so she can retell her story about David and the video calls to her self in ways that symbolize *love, peace, forgiveness, gratitude,* and *service.* If she does this, she will actively be able to help her self move away from egocentric seeing to inclusive seeing. Inclusive seeing will allow her to interpret David and the situation in wider ways. For example, she may recognize how she is obsessing over an event that takes fifteen minutes once every two weeks and how she has the option of running an errand for those fifteen minutes while David video calls his brother.

Lauren doesn't need to give up her *spoiled only child* feelings, but she does need to shift what she does with them. Instead of using them as a basis for justifying her resentment and anger, she can choose to clarify and address her underlying need in a way that includes David's needs and interests. If she confronts how her *spoiled only child* negatively biases her interpretation of the situation, she may be able to recognize her need for David's attention and time. If she does, she will then be able to re-script her story to herself, which will enable her to redirect her oppositional force of mind as compassionate cooperation. Calling on *Big You,* she may be able to re-script her story as follows:

I don't like the way I feel when my spoiled only child causes me to be self-centered! I choose to let go of my resentment about the video calls. David is always doing his best to help me out. This is how I can do something for him. I'm going to ask him to give me a heads up on the calls so I can plan.

Consider another example that shows how calling on *Big You* can help you redirect the *small self* "seeing" of negative perception. In this example, Hanna's *green with envy* self engages every time she thinks about her sister-in-law, causing her to see her sister-in-law as shallow and narcissistic:

I can't stand being around her! I hate the way she parades around. She's a narcissist! So shallow! Who wants to be around that! I have nothing in common with her.

Hanna's *green with envy* self has generated such an intensely polarizing force in the dynamic she shapes with her sister-in-law that they barely talk. When they're together, Hanna rarely makes eye contact with her and can only focus on the negative story she tells herself, reaffirming how awful it is to be around her and how narcissistic she is. In her private interaction with her self, Hanna gives a lot of negative attention to thoughts, recollections, and imaginings that prove to her how shallow and narcissistic her sister-in-law is.

By calling on the *Big You* part of her self, Hanna can reshape the story she tells herself about her sister-in-law. She can also come to take responsibility for the *green with envy* part of her that engages when she feels threatened or offended. By confronting how *green with envy* engages when she doesn't feel good enough, or when she feels inadequate in some other way, Hanna can try to better understand her self. Although *green with envy* may continue to come forward to protect Hanna when her brain perceives a threat or offense, Hanna will be better able to move away from her own self-centered seeing to inclusive seeing, which will allow her to release from trying to control how her sister-in-law behaves.

By calling on *Big You*, Hanna can help herself shift from egocentric "seeing" to inclusive "seeing" so she can reframe her story about her sister-in-law. This will enable her and others in her family to experience her self as a loving person. It will also help her avoid negative venting about her sister-in-law and avoid baiting others into aligning with and intensifying her own negative story about her sister-in-law. In making a deliberate choice to call on *Big You*, Hanna makes the choice to actively shape her emerging process of self in a positive and unifying way that serves her self, her sister-in-law, and every other person tied to their lives.

Whatever parts of your own *small self* tend to engage when your brain perceives a threat or offense, try identifying them and understanding them. Maybe you have an *always right* self that causes you to spin negative stories in your interaction with your self and others, causing you to feel miserable with others because no one but you really knows what they're talking about. Or maybe you rely on the part of your self that is a *victim forever,* the part of you that sees everything your mother says or does as manipulative and controlling and refuses to let go of past hurts.

Understanding how different parts of your *small self* interfere with you ability to generate the positive and unifying force of mind that produces connection can help you recognize when to step in and actively call on the *Big You* part of your self. Recognizing and acknowledging all the different parts of your self is core to wellness. While you probably won't ever completely stop those parts of *small self* that engage automatically, you can definitely learn to understand them and redirect the negative and polarizing values they generate when your brain perceives a threat of offense. As you do so, you can call on the *Big You* part of your self, the part of you that "sees" through the eyes of pure consciousness, to help you reframe the negative story you tell yourself and others about a relationship partner or situation so it generates the positive and unifying force of mind that is compassionate cooperation.

Avoid Taking the Bait

You are especially vulnerable to supporting a negative and polarizing *me-against-you* relationship dynamic when a person "baits you" to engage in struggle. Typically with a spouse or domestic partner, it's easy to take the bait and evolve familiar patterns of attack-and-defense, recognizable themes that often come to dominant how partner see a relationship partner and their entire relationship together. Increasingly, though, in the United States, you are also at risk in service encounters and other public settings for being enticed to take the bait and engage openly in predictable patterns of attack-and-defense that support negative *me-against-you* struggles.

Twenty-five years ago, exchanges like the one below between acquaintances or strangers in service encounters were uncommon. Today, they seem to be everywhere. This particular exchange occurred at an upscale hair salon between a client who was unhappy with the haircut she received and the stylist who gave her the haircut. The client baits the stylist by rejecting the stylist's request for payment with an attack:[53]

---

53 D'Amico-Reisner, *An Ethnolinguistic Study of Disapproval Exchanges,* 201.

Stylist: That'll be [sixty-five dollars].

Client: I'm sorry, it's a lousy job and I'm just not going to pay for it! [Attack]

Stylist: Look, you came to me for a haircut and I gave you one. The cost or a haircut is [sixty-five dollars]. [Defensive]

Client: Fine. When I get a haircut worth [sixty-five dollars] I'll be happy to pay for it. [Attack]

Stylist: I don't know what you expected. [Defense]

Client: No? How about a shampoo and a trim! I said, "Don't touch the top. I'm trying to grow it in." Look at this! [Holds up hair] There's nothing left! [Attack]

Stylist: If you want a trim, you don't ask for a senior cutter. I'm an artist, not a mechanic. [Defense]

Client: An artist? Look at me! You call this art? I can't believe this. This is really unbelievable. I'm not paying for this, I'm sorry. [Exits the shop] [Attack]

Once the stylist takes the bait, responding to the client's criticism with her own defensive justification, the interaction spirals into an overt struggle. If the stylist had not allowed himself to be drawn into the struggle, he could have responded differently to the client. Instead of becoming defensive in response to her criticism, he could have used cooperative problem-solving to come up with a solution that satisfied them both as he engaged in compassionate listening. Had he responded to the client's bait with a response that reflected compassionate listening and inclusive seeing, the exchange would have evolved much differently. Imagine if the client responded, *"I hear that you're unhappy about the haircut I gave you. What can I do to remedy the situation?"* instead of, *"Look, you came to me for a haircut and I gave you one."* This approach would have shown the client that her feelings were important, not necessarily that the stylist agreed with her. Instead, the exchange turns into a power struggle. The stylist doesn't get paid in the end anyway, but the impact of the exchange for both people extends beyond the moment of their struggle. It severs connection and leaves both people angry, resentful, and antagonistic. For sure the experience will shape their thoughts, recollections, and imaginings about each other and the situation.

To help you avoid taking the bait, remind yourself that *you are not your brain* and refuse to participate in a developing struggle. Instead, use inclusive seeing and rational cooperative problem-solving to explore the needs underlying an emotional reaction, and take the lead on redirecting the polarizing force of opposition.

Your capacity to avoid taking the bait is what makes you uniquely human.

Ask for What You Need

Don't expect others to know what you need or want if you haven't told them. In situations where it's appropriate to do so, if you want to make sure others meet your expectations, ask directly, clearly, and kindly for what you need. Kindness ensures balance and reciprocity in a relationship dynamic and limits power-grabbing and negative reciprocity.

Consider the following example where Amara has ordered a dress online from a department store that arrives at her home with stains on it. She is furious when she receives the stained dress, because she has to make a trip to the store to return it. When she does, she is very aware of her interaction with the store assistant who is helping her. When the assistant credits her account but neglects to reimburse her for the seventeen dollar shipping and handling charge, she feels herself react negatively. She stops herself from immediately reacting in her interaction with the assistant and begins to explore her real need, which she identifies as her desire to receive reimbursement for the shipping and handling charge.

She rehearses a script in her interaction with her self, focusing attention on asking the assistant directly, clearly, and kindly for reimbursement of the charge. As she does this, she releases herself from her initial negative reaction. Drawing on language elements, including body language and other non-verbal signals, she asks the assistant for what she needs, reminding herself that the assistant is doing her best and imagining how many difficult people the assistant has to deal with in a day:

> **Amara:** Excuse me [making eye contact and smiling as she leans on the counter toward the assistant], I just noticed that I wasn't reimbursed for the shipping and handling charge [genuinely smiling and making eye contact with the assistant]. I'm going to need to have that charge removed, since I am returning the dress because it was sent to me in unacceptable shape.
> **Assistant:** Oh, absolutely. I don't blame you. I'm afraid I'll have to get manager to sign off on that. I hope you don't mind waiting.
> **Amara:** Not at all. I appreciate all your help.
> **Assistant:** No, thank *you*. I'm very happy to help.

By asking directly, clearly, and kindly for what she needs, Amara invites the assistant to respond reciprocally with kindness, *"Oh, absolutely. I don't blame you."* Positive reciprocity continues in the exchange with Amara and the assistant emphasizing their respective appreciation to one another.

In contrast, consider the example below[54] between a swim coach and one of the swimmers on her team. The coach is frustrated and angry because the swimmers talk to her before the meet, but she hasn't told them that she needs time to herself before the start of the competition. As a result, they don't know what she expects and they don't understand her reaction. The coach's negative reaction is disruptive to keeping the team calm before they compete. If she had made her needs understood to her team before the meet, and used inclusive seeing rather than egocentric seeing, she would have been able to enhance everyone's experience. Instead, the coach reacts negatively to a swimmer's genuine question for information. She neglects to reframe her negative reaction, taking her power and disturbing reciprocity in her dynamic with one of the swimmers, evidenced by the apology the swimmer gives her:

> **Swimmer:** Cath, can I ask …?
> **Coach:** What is it?! If you girls don't leave me alone I'm going to scream … You're driving me crazy today and making me a nervous wreck.
> **Swimmer:** Sorry. I just wanted to know if I'm swimming.

The coach could have let her team know she wanted to be left alone before the start of the competition. She might have expressed her need directly, clearly, and kindly, in a way that would have allowed her to avoid polarizing her team:

> Girls, I feel nervous right before you swim, and I need some time by myself to calm down. I'll let you know who is swimming as soon as I know. But <u>I need you to leave me alone once we get out to the pool so I can focus on calming myself.</u> So, if you have questions to ask me, let's agree that you'll ask them before we get out to the pool. Agreed?

Say No with Kindness

You may find it hard to *say no* when a friend or someone else asks you for a favor. You may end up agreeing to help because you feel obligated, are concerned about how others see you, or feel that by *saying no* you will hurt someone's feelings. But, by *saying yes* when you want to *say no*, you end up creating an inauthentically positive relationship experience. When this happens, it causes

---

54   D'Amico-Reisner, *An Ethnolinguistic Study of Disapproval Exchanges.*

resentment. You end up resenting the person who asked you for the favor as well as you self for agreeing to do something you didn't want to do.

Saying *yes* resentfully reflects narrow vision because you can only see two possibilities, agreement or disagreement. If disagreement makes you uncomfortable, you will likely choose to agree even if you do so resentfully. By neglecting to see a request for a favor as an opportunity for cooperative problem-solving, you overlook an opportunity for getting your own needs and wants met while you help others.

Say No with Kindness

1   Express your desire to agree and clearly state your inability or unwillingness, using phrases such as *"I would love to be able to help but ..."* or *"I'm afraid I won't be able to agree because ..."*

2   Propose at least one option for cooperative problem-solving related to the request.

Consider a situation where Kiran asks her friend Pat if an acquaintance of hers can borrow her bike. Pat owns an expensive bike, which she doesn't want to lend. However, that's not what she tells her Kiran:

Saying *Yes* When You Want to Say *No*

> **Kiran:** Hey, do you think I could borrow your bike for one of my housemates? His wife is coming to visit for a week and they want to do site seeing and spend time outside, and he needs a bike for her.
>
> **Pat:** [hesitates] Well, my bike's kind of expensive ... I don't want him to have to worry about it ...
>
> **Kiran:** Oh, don't worry. He'll take good care of it. He's a really nice guy.
>
> **Pat:** I just hope nothing happens to it. My son's seat got stolen last year. He had a lock on it and someone still stole his seat.
>
> **Kiran:** Oh, don't worry. He's very responsible. He'll take good care of it. He's a real gentleman. I've known him for six months. He's a great guy.
>
> **Pat:** Okay ...

Pat agrees to lend her bike, but she really wants to *say no*. In fact, she tries to *say no* to lending her bike when she says, *I just hope nothing happens to it. My son's seat got stolen last year. He had a lock on it and someone still stole his seat.* The problem is that she does not clearly *say no* because she feels she can't say *no* to Kiran. Every time she tries to offer an excuse, Kiran rejects it. Finally, Pat just gives in and agrees.

Pat could have been deceitful and made up an excuse to avoid saying *no:*

> "I wish I could help you out, but my bike seat is broken" (or "the brakes don't work" or "I left it at the beach" or "it needs to be tuned").

But, in doing so she would be dishonest with herself because she would be betraying her feelings as well as not helping Kiran out. While she would avoid overt conflict or an unpleasant encounter, she would not be supporting a genuinely positive relationship experience with Kiran. Unfortunately, Pat narrows her vision so much that excludes the limitless options for collaborative problem-solving.

Reconsider how the interaction might have developed if Pat recognized the opportunity she had to help Kiran without lending her the bike by using the *say no with kindness* guidance:

> **Kiran:** Hey, do you think I could borrow your bike for one of my housemates? His wife is coming to visit for a week and they want to do site seeing and spend time outside, and he needs a bike for her.
>
> **Pat:** <u>I would love to be able to help you out</u> [Desire to Agree], but I don't feel comfortable lending my bike. I've got a lot invested in it, and I would hate to hold anyone responsible for replacing it.
>
> **Kiran:** I completely understand. Anyway, I'm just looking for an old bike that he could use, not anything expensive.
>
> **Pat:** That's definitely not my bike! And I'd hate for anything to happen to it while he had it.<u> I just thought of something. There's a bike place right on Monroe and Curtis that does rentals. That might be a good option for him. He can probably get a deal on a weekly rental, or just rent it for a few days</u> [Solution].
>
> **Kiran:** I forgot about that place. If I can't find an old bike for him, I'll tell definitely him to check it out.

Saying no with kindness is typically most challenging when you feel "put on the spot" and asked directly for a favor. Preparing and practicing scripts in your interaction with your self can help prepare to *say no with kindness* in your interaction with others.

Consider another example, which suggests the challenge of *saying no with kindness* to a friend or acquaintance who "puts you on the spot." Meg and Jen met in a class they are both taking. They exchange small talk during the class and sometimes get coffee together during the break or after class. One day, just before class begins, Jen approaches Meg and asks,

> **Jen**: Is there any way you can give me ride home after class today? If you can't, it's okay. I can take a cab, but I thought I'd ask.
> **Meg:** Where do you live?
> **Jen:** In DC, near Foggy Bottom [about 25 minutes away].

In the situation described, Meg may have many reasons for needing or wanting to *say no with kindness* to Jen's request, but it's important for her to understand her own resistance to helping. Maybe she knows there will be rush hour traffic and it will take her at least an hour and a half to make the round-trip, which she is unwilling to do. Or, maybe she wants to be home to cook dinner for her family. Whatever her reasons, she can use the guidance for *saying no with kindness,* which will allow her to acknowledge her own needs and help Jen with a solution. If Meg really does not want to drive in rush hour, she might *say no with kindness* as follows:

> **Meg:** I would really like to drive you home, but the traffic at this hour is ridiculous. If you want, you can come back to my house with me now, and I'll give you a ride home after dinner once rush hour is over. Or, if you need to leave now, I can help you get a cab or drive you to Metro.

While it is a mistake to *say yes* resentfully, it is also important to recognize when egocentric seeing is causing you to resist helping others. You can challenge yourself to *say no with kindness* as practice creating options for cooperative problem-solving that generate the attitudes and emotions of love and service.

Command Yourself to *Stop-and-Reframe*

Be vigilant for thoughts, recollections, and imaginings that reflect negative perception, commonly symbolized by fear, anger, resentment, criticism, and entitlement. When you feel yourself being pulled into an oppositional force of mind, give you self an explicit cue to reframe. By prompting yourself to redirect opposition, you can help yourself shift from a *me-against-you* dynamic to a *me-and-you* one as you reshape your thoughts, recollections, and imaginings to reflect positive perception, symbolized by stories reflecting love, peace, gratitude, forgiveness, and service.

Consider the following example. Jordan is reading in bed with her husband, who says something to her that causes her mind to resist and posture her for opposition. Saying nothing, she gets out of bed and goes into the living room with her book, passive-aggressively communicating her anger to her husband. As she sits on the couch in her own pool of negative thought, she remembers the *command yourself to stop-and-reframe* strategy, which prompts this story she tells herself,

> Stop-and-Reframe! I feel anger and resentment. How is this serving me? It isn't! I don't want to me here on the couch alone. What do I need? I need to be in bed, reading with him. I choose forgiveness because I choose to release myself. I choose to let go of my anger and resentment. I'm going to name three reasons for holding gratitude toward him ... He's always concerned with my wellbeing. He brings me breakfast in bed when I ask for it. He loves my parents ... I'm going back to bed ... forgive me, I'm sorry, I love you, thank you ...

Say *Rewind*

You are human, which means you are imperfect and fallible. You make mistakes, but you also have the capacity to learn and change. The process of striving to be your best self involves recognizing that you always have the chance to acknowledge error and apologize, whether you do so immediately, or hours, days, months, or years after an event. You can do this in your interaction with your self as well as with others. Since forgiveness releases you from anger and resentment, it serves compassionate cooperation and will help you redirect opposition and evolve a unifying relationship dynamic with a partner.

By saying *rewind* to your self or others, you allow your self the chance to create a more productive story. This gives you the chance to change your mind about taking the bait when a partner tries to engage you in attack-and-defense struggle, which will allow you to rebalance an evolving negative and polarizing dynamic.

Consider an earlier example to see how using the strategy of *rewind* can help you shift from opposition to compassionate cooperation:

> **Husband:** Why the hell didn't you stop and get milk? Didn't you see we don't have any? Now, I have to go out and get it!
> **Wife:** I didn't realize we needed milk. Don't you think I would have gotten it?
> **Husband:** <u>Rewind. I don't care about the milk. I'm frustrated because the kids need milk in the morning and I don't want to go out now and get it.</u>

Wife: I understand. I'll run out and get it first thing tomorrow. They can have juice in the morning and they'll be fine.

In the example, the husband realizes he is baiting his wife to engage in a struggle. He also knows that if he redirects his oppositional force of mind, that he will be able to reshape the negative dynamic he has invited. When he realizes what he is doing, he says *rewind,* which allows him to start the interaction over. He then takes steps to confront his feelings and acknowledge his real need so he can move beyond his emotional reaction to get his needs met. Using *rewind* as a strategy, he is able to shift away from his initial *me-against-you* orientation toward his wife, positioning himself instead "on his wife's team." His wife's response, "*I understand. I'll run out and get it first thing tomorrow,*" shows how successful he's been in rebalancing the dynamic he disturbed. In so doing, he avoided an argument and was able to allow himself to enjoy the evening with his wife, which might have ended very differently if he had not actively decided to *rewind.*

Ask for Forgiveness and Apologize

"*Forgive me, I'm sorry.*"

Forgiving and apologizing are a *decision to let go.* They are *not an admission of wrongdoing.* They require you to step away from egocentric seeing that causes you to assign blame and to see a winner and loser. Instead of making forgiveness and apology a choice between right and wrong, think of it as a choice to release from egocentric seeing. "*Forgive me, I'm sorry … I choose to let go.*"

Forgive and apologize to others regularly in your interaction with your self as well as in interaction with others. Because these words can help you redirect an oppositional force of mind, they help correct power imbalance and lack of positive reciprocity in a relationship dynamic. In saying these words, you help yourself move to *seeing differently.*

The next time you find yourself resisting forgiveness and apology, recognize how your *small self* is interfering with you ability to connect, and call on *Big You.*

Agree to Disagree

You can *agree to disagree* with a relationship partner when you recognize an interaction is beginning to spiral into overt argument. As long as your intention is to redirect opposition as compassionate cooperation, and not sarcastic or disingenuous, you can *agree to disagree* and move on to productive talk.

Typically, you become emotionally invested in religious and political views because they reflect your core values. When this happens and your brain reacts and positions you for opposition, your *small self* engages protect your boundaries. Before you know it, you're taking someone's criticism of your favorite political figure as a personal attack. When you do, it is very easy to become entangled in emotional struggle where your goal is to prove yourself more worthy and deserving and the other person less worthy and deserving simply because of their political or religious preferences.

Consider an example of a conversation at a community event dinner between Ben and Isabella, who were dining at a table with mutual friends, when their talk turned to a discussion of the President:

> **Ben:** You didn't just say what I thought you did, did you.
>
> **Isabella:** Yep, that's what I said. He's my man! Always was, always will be!
>
> **Ben:** You've got to be kidding me. After all the promises he made and didn't keep.
>
> **Isabella:** How could he get anything done with Congress?
>
> **Ben:** How can you even consider voting for him? You must be a socialist.
>
> **Isabella:** Well, if being a socialist means being concerned with social justice, immigration, and the poor, well, I guess I must be a socialist! [Takes the bait] We seem to have different views on the issue. Let's just agree to disagree and enjoy this lovely evening and dinner. The music is great, isn't it? [Smiles genuinely and makes eye contact with Ben] Have you been here before?

In the example, Ben's overtly expressed opposition signals to Isabella that he's inviting her to engage in a struggle, which begins to become more intense as the discussion continue. Although she initially takes the bait when Ben accuses her of being a socialist, she catches herself and chooses to reframe. Her success in re-scripting and redirecting to the values of *compassionate cooperation* are reflected in her words "*We seem to have different views on the issue.*" She uses the *agree to disagree* strategy to help her refocus the topic of their talk. It moves them away from struggle, enabling her to actively shift to a different discussion.

Agree to disagree forces topic closure and invites a boundary with others. It can be off-putting when your intention to preserve connection is disingenuous.

Create a *Space for Grace*

The word *grace* comes from the Hebrew root *bend*, which suggests willful release. You can allow yourself a *space for grace* so you can move from being a passive participant-observer in your interaction with your self to an active one.

Space for grace buys you time to regroup. When you catch yourself reacting negatively, or you are having trouble making the shift to a *me-and-you* orientation, it can be useful to give your self a few moments. Especially when you feel provoked by something a person says, or you aren't sure how to respond, you can pause and take the time to reframe and re-script. When you claim a space for grace in conversation with others, you buy time to redirect opposition as compassionate cooperation:

Taking a Space for Grace

- I feel grumpy right now. Sorry. Can we talk about this later?

- I'm not in the right mind frame to talk about that now. Sorry. Do you mind?

- I need some time to sort out my thoughts. Is that okay?

- I need a few minutes to think about that before I respond.

- Is it okay if we talk about this later? I need to think about it.

- Let me think about that and we can talk about it tomorrow after I'm home from work.

- Do you mind if we talk about this tomorrow when I'm in a better space?

- I'd like to think about that and get back to you if I can.

Creating a space for grace gives you time to confront the triggers that posture for opposition and acting out negative values such as fear, resentment, anger, criticism, and entitlement. If you learn to discuss emotionally charged issues when you are relaxed, unhurried, rested, and fed, you will be more able to shift from opposition to compassionate cooperation.

Recognizing that you can postpone a discussion until you are relaxed and recharged can help you engage take active steps to revalue a negative story to align with the values of love peace, forgiveness, gratitude, and service. With practice, you can become skilled at taking a space for grace whenever you need time to make the transition from a *me-against-you* orientation to a *me-and-you* one.

Create the Habit of Compassionate Cooperation

Habit is a neurological pattern produced by your brain. You can cause your brain to create the habit of producing positive and unifying thoughts, recollections, and imaginings by striving to redirect opposition on a moment-by-moment basis in your interaction with your self and others.

As you strive to transition to perception reflecting the positive and unifying values of compassionate cooperation, it may help to actively imagine the symbols of positive perception: *love, peace, forgiveness, gratitude,* and *service.* By bringing these words into your thoughts, recollections, and imaginings about a person or relationship situation, you can help your brain create the habit of compassionate cooperation.

The symbols *love, peace, forgiveness, gratitude,* and *service* are inherently positive. Just bringing them into consciousness when you think about a person or relationship situation will help you redirect the force of mind that is opposition and help rebalance a negative and polarizing relationship dynamic.

Try doing this when you first wake up in the morning, at midday, and at bedtime. Observe the impacts.

Breathe Deeply and Slowly

By breathing deeply and slowly you calm the involuntary nervous system, including heart rate, digestion, respiratory rate, and hormone release. When you feel yourself generating the force of opposition, try taking long, deep breaths to slow down your reaction so you can actively choose to reframe the fear, anger, resentment, criticism, or entitlement you are feeling. Try counting slowly to four as you deeply inhale, then again as you slowly exhale.

Breath awareness can calm, dissolve anger, and foster positive perception. Even in the face of violent threat, techniques for breath awareness have been proven effective. As you breathe slowly, you can help direct your mind toward the values of compassionate cooperation, bringing to mind the word symbols of love, peace, gratitude, forgiveness, and service as you think about the people and situations that frustrate you.

Meditate

Intensive meditation has been found to produce perceptual discrimination[55] as well as altered states of awareness. There are many different ways to meditate. However you practice it, meditation

---

55   Katherine A. MacLean, Emilio Ferrer, et al., "Intensive Meditation Training Leads to Improvements in Perceptual Discrimination and Sustained Attention," *Psychological Science* 21, no. 6: 829–839.

is an invaluable tool because it leads you to a place of mindfulness and calmness where you are more apt to be able to let go and release from the biases of perception. As you sit quietly and direct your attention to consciousness, you open to the part of you that is *Big You*, the pure perception that is free from the fear, anger, resentment, criticism, and entitlement of egocentric seeing.

Meditation can help you relax, let go of *small you* struggles and take a more active role in shaping your emerging self. By turning attention inward and closing your eyes, you limit the external stimuli to your brain, which means you focus the brain's attention on internal stimuli. This gives you an opportunity to actively calm the automatic nervous systems and your body's responses to stress, to slow your heart rate, and to reduce the release of adrenaline. In this calmness, you can actively and effectively shape your perceptions and people and situations. Because you are limiting distractions to your brain, you have more active control over molding your consciousness and your emerging self to reflect the values of compassionate cooperation.

If you are new to meditation, try sitting quietly and comfortably for ten minutes with your eyes closed as you imagine the words *love, peace, forgiveness, gratitude,* and *service*. Continue repeating these words and just see what happens. See who comes into your awareness and observe your creative power.

Laugh and Be Playful

You can help yourself move away from the force of mind that is opposition by learning to laugh at yourself and be playful.

Humor can lighten serious situations and help you rebalance a relationship dynamic. If you can learn to laugh at the various aspects of your *small self* that tend to engage to do your battles, you can embrace your vulnerabilities and your humanness as you learn to take yourself more lightly. Learning how to be playful about your shortcomings as you strive to redirect opposition is a way to help yourself redirect your negative and polarizing thoughts, recollections, and imaginings:

Rewind. There goes my spoiled only child again, always getting me into trouble!
Let me take that back. Here's what I really want to say ...

Next time your spouse or domestic partner does something that causes your brain to react negatively, try saying out loud, "*I love him, I really do.*" This can give you the opportunity to calmly identify and explain your underlying need instead of attacking your partner ("*How could you ...?*" "*Why did you ...?*") and provoking overt struggle.

Remind yourself that you can choose how you interpret relationship situations. When your mother-in-law corrects the way you're cooking eggs or comments on how much sugar you're giving the kids, you can allow your brain to engage your *small self,* get angry and build resentment toward her. Or you can choose to be playful as you strive to create emotional linkages with her. The story is yours to shape.

As long as your intention is to create and sustain compassionate cooperation, you will posture your mind to invite and support it.

CHAPTER 5

Conclusion

If learning aims at change, and that is always its purpose,
are you satisfied with the changes yours has brought you?
… If the outcome of yours has made you unhappy,
and if you want a different outcome,
a change in the curriculum is obviously necessary.

—*A Course in Miracles*[56]

Learning is an inevitable outcome of *being*. From the moment you are born, "you" begin emerging through an interactive dialogue with others, where the most important people in your personal life play a starring role. Your learning and "you" in any given instant reflect your brain's emotionally symbolic interpretations and adaptations to new experiences. Through your intricate network of relationships, you shape your learning and this emerging process of your *self*, which is a creative and evolving process of consciousness.

Your every instant of consciousness, every thought, recollection, and imagining reflects what you've learned, who you are at any given moment, and what kind of relationships and life you are shaping. If your goal is to be "happy," genuinely satisfied, and fulfilled with the people in your life but you feel frustrated or dissatisfied, your learning has failed you. It has taught you to think, recollect, and imagine through the veil of negative perception, and to shape the stories you tell yourself about others with negative and polarizing emotional values such as fear, anger, resentment, criticism, and entitlement. Whether or not you share your negative stories in interaction with others, they shape your experience of your self, others, and life.

To be "happy" and genuinely satisfied with people and life, *redirect your learning*. Make the commitment and willful choice to engage a mind-set symbolizing emotional values such as love,

---

56   Doug Thompson, ed., *A Course in Miracles* (Jaffrey, NH: Miracles in Action Press, 2008), 1–84, T8 B2, T8 B3.

peace, forgiveness, gratitude, and service that is capable of producing the positive and unifying force of mind causing the "song of heart" that is connection. By making the moment-by-moment choice to use your mind to redirect the negative stories you tell you self about others and the polarizing thoughts, recollections, and imaginings that inform them, you can control what your brain "believes it sees." This is how you can accommodate the paradox between your brain's predisposition to negativity and errors in mental processing that cause you to push others away, as well as your core human need to connect with others.

The choice is yours. Allow your brain to decide for you, and accept its predisposition to negative bias and errors in mental processing. Or use your mind to fabricate creations that will "rewire" your brain to produce thoughts, recollections, and imaginings consistent with the mind-set of positive perception that will always produce the unifying force of mind that is compassionate cooperation.

By doing nothing, you agree to learn opposition and to allow your brain to decide for you. Your brain will always "see what isn't there" and cause you to believe and defend what you "see." It will extend and deepen the negative emotional value of your every single negative thought, recollection, or imagining and lead you to invest in its negatively biased assumptions and premises. Even physically, your brain will shape its neural pathways to accommodate your negative learning, "wiring" you to feel frustrated and dissatisfied with the most important people in your life and with life in general.

However subtle and covert, the force of mind that is opposition always and reliably, to some extent and intensity, will inhibit connection and cause separation in a relationship dynamic. By doing nothing and allowing your brain to decide your learning for you, you give up your creative potential for shaping your emerging process of *self* that is consciousness, the mirror for "you," your relationships, and life.

You are human and imperfect, but striving to take responsibility for every personal relationship in your life in a way that serves collective wellness is a worthy and purposeful goal, one that serves you, your relationship partners, and your communities. It is what causes you to flourish, and how you can propel yourself toward self-actualization, and more joyful living as you promote a kinder and more cooperative and productive world.

PART 3 – APPLYING THE GUIDANCE

SHAPING RELATIONSHIPS, SELF, CONSCIOUSNESS, AND CONNECTION

Part 3 of *Force of Mind, Song of Heart* provides you with scenario exercises so you can practice applying the guidance in part 2. Each exercise contains a scenario, a series of inductive problem-solving and decision-making challenges, and discussion input.

CHAPTER 6

Exercises: Relationship Scenarios

The personal relationship scenario exercises in this section of *Force of Mind, Song of Heart* are intended to provide guided practice opportunities to help you improve the personal relationships in your life through the process of shaping self and consciousness[57]. For each exercise, read the *scenario description* and *discussion* sections. Respond to the questions on your own or with others before you read the *discussion input*.

1 The Force of Mind That Is Opposition

Scenario Description

Alicia has a calm demeanor. While she's easy to get along with, she has trouble saying "no" and setting boundaries, generally going along with what others want and then resenting them for it. When she does this with her husband, her way of expressing her resentment is to withhold conversation so he'll "get the message." Sometimes when she feels angry or hurt, she can go days without talking to him. The exchange below between Alicia and her husband Jack is typical:

> **Alicia:** [Shifts her body posturing and facial expression away from what is "normal" for her in her interaction with Jack]
> **Jack:** What's wrong? Now, what'd I do?
> **Alicia:** Nothing.
> **Jack:** Then why aren't you talking?
> **Alicia:** [Silence, no eye contact, crossed arms]

---

57 The scenarios used in the exercises are based on authentic interactions. Names and other identifying information have been removed, and adjustments have sometimes been made to make the examples more generic.

Discussion

1. What clues in the interaction allow you to understand Alicia's negative and polarizing force of mind?
2. How do you know Jack understands her intended message?
3. How successful is Alicia in her goal of making sure her husband "gets the message"? How does this goal serve her? How does this goal *not* serve Alicia? Does it serve Jack? How/ how not?
4. Why can't Alicia's goal of making sure Jack "gets the message" invite or support connection with Jack?

Discussion Input

1. Her shifts in body posturing and facial expression from what is "normal" for her in her interaction with Jack; her refusal to speak when Jack asks her why she isn't talking.
2. You know Jack understands Alicia's intended message because he says, "*What's wrong. Now, what'd I do*," suggesting that this is a familiar struggle for them.
3. Alicia successful accomplishes her goal of making sure Jack "gets the message," which serves her egocentric seeing. In her eyes, she's "won" the struggle by refusing to speak to Jack. Her goal does not serve her, because it causes separation between her and Jack. It definitely doesn't serve Jack, because he has no idea what she really needs or wants from him.
4. Alicia's goal is punitive. She wants to punish Jack and takes her power and removes reciprocity in the exchange by refusing to talk to him. She has created imbalance in the dynamic between them, which cannot lead to connection, only separation.

2 Negative Story Julia Tells Her Self

Scenario Description

Julia is constantly obsessing about her mother-in-law, wishing that she didn't have to deal with her. Although she sees her infrequently, she spends a lot of time spinning negative stories about her in her interaction with her self and talking about her mother-in-law to her friends. The following is a familiar theme in Julia's interaction with her self:

> Why do I have to deal with her? I hate it when she comes over. Why can't he just tell her to stay home! Her voice is so annoying! I wish the kids didn't like her. She drives me crazy!

Discussion

1. How and why will Julia's negative script cause her to generate an oppositional force of mind and only an oppositional force of mind? How and why will it inhibit Julia from connecting with her mother-in-law even if she is polite and appropriate when she interacts with her?

2. How will the emotional value of Julia's present thoughts shape the larger melody of her relationship with her husband, and why? What will be the impact on her relationship with her mother-in-law? What other people will be affected by her oppositional force of mind, and why?

Discussion Input

1. The negative attitudes and emotions characterizing Julia's negative story create an oppositional force of mind that postures her in a *me-against-you* relationship dynamic with her mother-in-law, which can only inhibit connection and cause separation even if Julia is polite and appropriate to her mother-in-law when she interacts with her.

2. Julia's negative script will shape the larger melody of her relationship with her husband because she will probably come to blame him for not telling his mother to stay home, or for siding with his mother. As she builds her case against her mother-in-law, she will be likely to blame her husband in some way, unless he "writes his mother off." The more negative attention Julia gives to her mother-in-law, the more negative impact it will have on her relationship with her mother-in-law (and probably with her husband). Julia's oppositional force of mind will affect alignments with her children and with other in-laws, such as a sister-in-law or her husband's other siblings.

3 Redirecting an Oppositional Force of Mind

Scenario Description

Olivia and Josh have been married for several years. Olivia has been under a lot of pressure at work lately and feels tired and often impatient with the people around her, especially Josh. When Josh asks her, *"Hey, Olivia, have you seen my sweater around?"* she answers, *"Check on the back of chair in the den."* As she answers, she's thinking to her self,

> He is so annoying! Doesn't he see I'm busy? Why doesn't he just shut up and leave me alone? Does he really have to ask me such stupid questions when he sees I'm busy?

Discussion

1. Describe the negative emotional values characterized by the conversation in Olivia's mind. What mind-set does it reflect—the PIT or the positive perceptual paradigm that creates the "song of heart" that is connection?

2. Is Olivia creating a genuinely positive, authentically negative, or inauthentically positive relationship experience with Josh when she generates the force of opposition while pretending to be cooperative in her interaction with him? How will the authenticity of her relationship experience affect her relationship with Josh?

3. If Olivia redirects her force of mind to generate the attitudes and emotions of compassionate cooperation, what might her story to her self look like? How would it affect the authenticity of her relationship experience with Josh?

Discussion Input

1. Olivia's mind-set reflects the negative attitudes and emotions associated with the perceptual inattention trap (PIT) mind-set—values such as fear, resentment, anger, criticism, and entitlement.

2. Olivia creates an *inauthentically positive* relationship experience with her husband because she generates the force of mind that is opposition but pretends to be cooperative. Olivia will deepen and extend her negative and polarizing feelings toward her husband unless she redirects the force of her mind. The extent to which it disconnects her from him will depend on how invested she is in the issues causing her to deepen and extend her negative perceptions.

3. If Olivia redirects the force of opposition as compassionate cooperation and reframes the story she tells her self, it might look like this: *"He is annoying! But, the truth is that he is always doing things for me. Let me be of service and take a minute to help him out."* By changing the emotional value of her story to reflect positive perception, Olivia would be creating a *genuinely positive* relationship experience with Josh.

---

4 Predicable Outcome over Time

Scenario Description

Laura has a tendency to order Larry around: *"Can you empty the trash?"* *"The dog needs to be taken out."* *"Put your clothes away."* To avoid arguing, Larry complies with her need to control, but the conversation in his mind is anything but compliant:

How did I ever marry her? What was I thinking? I can't stand the way she orders me around. Why doesn't she put the clothes away herself?

Discussion

1. How do the negative emotional values in Larry's narrative threaten his connection to his wife?
2. If Larry doesn't reframe his story, what will happen?

Discussion Input

1. Larry's words, *"How did I ever marry her? What was I thinking?"* reflect his brain's emotional responses. If he doesn't reframe the emotional value of his narrative so it reflects positive values such as love, peace, forgiveness, gratitude, and service, his brain will posture him to see everything his wife does as controlling.
2. If he doesn't reframe his story, Larry's brain will cause him to push Laura away and work tirelessly to accumulate evidence that justifies him to push her away.

5 Productive Use of Negative Feelings

Scenario Description

Derrick and Dan are domestic partners.

> **Derrick:** I'm starting to feel frustrated. I really need you to stop and listen to what I'm trying to say.
>
> **Dan:** Okay, sorry. I'm listening.

Discussion

1. How does Derrick productively use his feelings of frustration to help redirect the force of mind that is opposition?
2. How does Dan's response show that they have redirected opposition and restored balance to the relationship?

Discussion Input

1. Derrick rationally tells Dan how he feels instead of acting out his feelings. This enables Dan to get to know him better while it supports a *me-and-you* dynamic that maintains balance between them and keeps them connected.

2. Dan's acknowledgement ("Okay") and apology ("sorry") indicate that he accepts the redirection that Derrick suggests. When he says, "I'm listening," he relinquishes his power in the exchange and gives Derrick the floor, which sustains *me-and-you* posturing.

6 Implied Expectations

Scenario Description

Eli's mother has a passive-aggressive way of making him feel as if she expects him to show up at family events, such as his cousins' birthday parties. Her way is to make comments that indirectly reflect her expectations of him. Eli reacts negatively to her comments in his mind, feeling angry and resentful toward her. But he never says anything to his mother about the way he feels. He complains to his sister, but he still shows up at the family events.

Discussion
1. Why does Eli's anger and resentment produce an oppositional force of mind?
2. What effects will his oppositional force of mind have on his relationship with his mother?
3. How does anger and resentment cause imbalance to a relationship dynamic? How will Eli's oppositional force of mind affect the quality of his relationship with his mother?

Discussion Input
1. Because negative emotional values *only* and *always* generate the force of opposition.
2. It will cause him to push her away, accumulate "evidence" in his mind against her, and justify his own negative perceptions, deepening his dissatisfaction with her.
3. It will invite and sustain a negative and polarizing relationship dynamic and will inhibit connection. If he continues to pretend everything is fine, he will continue to create *inauthentically negative* relationship experiences with her, which cannot produce connection.

7 Criticism Won't Make You Feel Connected

Scenario Description

Emily and Henry are married and feel satisfied in their relationship although they bicker a lot about petty things, criticizing and blaming one another when they do.

Discussion

1. How long do you think Emily and Henry have been married and why?
2. What kind of relationship do you think they will have in twenty years if they stay together but don't learn how to redirect the negative relationship dynamic they create?

Discussion Input

1. If Emily and Henry are bickering a lot about petty things *and still feel satisfied*, chances are they've been married no more than a few years, since study evidence suggests that couples who are satisfied initially after marriage often become dissatisfied within the first three years, a consequence of verbal arguments marked by criticism and sarcasm.
2. If Emily and Henry stay together, they will probably feel dissatisfied with the relationship, and possibly comfortable if the dynamic they jointly create is one that is familiar from childhood.

8 The *People Pleaser-Always in Control* Dynamic

Scenario Description

Ethan and Heidi complement each other as a couple. Ethan, a philosophy professor, is laid back and calm. He was raised without too many rules as a child, but as a result of his reaction to his parents' divorce and the fact that he was constantly being pushed and pulled between his parents different homes in different states, he developed a *people pleaser* trait. Heidi, on the other hand, grew up in a stable two-parent home, but her father was sick most of her childhood and money was a problem for the family. As the oldest child, she felt responsible for her mother and her siblings and powerless to solve their problems. She worried a lot in childhood, feeling frustration over the family's situation. As a result, she developed an *always in control* self. Today, she runs a highly successful business and is in complete control of her financial situation.

The dominant relationship dynamic that Ethan and Heidi engage in is a struggle between Ethan's *people pleaser* self and Heidi's *always in control* self. Ethan hates that Heidi is constantly ordering him around as if he's one of her employees, and he also hates the fact that he gives in to all of her orders. Heidi, on the other hand, hates that she has to take care of everything and resents Ethan for not taking initiative. Before they were married, they enjoyed their time together, but now it seems that every interaction they have together is a struggle between her *always in control* self and his *people pleaser* self.

Discussion

1. How do Heidi and Ethan's childhood experiences contribute to the negative relationship dynamic they create? What qualities do you think attracted them to each other when they met, and why?

2. Why is it likely that Heidi and Ethan didn't engage the same way with each other at the beginning of their relationship? What happened to cause them to engage in a negative relationship dynamic?

3. How does Heidi's own egocentric "seeing" strengthen the polarizing relationship dynamic she invites and supports with Ethan? How might inclusive "seeing" help her to redirect the negative dynamic?

4. How does his own egocentric "seeing" strengthen the polarizing relationship dynamic he invites and supports with Heidi? How might inclusive "seeing" help him to restore balance to their dynamic?

Discussion Input

1. Heidi and Ethan were probably attracted to each other at a nonconscious level, where their respective brain's recognized how they could enable each other to extend a familiar dynamic from childhood. His *people pleaser* self was the perfect choice for her *always in control,* self because their respective *small selves* can provoke the other to respond in familiar emotional ways.

2. In the beginning of their relationship, Heidi and Ethan put their best selves forward and were very watchful to make sure they didn't let down their guards. The more time they spent together, the more their brains perceived threats and offenses, and the more they defended their own selves. Because spouses and domestic partners feel more entitled to control each other than other kinds of relationship partners, it isn't surprising that Heidi and Ethan struggle, using their familiar *small self* emotional patterns to defend their respective boundaries.

3. Heidi's own egocentric "seeing" strengthens the polarizing relationship dynamic she invites and supports with Ethan. She becomes very accusatory (*"Why didn't you ...?"* *"How could you ...?"* *"Why do you always ...?"*) and becomes invested in "winning" and proving Ethan "wrong" and herself "right." Her controlling approach disempowers Ethan and makes him feel that he can never win and is always losing the battles with her. It also imbalances their dynamic, making clear there *you-against-me* posturing. If Heidi moved to more inclusive "seeing" and put herself in Ethan's position, it would help her understand how her own behavior pushes Ethan away emotionally. She would begin to

explore strategies for connecting with him, such as *true-for-me statements* and *ask for what you need*. She might also use compassionate listening so she can learn what Ethan's real emotional issues are and how they could use cooperative problem-solving to meet each other's needs.

4. Ethan's egocentric perspective and his *people pleaser* self causes him to feel victimized by Heidi. A more inclusive perspective would allow him to see how his own role of *always giving in no matter what* allows Heidi to be *always in control*. The problem for Ethan is that he gives in and resents it, which is what causes him to generate the force of mind that is opposition and push Heidi away. Ethan will also benefit from learning how to use strategies, such *as true-for-me statements, ask for what you need,* compassionate listening, and cooperative problem-solving.

9 "How Can You Argue about Something So Silly?"

Scenario Description

Fay and Jay have been married for three years. When Fay puts a roll of toilet paper on the holder in the bathroom, she likes the roll to pull out from the top of the dispenser. When Jay puts a new roll on, he places it so the paper pulls from the bottom of the holder. Fay gets really frustrated with Jay because she keeps asking him to put the roll on the way she likes it, but he doesn't do it. Jay thinks it's ridiculous to make the toilet paper such an issue between them. Fay has started many arguments over the toilet paper, and Jay has taken the bait of opposition. Their arguments always leave them feeling frustrated and angry, and cause them to stop speaking to each other sometimes for hours. The issue causes Jay to see Fay as controlling and selfish and Fay to see Jay as incompetent.

Discussion

1. What's the real issue for Fay that causing her negative emotional reaction?
2. Instead of starting arguments over the toilet paper, what might Fay do with her feelings that would be more productive and preserve a balanced relationship dynamic? What might Jay do differently to make sure they maintain a balanced relationship dynamic instead of arguing over the toilet paper?

Discussion Input

1. The real issue for Fay is her need to control Jay and prove herself "right." The toilet paper issue triggers her *always in control* self to act out. Jay really doesn't care about the toilet

paper and thinks Fay's view is ridiculous, which causes him purposely o resist giving in to her. Jay's *resistor* self causes him to react passive-aggressively and take his power by not putting the toilet paper on the way Fay likes it. He knows it irritates her, but he does it anyway, knowing it will lead to a struggle between them.

2. Fay could recognize her own egocentric "seeing" and decide to use *collaborative problem-solving* to shift away from resentment and anger to include Jay in her need and a decision to address it. She might say something like, "*I know it's silly to be so invested in the toilet paper issue, but it would really make me feel like you care about me if you could make sure the roll pulls from the top.*" On the other hand, Jay could also initiate *collaborative problem-solving* to show Fay he cared about her needs and interest. He could say something like, "*I can see the toilet paper issue means a lot to you, and even though I think it's ridiculous, I'm going to try to make sure the roll always pulls from the top, because that's how much I love you.*" He could also be honest with himself and say, "*Part of me doesn't want to give in to you when you react emotionally, so it would really help me if you could tell me what you need.*" Either way, instead of buying into the familiar and negative relationship dynamic that always takes shape whenever one of them generates the force of mind that is opposition, they could try to understand each other's real emotional needs and interpret the situation more inclusively.

10 *"If I Say It's Black, He Says It's White"*

Scenario Description

Gail and Jim have been married for decades. Gail treats Jim like her son instead of her husband, directing him and criticizing his every move. Jim never directly contradicts Gail or says "no" to her. He always treats her politely. Gail feels that Jim is always making her "wrong." For fifty years, their daughter has been hearing her mother say, "*If I say it's black, he says it's white,*" referring to the father, although the daughter doesn't see it that way.

Discussion

1. What do you think is going on? What attitudes and emotions might Jim have toward his wife that might cause her to feel as she does? How do you explain the discrepancy between Gail's perception of Jim's intention to make her wrong and his politeness in outward conversation?

2. Can their relationship dynamic be fixed? Or is it too late after fifty years of marriage?

3. Assuming Gail wants to cause the relationship dynamic with her husband to change, what words could she used to take active steps to *connect* with Jim when she disagrees with what he says instead of accusing him by saying, *"If I say it's black, he says it's white"*?

Discussion Input

1. Gail and Jim's dynamic resembles a parent-child interaction, where Gail tells Jim what to do and Jim does it. While Jim feels comfortable with letting Gail take charge (having been raised by a domineering father), he also resents her because she takes away his power in the dynamic. Although Jim never contradicts Gail directly or neglects to follow her orders, he takes his power passive-aggressively by making indirect comments that he knows will make her mad and cause her to react. But because he uses language that's ambiguous (a comment sentence pattern without any confrontational word choices), he routinely denies his intention, which is really to provoke Gail. Jim *sets the dynamite* by baiting Gail indirectly to generate the force of mind that is opposition. Gail always *takes the bait*, which "ignites the dynamite," attacking Jim or accusing and blaming him. While Gail looks like the "bad guy," and Jim thinks she is, he neglects to see his own role in their joint negative relationship dynamic.

2. One or the other of them would have to be fully committed to changing a stubborn pattern that their respective brains have engaged in for fifty years. Gail and Jim "rewire" their brains, but after fifty years of reinforcing the same negative response patterns, they would need to be highly motivated to change.

3. Gail could learn to use phrases that show Jim she hears his point of view before giving her own, phrases such as, *"What you say is sometimes true, but I also think that ..."* or *"You have a point, but don't you think that ..."* or *"I see what you mean, but ..."* or *"What you say makes sense, but ..."* Whatever phrases Gail uses to shift her perspective to more inclusive seeing, the point is to show Jim that she hears him and wants to keep the stories she tells herself within the mind-set of positive perception. Gail does not have to make Jim wrong in order to share her opinion. Also, they can have different opinions and maintain a balanced relationship dynamic that preserves their connection, and actually intensifies it, if they create their respective stories with the emotional symbols of compassionate cooperation – such as love, peace, forgiveness, gratitude, and service.

Scenario Description

Sharon to her friends at lunch:

My mother-in-law is so annoying! I definitely wouldn't pick her to be in my life. All she does is shop, and worse, she keeps giving us things we don't want, need, or have a place for. Every time you turn around, another package arrives in the mail. None of it is anything I'd pick out myself. She's wasting her money. I'm going to ask her to stop sending things. She's just wasting her money.

Discussion

1. How does the narrative reflect Sharon's egocentric perspective of her mother-in-law? How does it influence the way she postures herself toward her mother-in-law and the dynamic she invites?

2. How would a more inclusive perspective of her mother change Sharon's interpretation of the situation described? How would it impact the way she postures herself toward her mother-in-law and the dynamic she invites?

3. Do you think it's a good idea for Sharon to ask her mother-in-law to stop sending them things? Explain.

4. How does Sharon's perspective reflect *entitlement*? What could she bring to mind instead to replace her feelings of entitlement?

Discussion Input

1. Sharon's egocentric perspective of her mother-in-law reflects her biased interpretation of the situation that are based on negative judgments about her mother-in-law's shopping, gift-giving, taste, and waste of money. She sees everything with the emotional symbols of opposition, the attitudes and emotions of negative perception, which cause her to posture and invite a *me-against-you* dynamic with her mother-in-law. Her emotional values cause her to generate the force of mind that is opposition, which will make it likely that she will see the gift-giving issue negatively, perhaps coming to see everything her mother-in-law does or says as wrong or invaluable.

2. A more inclusive perspective of the situation would allow her to see things through the eyes of her mother-in-law. It would allow her to recognize that although her mother-in-law might not have much in common with her, she is really trying to do her best to show her kindnesses by sending her gifts, regardless of what they are.

3. Telling her mother-in-law to stop sending things would be extremely selfish and confrontational, especially since her mother-in-law is trying to do a kindness by sending the gifts. Sharon's own negative attitudes and emotions are causing her to reject the gifts and preventing her from seeing them as a loving gesture. To transform how she "sees" the situation and her mother-in-law, she would need to reframe her story and re-script using the positive and unifying attitudes and emotions of compassionate cooperation. Sharon could choose to see with her mother-in-law with gratitude. She could thank her mother-in-law for her thoughtfulness and put the gifts away or donate them if she had no place for them.

4. Sharon's perspective reflects entitlement because it does not reflect gratitude. You cannot simultaneously feel entitlement and gratitude. By thinking about her mother-in-law's gift sending in a way that reflects appreciation, Sharon could transform her feelings of entitlement.

12 "Let Me Be Brutally Honest ..."

Scenario Description

Lauren has always felt that her husband's teenage girls don't like her and that their mother, Michelle, his ex-wife, has done her best to make sure they don't give her a chance to get close to them. When their mother calls to talk to one of the children on a weekend they are scheduled to visit their dad and Lauren answers the phone, here's the conversation:

> **Lauren:** Michelle, I would really like for us to have a better relationship.
> **Michelle:** A better relationship? That's not gonna happen.
> **Lauren:** Can't we just put the past between us and start from today?
> **Michelle:** Let me be brutally honest here. No one likes you. They think you're selfish and self-serving, and they don't want to have a relationship with you.

Discussion

1. Lauren attempts to restore balance to the dynamic she jointly creates with Michelle. How does Michelle's response to Lauren comment, *"A better relationship? That's not gonna happen,"* support or interfere with Lauren's attempt?

2. How is Michelle's attempt to be "brutally honest" support her own oppositional force of mind and egocentric seeing? How can being "brutal honesty" be harmful?

3. What's the difference between being "brutally honest" and expressing *true-for-me statements*?

4. How does Michelle's oppositional posturing influence other lives connected to theirs?

Discussion Input

1. Michelle rejects Lauren's attempt to *"have a better relationship."* She is committed to egocentric seeing and a perspective generates negative attitudes and emotions and is incapable of producing connection and a balanced dynamic.

2. Michelle is brutally *hurtful*. Honesty is about taking ownership for your own negative feelings and trying to understand your real underlying emotional need so you can work toward creating linkages and collaborative problem-solving. Michelle criticizes Lauren with *accusatory you statements ("You're selfish and self-serving")*, aligning her daughters' opinions with her own (*"No one likes you. They think ..."*). "Brutal honesty" is harmful when you criticize and blame others and neglect to look inward at your own egocentric seeing. Michelle neglects to put herself in Lauren's position and to try to see things from her perspective as an outsider to the family where her husband's children won't give her a chance because they fear their mother will be hurt or angry.

3. Michelle doesn't "own" her own feelings or emotional needs. She uses "brutal honesty" as an excuse to accuse and criticize Lauren. Honesty that is shaped using the positive and unifying emotional values of positive perception is never "brutal." If she used *true-for-me statements* and took an honest look within herself to shape them, she might discover that she is angry at her ex-husband for leaving her and is punishing Lauren as a way to get back at him. She might also see that she is encouraging her daughters to be unloving and unforgiving, which will contribute to their own negative thinking patterns.

4. Knowingly or unknowingly, Michelle influences negative alignments with her children against Lauren. She also strengthens the force of opposition she shapes with her ex-husband, which has a negative impact on their children's lives.

13 *"How Can I Connect with Him When He's Being a Jerk?"*

Scenario Description

Cassandra about her father-in-law

When I first got married, I thought my father-in-law was a great guy. I thought he was smart, successful, well educated, and well off. We really hit it off. I knew he was opinionated, but for some reason, it didn't bother me. There's a lot of stuff going on between him and my mother-in-law. They each kind of do their own thing. Definitely not the marriage I want. I think they just stay together for the kids, even though all the kids are grown and married. We only see them once or twice a year on holidays, but I hate going there. The only thing his father talks about is politics, and we really get into it when we start disagreeing. He's really conservative and right wing, and I can't just sit there when he's giving his ridiculous opinions. He argues against everything I say about women's rights. I try to be polite, but it's really hard because I'm not one to back down. Really, I can't talk to him about anything.

Discussion

1. How has Cassandra's perception of her father-in-law changed since she first got married? Why?
2. How has Cassandra equated her father-in-law with his views?
3. What can she do to rebalance the negative dynamic she shapes with her father-in-law?

Discussion Input

1. When Cassandra first got married she saw him through the eyes of positive perception, telling herself stories about him that generated compassionate cooperation with her father-in-law, which is why she *thought he was a great guy* even thought she knew *"he was opinionated."* Since then, she has changed her feelings about him because his views trigger her brain to react and position her to defend and attack.
2. She opposes his views and extends her opposition to her feelings *about him*. Because she is invested in making herself "right" and her father-in-law "wrong," a consequence of egocentric "seeing," she rejects him instead of his views. Cassandra can benefit

from separating her feelings about her father-in-law's views from her feelings about her father-in-law.

3. Cassandra can restore balance to their dynamic by telling herself stories about him that reflect positive emotional value. She can use language symbols to create linkages with him even though her opinions differ from his. She can make sure her father-in-law feels heard, by using phrases such as, *"You have a point, but I also feel that …," " I can understand why you feel that way, but for me …,"* and *"I see what you mean, but for me …"* Once Cassandra generates the force of mind that is compassionate cooperation with her father-in-law, she will show him in subtle ways (the way she sits and positions her body) that she wants to draw him closer to her instead of push him away. Right now, she sees everything he says and does as a threat or offense because her brain reacts and she allows herself to root more and more deeply in her negative perceptions. She can also talk to him, genuinely asking him how he's doing and feeling. By finding other ways to connect with him, she can help herself invite balance to the dynamic they create, change what she "sees," and separate her father-in-law as a person from his views.

14 Saying "No" with Kindness

Scenario

Gia and her husband are newlyweds. Gia's parents bought a house two streets away from where they live, thinking it would be perfect for Gia and her husband. Gia and her husband had been talking about relocating to a different state and had been looking for job opportunities, which her parents knew about. When Gia's parents told them they bought them the house, Gia told them they weren't sure if they were staying in the area. Gia's mother said it was too late for them to decide to move because she and her husband had already put a large down payment on the house and they needed Gia and her husband to take over the mortgage payments. Gia feels anger and resentment that her mother didn't talk to her about involving her in such a big commitment and did not consider that Gia and her husband wanted to relocate. She knows that if she and her husband move into the house and take over the mortgage payments, her resentment and anger will deepen.

Discussion

1. How can Gia redirect her anger and resentment with an inclusive perspective where she sees her parents with the attitudes and emotions of compassionate cooperation that will

allow her to *say no with kindness* to her parents on the house issue without posturing, creating a *me-against-you* dynamic with them?

Discussion Input

1. Gia might *say no with kindness* by using the positive and unifying mind-set of positive perception and creating her narrative with emotional values such as love, peace, forgiveness, gratitude, and service, which generate *compassionate cooperation*. This will position her in a *me-and-you* orientation that invites a power-sharing and positive reciprocity their relationship dynamic. She can connect with her parents and use inclusive "seeing" to try to collaboratively problem-solve an emotionally charged relationship situation. She might script out the following as a preparatory step to help her before she sits down to talk to her parents: *"Mom and Dad, thank you so much for trying to help us out by buying the house and putting in the down payment. We are so very grateful for how much you must love us and care about us to have done that, but we've decided that we really want to relocate for work. But please don't worry about your down payment. We will contact the real estate agent and have her put the house back on the market immediately, and we'll move in temporarily and make the mortgage payments until it's sold if we need to."* While her parents might react negatively at first, if Gia continues to stay within the parameters of positive perception and *avoid taking the bait* of negative perception, she will invite her parents to sustain a balanced relationship dynamic. However, if she allows herself to be pulled into a polarizing dynamic, the situation is likely to cause overt struggle and to spiral out of control.

15 The *Control Freak* and *Doubting Thomas* Dynamic

Scenario

Seana and Sean are married. They have complementary personalities, which is what attracted them to one another when they first met. Seana is highly energetic, organized, detail oriented, and proactive. Her take-charge attitude makes her a highly valued employee at work and an excellent supervisor. Although Sean is responsible and dependable, he takes things as they come and is laid back.

Seana routinely takes care of almost everything around the house, including the dog, the bills, service work, cleaning, and organizing. The frustration and anger she feels toward Sean for leaving everything for her has contaminated how she feels about their entire relationship. She is constantly blaming him and criticizing him. However, Seana hasn't realized and accepted that she has a *control freak* aspect to her *small self* that wants everything done her way, or that she is so proactive in getting things done that she doesn't give Sean a chance to help. She also doesn't recognize the *perfectionist* part of her *small self* that causes her to see everything Sean does as *wrong*. Sean, on the other hand, has a *doubting Thomas* aspect to his *small self* that engages with the power dynamic Seana sets up. Because he feels he can never do anything right in Seana's eyes, and because he feels she nags and bosses him around, he has given up trying to please her and passive-aggressively withdraws, which only annoys her more. Sean's view is that no matter what he does around the house, it's never enough or done well enough for Seana. Sean and Seana say they love each other, but they feel dissatisfied with one another and their relationship.

Discussion

1. How do the various parts of Seana's *small self* position her to push Sean away?
2. What causes Sean and Seana to feel dissatisfied with each other and their relationship?
3. How can Seana move away from criticism and *accusatory you statements* to stop blaming Sean when she feels herself reacting with negative attitudes and emotions?

Discussion Input

1. The various parts of Seana's *small self* position her to push Sean away because the *control freak* in her causes her to see her way as the only "right" way and the *perfectionist* in her sets impossible standards that no one can satisfy. Sean will never be able to please Seana unless they rebalance their polarizing relationship dynamic, which will require them to restore power-sharing and positive reciprocity.
2. The more Seana sees Sean's imperfections and errors, the more his *doubting Thomas* prevents him for feeling he can do anything "right" and the more he withdraws from trying. Their familiar struggle can only spiral them away from each other, not draw them closer to one another. Negative perception always causes separation and dissatisfaction, which they would need to heal by reframing.
3. When Seana feels herself reacting and generating the force of opposition, she can move from pointing blame at Sean to creating *true-for-me statements*. By focusing on her own real underlying emotional need, she can take responsibility for her own feelings, instead of blaming him, then move on to collaboratively problem-solve her needs with Sean. She could also say to Sean, "*Let me tell you what I need,*" so he doesn't have to guess.

16 Transforming Negativity

Scenario

Ben's girlfriend, Adele, doesn't want anything to do with his ex-wife. Adele doesn't understand why his ex-wife wants to involve her and Ben in spending Christmas together. She doesn't care if Ben and the ex-wife have three kids and the ex-wife wants them all to be together. She is worried that Ben will get back together with his ex-wife and wants to make sure that doesn't happen. She spends a lot of effort on generating negative thoughts, recollections, and imaginings about the ex-wife, even though she doesn't know her well and rarely sees her. Also, she routinely criticizes her when she's talking with her friends. She doesn't want anything to do with the ex-wife, and she doesn't want Ben to have anything to do with her. She doesn't care how long they were married or how many kids they have together.

Discussion

1. Describe how Adele's attitudes and emotions toward the ex-wife generate the force of mind that is opposition.
2. How can Adele reframe her interpretation of the situation with Ben's ex-wife, using the attitudes and emotions of compassionate cooperation, values such as love, peace, gratitude, forgiveness, and service?

Discussion Input

1. Adele's negative feelings are driven by her fear that Ben will get back with his ex-wife. The more she worries about that that possibility, the stronger her feelings of resentment and anger toward the ex-wife for the fact she is still in Ben's life. Adele feels entitlement toward Ben, that he is hers now and that he has no right to have a relationship with his ex-wife, even if it is helpful to the kids.
2. Adele can *reframe* her interpretation of the situation with Ben's ex-wife by taking an honest look within herself to identify how her *small self* is causing her egocentric perspective. She might come to recognize how the *green with envy* part of her *small self* is causing her to be selfish. This could help her recognize that the real underlying emotional issue for her is her fear of losing Ben. It might also allow her to see that her fear of losing Ben is causing her to push him away. By shifting to more inclusive "seeing," she would be able to look at the

situation from the perspectives of everyone involved (Ben, the kids, and Ben's ex-wife) to see how spending Christmas together could benefit them. She could see the situation as an opportunity for her to show love to Ben and his kids, and as a way to support peace in the family, knowing Christmas is always an difficult time for everyone. She could forgive the ex-wife for wanting to continue to have a relationship with Ben and choose to release her negativity around the issue. She could also generate a gratitude list, focusing on how she appreciates the ex-wife's openness and willingness to include her in family events. Then she could choose to agree to counter every criticism that comes into her mind about the ex-wife with a positive point as an act of service.

17 Watch Your Mind

Scenario

Susan is having dinner with her brother and his new girlfriend, whose fashion style is completely different from hers. Susan is very conservative in the way she dresses, doesn't like nail polish, and wears only designer clothes. Her reaction to her brother's girlfriend is reflected in her interaction with her self:

> Wow, that dress is ugly. She looks awful. Doesn't she have a mirror to see herself? Terrible hair. Frizz. I hate frizz. What a mess. Cheap clothes. Bad colors. What does he see in her?

Discussion

1. Explain how Susan came to have her values and why you think she reacts negatively to her brother's girlfriend's fashion style.
2. Why is the story Susan tells herself harmful to her, the girlfriend, and her brother?
3. How might Susan reframe the story she tells her self as soon as she realizes it's unfolding in her mind?

Discussion Input

1. Susan came to have her values (tendency to "see" as she does) through socialization into culture, family, and her own idiosyncratic ways of "seeing." Based on a largely nonconscious desire to identify with different in-groups within her culture (school,

neighborhood, professional, church) or reject being associated with them, she came to her own biased perception of people and the world around her. When Susan perceives someone or something that threatens her own values, beliefs, and expectations, her brain reacts by posturing her for opposition, generating negative scripts in the interaction she has with her self.

2. Negative stories like Susan's are harmful to the person producing them, because they reinforces emotionally negative thought patterns and extend them across other relationships and situations, strengthening negative perception in consciousness. Negative stories are harmful to others because they are subjective and unfair, based on biased and egocentric "seeing." They also invite harmful negative alignments, drawing others into an unproductive and harmful dynamic.

3. Susan might reframe her story to align with the positive emotional values of compassionate cooperation—love, peace, gratitude, forgiveness, and service. She can redirect her negative emotional values in any way that reflects positive perception. For example, she might re-script as follows: *"What does my view of her dress matter if she likes it? She must be trying her best to look good. She can't help what kind of hair she has. She seems as if she genuinely cares about my brother. She is very outgoing and kind."*

18 *"I'll Never See Him Again Anyway ..."*

Scenario

Bob is driving on a busy expressway when another driver cuts him off at the entrance where cars are merging into a single lane. As the other driver passes Bob, he angrily mouths words and thrusts his middle finger at him. In response, Bill mouths,

Idiot! Screw you too! Scumbag.

Discussion

1. How has Bob allowed himself to be pulled into opposition by the other driver? How does he cause himself harm?
2. How could the *stop-and-reframe* technique have helped Bob?
3. How could inclusive "seeing" help him reframe?

Discussion Input

1. Bob shares the negative story he tells himself before he can reframe it. In doing so, he causes himself stress that is not good for his health. He also reinforces his negative reaction and response pattern.

2. Bob could have commanded himself to *stop-and-reframe,* which would have given him time to create a *space for grace* in order to reframe his automatic negative reaction.

3. Inclusive "seeing" would have helped Bob think about why the other driver may have been having such a bad day that he cut him off and so rudely confronted him. He might have thought about how he's had bad days too, and how bad he's felt when he's realized he's lost control of his own emotions and reacted.

19 *"Let Me Tell You What I Need ..."*

Scenario

Pearl asks Steve what he wants for dinner, but what she really wants is his help deciding what to make and preparing it. She is irritated with him for not knowing what she needs:

> **Pearl**: What do you want for dinner?
> **Steve:** I don't care.
> **Pearl:** Tell me.
> **Steve:** I said, I don't care.
> **Pearl:** [Signs deeply] I really can't do this!
> **Steve:** Do what?
> **Pearl:** [Marches out of the room, clearly irritated with Steve]

Discussion

1. How might Pearl ask for what she needs or let Steve know what she needs?
2. What effect does "marching out of the room" have?

Discussion Input

1. Pearl might say, *"Steve, I need you to help me decide what to cook tonight and to keep me company in the kitchen or help me prepare it."* She might also say, *"Let me tell you what I need so you don't have to guess."*

2. Marching out of the room is passive-aggressive and serves to clarify Pearl's force of opposition. Although she clarifies her irritation, she does so in an unproductive way that reflects power-grabbing, clearing creating imbalance in the relationship dynamic.

20 Damaging Negative Alignments

Scenario

Pamela and Margo were best friends and so were their teenage daughters until Pamela's daughter had a sleepover and didn't include Margo's daughter. Margo was so angry because her daughter felt excluded that she broke off her friendship with Pamela. Neither Margo and Pamela nor their daughters have spoken since.

Bobby is friends with both Pamela and Margo. He met Pamela through Margo. Margo has asked him not to talk to Pamela, telling him she expects him to be loyal to her because he's *like a brother* to her. She asks him to agree with her request not to talk to Pamela to show his loyalty to her because they're *like family*. Bobby feels very uncomfortable with Margo's request.

Discussion

1. Why is Margo's request to Bobby unreasonable and harmful to Bobby as well as to Pamela?
2. How might Bobby *say no with kindness* to Margo's request? Give an example of what he might say to Margo.
3. What are the possible scenarios if Bobby doesn't *say no with kindness*?

Discussion Input

1. Margo's request to Bobby is unreasonable and harmful because it is an attempt to align Bobby negatively against Pamela. Her request represents her attempt to align Bobby's against Pamela, and strengthen her own oppositional force of mind. Margo's request is unreasonable because it unfairly tries to posture Bobby to disconnect from Pamela. Margo uses her force of opposition toward Pamela to try to create connection with Bobby.
2. It is important for Bobby to *say no with kindness* to Margo's request because it is harmful to him and to Pamela. It will also extend and strengthen Margo's opposition, and will not serve Bobby's relationship with Pamela. Bobby might say to Margo, "*I hear what you're saying, and I also feel we are family* [Acknowledgment]. *Because I do love you, I can't agree to do that. I love you both* [True-for-Me Statement] *and I won't feel good about myself if I agree*

to do that [True-for-Me Statement]. *You also won't be able to trust that some day I won't turn my back on you as well. I hope you understand and I also hope you reconcile with Pamela* [True-for-Me Statements]."

3. If Bobby doesn't *say no with kindness*, he is likely to create an *inauthentically negative* situation with Margo, where he pretends to agree with her request, but feels negative emotions about it and tells himself negative stories about Margo that will negatively bias his thoughts, recollections, and imaginings about her. This is how he will do harm to himself.

---

21 Subtle Opposition

Scenario

Fran and her baby sister are adults, talking about the need to cut down on carbs and desserts.

> **Fran**: It doesn't help when we go out and they put that delicious bread on the table.
>
> **Fran's Sister**: Sometimes, I ask them not to put bread on the table so I won't eat it. Otherwise, it's hard to resist.
>
> **Fran**: I can't do that with ten other people at the table.
>
> **Fran's Sister**: I'm not saying you should do that. Of course you can't do that with ten other people. I do it when it's just the two of us.
>
> **Fran**: I can't do that.
>
> **Fran's Sister**: I'd just have them put it down at the other end then.
>
> **Fran**: Dave sits next to us and he devours that bread, even when he has pasta. I never saw anybody eat bread and pasta like that.
>
> **Fran's Sister**: Well, I'd just tell him you need to stay away from the bread and ask for his help.

Discussion

1. Where is opposition first expressed in the conversation between Fran and her sister? How does it affect the rest of the conversation? What could Fran have been said instead to redirect opposition as compassionate cooperation, creating an emotional linkage with her sister?

2. What does the conversation suggest about the dynamic Fran and her sister engage in regularly with one another? What does it suggest about their relationship?

3. How do you think the sisters see their relationship?

Discussion Input

1. When Fran says, *"I can't do that with ten other people at the table,"* Fran completely negates her sister's suggestion, which causes more opposition: *"I'm not saying you should do that."* Fran could have said to her sister's suggestion of asking them not to put the bread on the table, *"That's a good idea, but it can be hard when there are a lot of other people at the table."* If she used the words, *"That's a good idea,"* she would have reflected the force of mind that is compassionate cooperation, maintaining balance in their relationship dynamic, which will preserve connection with her sister instead of subtly pushing her away.

2. The dialogue suggests that Fran and her sister shape a subtle negative and polarizing relationship dynamic, which is probably mirrored in all of these conversations together. It suggests that their relationship reflects a larger emotional melody representing the force of mind that is opposition, a struggle they act out in the same way on other most topics they come together to discuss.

3. Fran's sister likely feels disempowered in their relationship, an imbalance that was likely established in their childhood together because Fran is the "big sister," a role which has certain rights and responsibilities associated with it that *entitle her.* Fran still probably feels entitled to have control in their relationship, always taking her power to "have the last word" or prove her baby sister "wrong."

22 Detox from Negative Memories

Scenario

Millie is constantly reviewing in her mind all the things her mother-in-law has done to wrong her. Shortly after she takes a call from her mother-in-law, she says to her friend:

> My mother-in-law called and I made the mistake of picking up the phone. I should have just let it go to voice mail, but I made the mistake of picking it up. I was polite. She asked how I was doing, and I said, "Fine." Ugh! I don't know why I answered the phone.

Discussion

1. How do Millie's thoughts of all the things her mother-in-law has done to wrong her affect how she feels about her relationship with her mother-in-law? How do you think it affects her life?

2. What can she do to move beyond her negative feelings about her mother-in-law?

3. If her husband also has the same negative feelings about his mother, what kind of impact does it have on how they feel? Why? How does their alignment affect Millie?

4. Is cutting off communication with her mother-in-law the answer? Explain.

5. What other options does Millie have?

Discussion Input

1. By thinking about all the things her mother-in-law has does "wrong," Millie positions her mind in *me-against-you* posturing toward her mother-in-law, generating the force of mind that is opposition, which makes connection impossible. Millie strengthens the likelihood that she will interpret everything her mother-in-law stands for and does as negative. She also invites her mother-in-law to join a negative relationship dynamic, because although she is polite, her polarizing force of mind causes her to embody her negative feelings with negative symbols such as shifts in intonation when she talks, for instance, that invite negative reciprocity (negative kindnesses) with her. Millie's negative thoughts also predispose her to strengthening and extending the force of opposition through more negative thoughts and also recollections and imaginings about her mother-in-law and will reinforce how her brain will react in every next instant. This will predispose her more generally to negativity in her life.

2. Millie can move beyond her negative feelings about her mother-in-law by redirecting her negative thoughts, the story she tells her self about her mother-in-law, that generate her oppositional force of mind. She can engage in reframing and re-scripting to revalue the emotional significance of her story. Instead of allowing it to reflect negative values like fear, resentment, anger, and entitlement, she can reinterpret it to reflect positive perceptual values, such as love, peace, gratitude, forgiveness, and service. She can all call on the *Big You* part of her self that that is inclusive "seeing" to help her recognize her connection with her mother-in-law and see her own humanity in her. This might help her think about how devastated she would be if her own children didn't want to talk to her. It might also help her think how we all do our best as parents, and how she is holding her mother-in-law responsible for her husband's past hurts. She might also recognize the various parts of her *small self* that are interfering with her ability to generate a positive and unifying force of mind and a unifying dynamic that invites her mother-in-law to connect with her, address her own real emotional needs, and take steps to address them in ways that will serve the relationship.

3. Millie's husband has had a negative view of his mother his entire life. That's the only way Millie has ever heard him talk about her. For their whole married life, she has fed into her husband's negative feelings about his mother, helping him prove to himself that he has been right all along in how he feels about her. The two of them intensify the opposition he has toward his mother by their negative alignment. It serves Millie because she has a *spoiled only child* self that doesn't really want to share her husband with his mother, as she might have to do otherwise. Also, being able to gang up against his mother has been a bond between Millie and her husband. It has served as a common cause between them. In some harmful ways, it serves the relationship she has with her husband, even though it causes frustration and stress to both of them and hurts his mother. Their children also get to see their grandmother as the "bad guy," which interferes with their own perceptions about her, extending the negative alignments even further.

4. Cutting off communication will eliminate the need for Millie to interact with her mother-in-law, but it won't cause Millie to redirect her negative and polarizing attitudes and emotions toward her mother-in-law or to reprogram her brain to produce the force of mind that is compassionate cooperation. It is also harmful to her mother-in-law because it withholds love and intensifies negative alignments.

Millie might think about how she can be of *service* to her mother-in-law by sending her a sincere note once a year, thanking her raising such a wonderful son. She might also generate a gratitude list about her mother-in-law and review the list every morning when she wakes up. By actively generating the force of mind that is compassionate cooperation, by "seeing" within the mind-set of positive perception, she can "rewire" her brain to produce *me-and-you* posturing, not only with her mother-in-law but more generally. She will also be influencing her husband to align in a way that is positive and unifying with her own posturing toward his mother, which will also affect how their children align themselves toward their grandmother.

23 Relationship Frustration

Scenario

My sister's manipulative ... My mother's controlling ... I can't stand my brother's wife ... My mother-in-law's nuts ... I can't deal with my father ... My boss is an idiot ... She drives me crazy ... He's a jerk ... Why won't she listen ... Why does he keep on arguing ... Who does she think she is ... Why doesn't he get it ...

Discussion

1. How do your own biased negative perceptions, such as the ones suggested above, limit your ability to create and sustain *genuinely positive* relationship experiences?

2. More generally, how do such instances of negative thought affect the overall quality of a relationship?

Discussion Input

1. Every single negative thought, recollection, or imagining you allow to persist in your mind generates the force of mind that is opposition and serves a *me-against-you* dynamic. Because certain social situations predispose you to compliance in social interaction with some partners, when your force of mind is negative and you feign being positive, you will always create *inauthentically positive* relationship experiences, *and* you brain will use the negative thoughts, recollections, and imaginings related to them as premises and assumptions for more similar negative perceptions. *Genuinely positive* relationship experiences result when you generate thoughts, recollections, and imaginings with positive symbolic value, reflecting attitudes and emotions such as love, peace, gratitude, forgiveness, and service, because you will always embody what is in your mind. When you generate the force of mind that is compassionate cooperation, you project it.

2. Negative thought supports a negative and polarizing dynamic across the life of a relationship and enhances your risk for feeling dissatisfied with the overall quality of a relationship. Your brain will use a single negative thought to "prove" to you that you are justified in seeing a relationship partner with egocentric, *small self* "seeing."

---

24 *"Why Should I Have to Sacrifice?"*

Scenario

A divorced sixty-six-year-old woman who lives alone in a small apartment needs financial help to meet her monthly expenses. Her son gives her the money she needs every month without issue, but his wife resents it. Consider the daughter-in-law's argument to her husband about his mother:

> Why should I have to sacrifice because *she* was irresponsible. She got money from her divorce. It's not my fault she spent it on vacations and things. That's *her* problem, not *mine*.

Discussion

1. Which mind-set does the daughter-in-law use to shape her thoughts, recollections, and imaginings about her mother-in-law, the PIT mind-set or the paradigm for positive perception? Explain your answer.

2. Which sentence pattern clearly symbolizes the daughter-in-law's negative and polarizing attitudes and emotions toward her mother-in-law?

3. What is the problem with perception that punishes a relationship partner for a past error? How does it interfere with the force of mind that is compassionate cooperation and a relationship dynamic?

4. Explain how the daughter-in-law might reframe the situation so she can release her resentment.

5. How would a shift to inclusive "seeing" help the daughter-in-law find some other possible solutions besides giving money for addressing the mother-in-law's situation?

Discussion Input

1. The daughter-in-law's thoughts reflect the perceptual inattention trap (PIT) mind-set. She allows the attitudes and emotions of egocentric "seeing" to guide relationship problem-solving and decision-making. She creates a *me-against-you* dynamic with her mother-in-law (and her husband) on the issue. Her fear, resentment, anger, criticism, and entitlement cause her to think only of herself and see her mother-in-law as irresponsible with money. Her negative perception interferes with her ability to cause a positive and unifying dynamic with her mother-in-law and reflects power-grabbing, where she sees herself as more entitled and deserving, and negative reciprocity, where she withholds kindnesses. Her negative and polarizing force of mind also interferes with her ability to connect with her husband.

2. *"Why should I have to sacrifice because SHE was irresponsible."* The *wh-question* clearly symbolizes the daughter-in-law's negative perception and strongly postures her in a *me-against-you* dynamic toward her mother-in-law on the issue of giving her money.

3. The problem with punishing a relationship partner for a past error is that you allow yourself to perpetuate the attitudes and emotions of negative judgment that generate oppositional posturing and interfere with connection. You also harm yourself by strengthening and extending negative perception, which will strengthen the larger negative melody of your relationship and also affect your life, because you will intensify the likelihood that your brain will react in the same negative way in other situations where threat or offense is perceived.

4. She might reframe her resentment by focusing on gratitude and bringing to mind her mother-in-law's contributions. She might thank her mother-in-law for raising such a wonderful son, for sharing him with her, for the sacrifices she made to send him to college, for the times she took care of the grandchildren, or for always remembering her birthday. She might also discover upon introspection that the *green with envy* aspect of her *small self* perceives scarcity instead of abundance and causes her egocentric seeing. By calling on the inclusive "seeing" of *Big You,* she would be able to imagine herself as her mother-in-law and see her own vulnerability, realizing that, like all of us, she did the best she could.

5. A shift to inclusive "seeing" would help her move away from her *small self* perspective to confront her real emotional issue, her resentment about the money. It would lead her explore the source of her feelings and her real emotional interest. She might be able to recognize her fear of not having enough as she describes her feelings rationally to herself instead of reacting negatively to the trigger of her mother-in-law's need. By focusing on inclusive needs and interests, she would be able to explore other ways to help. She might buy her mother-in-law's groceries or have meals delivered to her. She might also be able to help find options for a better living situation for her mother-in-law. (Holding on to her mother-in-law's past error of judgment and causing herself to experience resentment is how she harms her self, her mother-in-law, and her husband. It does not serve collective wellness and will not make her "happy").

---

25 "He Really Liked My Potato Salad …"

Scenario

Daughter: Mom, what was the secret to your long and happy marriage to Dad?
Mother: He really liked my potato salad.

Discussion

1. How is the mother's potato salad a positive emotional symbol that generates the force of mind that is compassionate cooperation that causes connection with the husband? How does it affect the relationship dynamic between the couple?

Discussion Input

1. The potato salad is an emotional symbol of positive perception. By taking the time and effort to prepare something she knows her husband likes, the woman practices love. She

may also have prepared it at times over the years as a gesture of peace and forgiveness when they had an argument, or to show her gratitude to him. It also represents a gesture of service, because she probably went out of her way to make it even when she didn't feel like, just to please him. It allows her to generate attitudes and emotions shaping a *me-against-you* dynamic with her husband and represents *positive reciprocity,* an act of kindness that will draw him closer or keep him close to her. *Any positive emotional symbol will generate the force of mind that is compassionate cooperation and serve connection.*

26 "I Cut My Brother Off"

Scenario

Marion is a middle-aged American woman, who is married with college-age children. She has a brother, Don, who is also married with children. Marion's daughter (Don's niece) and his wife's sister's daughter (his wife's niece) unknowingly planned their daughters' weddings for the same day at the same time in different states. Don and his wife went to his wife's niece's wedding. They did not attend Marion's daughter's wedding, although they did send her a gift.

Marion is so angry with Don because he didn't attend her daughter's event that she stopped speaking to him. When she met with a friend shortly after the wedding, this is how the conversation went:

> **Marion**: I cut my brother off.
> **Friend**: What do you mean?
> **Marion**: I cut him off. He didn't come to my daughter's wedding so I cut him off.
> **Friend**: You're not speaking to him?
> **Marion**: Nope.
> **Friend**: What happened?
> **Marion**: He didn't come to the wedding.
> **Friend**: What? You're kidding! I can't believe it. That's terrible! Why not? That is totally unacceptable. I wouldn't talk to him either!

Discussion

1. What affect does Marion's anger have on the way she postures her self toward her brother? How does it affect their dynamic?

2. What do you think the real underlying issue is for Marion? What's going on beneath her emotional reaction to her brother's decision not to attend her daughter's wedding? Will "cutting him off" address her real need? Explain.

3. What *negative assumptions* do you think Marion makes about why her brother didn't attend her daughter's event? How might her interpretation of the situation, her negative perception, cause her to incorrectly draw conclusions (unstated, but implied by the fact that she stopped speaking to him)?

4. Name at least two specific biases that are interfering with how Marion sees the situation with her brother, caused by the brain's predisposition to errors in mental processing.

5. What effect does the friend's alignment with what Marion is saying do harm to Marion's brother?

6. How could you re-script the friend's message so that it aligns with the attitudes and emotions of compassionate cooperation and helps Marion rather than harms the relationship she has with her brother?

Discussion Input

1. Her anger generates the force of mind that is opposition and invites her brother to join her *me-against-you* dynamic. It creates a negative and polarizing force that cannot cause connection, only separation.

2. The real issue for Marion is probably her disappointment, and feelings of rejection. She may feel as if her brother has abandoned her. *Cutting him off* won't address her real need, because it only contributes to strengthening her own negative perception and their disconnection, which is not what she really wants. Her real need is to know her brother is there for her and hasn't abandoned her. She can reframe the story she tells herself, which she can do by calling on the *Big You* part of her self. This will help her "see" the situation from her brother's perspective so she can move beyond her narrow, egocentric "seeing," which causes her to prove him "wrong" and punish him by rejecting him (negative reciprocity that causes an imbalance in their dynamic, a "reverse act of kindness"). She may realize that her brother couldn't possibly be in two places at once and that he and his wife have had more involvement with his wife's family than with her family, that his wedding gift was an expression of love and generosity and that she wasn't getting what she needed by withdrawing and punishing her brother.

3. Marion assumes that her brother doesn't want to attend her daughter's event. Her incorrect conclusion makes her angry and causes her to generate the force of mind that is opposition, which is rooted in egocentric "seeing." Her brain's error in mental processing causes her to narrow what she "sees."

4. Cause-and-effect bias: Marion incorrectly assembles evidence as to why he doesn't want to attend her daughter's wedding. Confirmation bias: Marion seeks or interprets information that is consistent with her own preconceptions and assumptions. Selective perception bias: Marion perceives what she expects to perceive.

5. In trying to show her support, Marion's friend encourages Marion *not to talk* to her brother and validates Marion's biased judgment of him. The *friend aligns negatively* with Marion, strengthening negative perception instead of helping her transform her negative story to align with the mind-set of positive perception, which will enable Marion to "see" the situation and her brother in a way that allows her to create peace within herself.

The friend could use compassionate listening. She could acknowledge that she heard what Marion said, and then offer a suggestion:

> "I hear you. I'm sure you must have been disappointed, but have you thought about talking to your brother about it? I'm sure he didn't want to miss your daughter's wedding."

27 "I Can't Stand His Parents"

Scenario

Ali and Cara are friends who haven't seen each other in a few months. They met for a glass of wine and are catching up when the following conversation about Ali's in-laws takes place:

Ali: I can't stand his parents. They're mean. They never liked me.
Cara: That's awful.
Ali: It's true, they never liked me.
Cara: You're kidding. I thought they did.
Ali: Well, they kinda did in the beginning, but it was more for show.
Cara: Really? They fooled me. I thought they came over all the time?
Ali: Not really. They visited. Now they don't come at all and I don't go there. The last time we were all together she hardly gave me the time of day. Screw her if she thinks I'm going back there.
Cara: I don't blame you. You don't need aggravation in your life.
Ali: That's for sure. I'm glad they live out of state.

Discussion

1. How might Ali use questions to prompt her self to reframe her story about her in-laws?
2. Think of Ali's in-laws. What might they be thinking of the situation and their dynamic with Ali and their son? What biases might they hold about Ali?

Discussion Input

1. Ali might use question prompts like the following to help her shift away from the PIT mind-set and negative perception of her in-laws in reframe. She might ask herself the following questions: Love: *Am I extending love? No! I'm sure it must be hard for his parents to give up interacting with their son on a regular basis. I would feel sad too if I were in their situation.* Peace: *I will choose to redirect my negative feelings about my mother-in-law into loving thoughts by moving to inclusive "seeing" and thinking about her needs and interests as well as my own.* Forgiveness: *I forgive his parents, because I choose to release myself from the negative feelings that are causing my resentment toward them.* Gratitude: *I am grateful to his parents for raising such a responsible son. I am grateful that I am the beneficiary of their hard work and sacrifice. I am grateful that they always want us to come and visit. I am grateful that they will come to our home if I invite them.* Service: *I will look for ways to extend love through service. Maybe I'll offer to help his mother cook or help set up their summer home. Every time a negative thought about his parents enters my mind, I will reframe it as a positive one, as an act of service.*

2. Ali's in-laws might be biased in wondering how their son chose Ali as his wife. They may see her as unwilling to participate in family functions and unwilling to share their son. They may feel that they've done everything in their power to make her like them, and feel frustrated that they do not feel connected to her. They for sure understand that the dynamic between them is not positive and unifying, and understand that their son is "in the middle" between them and Ali.

---

28 "I Don't Want to Visit Your Parents ..."

Scenario

Em and Jewel are domestic partners who have been visiting Em's parents once a month for the past two years. Jewel hates visiting Em's parents, although she hasn't talked to Jewel about it. Even so, Jewel knows how Em feels because she's always in a bad mood the week before a family visit, and when they are at her parents' house, Em is withdrawn and punitive. When Jewel notices the change in Em's mood after they plan a visit to her parents', she always asks, "*What's wrong?*" Em's standard answer is, "*Nothing's wrong. I'm just tired.*"

Em keeps her negative thoughts to her self, but spends a lot of time being distracted by the negative story she tells her self:

I do *not* want to go there this weekend. I hate being around them. Why do I have to go? If she wants to see them, she can go alone. They're *her* parents. Why should I have to sit there for hours with them? Her mother's voice irritates me. This is the last thing I want to be doing this weekend. I wish we could just stay home and spend time alone! I hate giving up give my time with Jewel to visit them. B-O-R-I-N-G!

Discussion

1. What might Em say to her self to help her shift away from her negative story?
2. Although Em never discusses the issue or her feelings directly with Jewel, how does her negative story about Jewel's parents interfere with her ability to connect with Jewel's parents? How does it impact her relationship with Jewel?
3. What might be the real underlying issue for Em, the real emotional issue beneath her negative story that biases her perception?
4. How might Em rationally describe her feelings and need, positioning herself for compassionate cooperation with Jewel, and Jewel's parents?

Discussion Input

1. "*I am going to go this weekend and commit to extending love through my thoughts and actions. Every time I feel the pull of opposition, I am going to command myself to stop-and-reframe. I will take a space for grace to transform my negative feelings and will work at trying to understand what my real needs are so I can address them in a way that includes others. I am going to show Jewel how much I love her by extending love to her parents.*"
2. It causes her to posture in *me-against-you* orientation toward Jewel and toward Jewel's parents. Because her thoughts are negative, she generates the force of mind that is opposition, creating a negative and polarizing dynamic, causing imbalance and interfering with connection.
3. Em may feel fear, anger, resentment, criticism, and entitlement because she doesn't want to share Jewel with Jewel's parents. Whatever emotional issue is driving her feelings, if she can identify it, she can address it without pushing others away. By reframing her negative story to reflect the emotional symbols of positive perception, she can generate the force of mind that is compassionate cooperation that causes a *me-and-you* balanced dynamic.

4. *"Jewel, I'm really having a hard time sharing you all weekend with your parents. I hate feeling this way. I want to be a loving person. <u>It would help me a lot if</u> we could plan to leave your parents' house a few hours earlier on Sunday so that we could plan something fun together, just with the two of us. What do you think?"*

29 "I'm Desperate, I Need $1,500"

Scenario

April was an administrative assistant at the company Noor worked for. Although April and Noor had nothing in common, April befriended Noor at a difficult time in Noor's life. By the time Noor figured out that April's relationship motives were disingenuous, April was no longer working at the company:

> April told me she had cancer and I believed her. She did a great job faking it, pretending to be sick after chemo. It was all very dramatic and convincing. I'd only known her a few months, but I felt for her. She said she was alone and divorced. I'd seen her apartment and knew she was struggling so when she said, "I'm desperate. I need $1,500 to pay for chemo," I believed her. She begged me for the money, and I saw how sick she seemed to be. We actually drove together to my bank and I withdrew the money and gave it to her. A few weeks later, I decided to surprise her at the cancer center, where she said she was having her treatments. When I showed up there, they had never heard of anyone by her name. They checked the patient logs and she wasn't listed for that day, or ever. I thought that she might have used another last name, but I was told that no one fitting her description had been in for treatment recently. That was the moment I knew I had been taken.

Discussion

1. Looking back, Noor finds it easy to see red flags that signaled April was trying to deceive Noor about her illness. What bias allows Noor to look back and make sense of the situation even though she was unable to see the red flags before she figured out what was going on?
2. When Noor realizes she's been taken for the money, she reacts with anger, furious that she has been deceived by April. After the initial reaction, she willfully commands herself to *stop-and-reframe*. She realizes that she will never recover the money, so she decides to tell

her self a different story about April and the situation. Create an example of a story Noor could create to help her see the situation differently, in a way that frees her and allows her to move on without agitating herself with negative attitudes and emotions and harming her self.

Discussion Input

1. Hindsight Bias accounts for the fact that Noor can easily identify red flags as she looks back on events.

2. "I choose to release my anger because I am punishing myself if I hold on to it. I will never get the money back, so I choose to detach from it and view it as a gift. I wish April well. I release myself from expecting a return of the money. When I gave it to her and believed she had cancer, I wasn't expecting her to return it. I am not going to expect it now. I choose to give myself peace in the situation. I am grateful that I have abundance enough to have been able to give her the money. I am grateful that I don't have cancer and that I wake up feeling great every day."

30 Oppositional Force of Fear

Scenario

In July 2011 Norwegian extremist Anders Breivik killed seventy-seven people in Oslo when he went on a bombing and shooting spree. Breivik was said to be a right-wing fundamentalist Christian who became obsessed with what he saw as the threats of multiculturalism and Muslim immigration. After the tragic events, it was discovered that he had prepared a detailed manifesto outlining his plans to call for a Christian war in defense of Muslim domination in Europe. A specialist at the Norwegian Defense Research Establishment reported that the manifesto bears an eerie resemblance to those of Osama bin Laden and other Al Qaeda leaders, though from a Christian rather than a Muslim point of view. Like Mr. Breivik's manuscript, the major Al Qaeda declarations have detailed accounts of the Crusades, a pronounced sense of historical grievance and calls for apocalyptic warfare to defeat the religious and cultural enemy.[58]

---

58   Steven Erlanger and Scott Shane, "Oslow Suspect Wrote of Fear of Islam and Plan for War," *New York Times*, July 23, 2011, http://www.nytimes.com/2011/07/24/world/europe/24oslo.html?_r=1&nl=todaysheadlines&emc=tha2.

Discussion

1. What conclusions can you make about perceptual biases, based on the similarities between Breivik and Osama bin Laden's perceptions about one another's values and views?
2. What can you say about Breivik and bin Laden's respective perceptions?
3. What does the situation described suggest about negative perception and opposition?

Discussion Input

1. Perceptual biases explain why we think we are "right" and others are "wrong," why we blame, and why we tend to cling to our own views, beliefs, and expectations.
2. Even though Breivik was said to be a Christian extremist and bin Laden an Islamic extremist, their different perceptions both reflect extremes of egocentric "seeing" that can only polarize and separate.
3. The situation described in the scenario implies how the negative symbols generating the force of mind that is opposition can only spiral into more opposition, extending and strengthening separation between and among people.

31 "I'd Ask Him Why He's So Angry ..."

Scenario

In November 2001, Ann A. Simpkinson interviewed the Vietnamese monk Thích Nhất Hạnh, who is a strong proponent of Buddhism in the Western world.[59] The following is a segment is part of his response to her interview question, *"If you could speak to Osama bin Laden, what would you say to him?"*

The first thing I would do is listen ... I would try to understand all of the suffering that had led him to violence ... deep listening, listening without reacting, without judging and blaming ... listening with great will to understand the roots of suffering that are the cause of the violent actions ... Only then will we have sufficient insight to respond in such a way that healing and reconciliation can be realized for everyone involved.

Discussion

1. How does Thích Nhất Hạnh's response to Simpkinson's question highlight the importance of compassionate listening in developing consciousness and self? Why is it important to

---

59 The interview appeared online at http://www.buddhismtoday.com/english/world/facts/Bin_Laden.htm.

redirect negative perception when you are practicing compassionate listening? If you do, what is likely to happen, and why?

2. What effect does *blaming* have on a conversation? How does it affect the direction of a relationship dynamic? Explain.

3. Thích Nhất Hạnh's response suggests that we each have pain and need to be heard in order to be able to release ourselves to move beyond it. Explain how you can use compassionate listening to help raise awareness of a relationship partner's emotional pain, the real issue underneath anger.

Discussion Input

1. His response illustrates how we need to be heard when we are emotionally invested in an issue or when we are suffering or in emotional pain. Developing your emerging process of *self* and consciousness in a way that embraces inclusive "seeing" serves collective wellness. It is important not to react when you are using compassionate listening because your role is not to judge or argue with what you hear, only to listen and allow the other person to feel heard. If you blame, defend, criticize, or accuse in response to what you hear, your partner will likely do the same, making argument likely because of the oppositional *me-against-you* dynamic that your force of mind will invite.

2. Blaming, like criticism, has negative emotional value that causes a relationship partner to defend, justify, or counterattack. It invites the force of opposition and emotional struggle and predisposes you to holding on to and deepening the negative stories you tell your self. The force of mind that is opposition interferes with connection and strengthens a *me-against-you* dynamic that can only separate and push others away.

3. You can use compassionate listening to help uncover a relationship partner's pain, which can help you both understand the real emotional issue causing the attitudes and emotions of opposition. This will enable you to work together to address inclusive needs in your relationship.

32 The Price of Bullying

Scenario

Bullying because of sexual orientation, sexual identity, or race is a national problem that occurs routinely in schools, communities, and workplace environments across the country. Hate crimes related to gender orientation are so prevalent that the US Department of Justice is now required by law to collect and publish statistics on them. According to the US Department of Justice, Community Relations Service,[60] rumors fuel more than two-thirds of civil disturbances.

In 2010 a talented college student jumped to his death from a city bridge. Apparently, his roommate and his roommate's friends secretly used a webcam to record him making out with another man, using the recording as evidence to torment him publically online:[61]

> I guess what he was doing was … he was in another person's room, with other people … and so I feel like it was "look at what a fag my roommate I" … other people have commented on his profile with things like "how did you manage to go back in there?" "are you ok?" … and the fact that the people he was with saw me making out with a guy as the scandal whereas i mean come on … he was *spying on me* … do they see nothing wrong with this?

After the spying and tormenting continued, the young man announced in a social network posting, *Jumping off the gw bridge sorry.* The impact of disconnection through rejection and public humiliation was too much for him to handle.

Discussion

1. Explain how rumors reflect perceptual bias and why they represent judgments that unfairly create a subjective and biased negative reality about a person.
2. Explain how homophobia is *inconsistent with* compassionate cooperation and attitudes and emotions of inclusive "seeing."
3. Describe the role the roommate's friends played in his death by aligning themselves with the roommate to torment the young man who killed himself.
4. Imagine if one of the roommate's friends had reframed her perception of the situation and instead of aligning herself negatively with the roommate, had told her self a different story, one reflecting the force of mind that is compassionate cooperation. What might she have posted online after seeing the video instead of saying, *"How did you manage to go back in there?"* which essentially shunned the young man publicly?
5. Have you ever been in a conversation when a person makes fun of someone (in their presence or absence) because the person is gay or transgender? Do you recall the

---

60 US Department of Justice, Community Relations Service: http://www.justice.gov/crs/pubs/crs_pub_hate_crime_bulletin_1201.htm.

61 http://www.justusboys.com/forum/showthread.php?p=6482311#post6482311.

conversation? How did you react? What did you say? Do you feel your reaction redirected or supported the conversation? Explain. Would you react the same way or differently today if the same conversation were started?

Discussion Input

1. Rumors are subjective and negative judgments that reflect a biased reality about a person. When you create a negative judgment about another person—regardless of what it is—you bias a relationship partner to align their thinking with yours. Since negative stories about others are so pervasive in American culture, this is an area of work that requires a lot of attention. Always remind yourself to *do no harm* and reframe when you mind begins to pull you into negative alignments that influence you to buy into negative stories about others.

2. Homophobia is inconsistent with the attitudes and emotions of compassionate cooperation. It reflects the faulty thinking of negative perception and uses *moral judgment* as a defense for proving others "wrong." It withholds love and is fear-based, because it threatens one's own self-identity. It interferes with collective wellness and causes extensive harm.

3. While the roommate's friends may not have been convicted, they played a significant role in his death. By aligning themselves with the roommate's negative stories, which consisted of taunting and pejorative criticisms, they caused harm by supporting the roommate and encouraging him to continue.

4. She might have posted, *"Please delete your posting. I find it unkind and a violation of his privacy. Thanks."*

5. It is often challenging to speak up in conversation where there are multiple people, especially when you are not the dominant personality or role. It is helpful to have a script ready so you don't have to come up with one on the spot. Creating a script can help you take more deliberate action toward compassionate cooperation, and to revise the automatic and impulsive reactions produced by your brain.

33 "Okay, So You're Still Not Talking to Me?"

Scenario

Husband [to his wife]: Okay, so you're still not talking to me? How long is this going to go on? How long are you going to punish me?
Wife: [Silence]

The two spouses spiraled so far away from each other in a verbal struggle that the polarizing force of their relationship dynamic caused them to break their connection with one another for several days.

Discussion

1. Explain the impact of the wife's passive-aggressive response of silence on the relationship.
2. Although it looks on the surface (because of the sentence patterns he uses to symbolize his negative feelings) as though the husband is asking his wife a series of questions, really he is criticizing her passive-aggressive reaction with an accusation (*you're still not ...*), which causes her to counter with her own symbol of opposition, more silence. What do you imagine is the husband's real underlying need when he asks his wife those questions?
3. How might the husband reframe his story to reflect his underlying need instead of reacting as he does?

Discussion Input

1. Her silence symbolizes her negative force of mind and postures her for opposition with her husband. Without saying a word, she attacks him by punishing him and withdrawing. The force of mind she generates can only cause an imbalance to their dynamic and inhibit connection.
2. It is likely that the husband wants his wife to talk to him and he to feel connected with her, that he feels unhappy when their connection is disrupted, and that he is frustrated by the fact that she is punishing him with her silence.
3. He could share his feelings: "*I feel sad and lonely when you don't talk to me. I want us to be connected again.*" He could also apologize: "*I'm sorry. I didn't mean to hurt you.*" Whether or not he feels he did anything to hurt her is not the issue. Apologizing means acknowledging another person's pain, and choosing to release your self from egocentric "seeing" that causes you to push others away.

34 "I'm Not a Mind Reader ..."

Scenario

After dinner, the husband sits down on the couch where his wife is sitting:

> **Husband:** [Sighs deeply, positions himself about a foot further away from his wife on the couch than he usually does, stares at his phone, and purses his lips]
> **Wife:** What's wrong? What's going on?
> **Husband:** [Silence]
> **Wife:** Now what'd I do? You're pissed about something. What is it? What'd I do now? ... You'd better tell me 'cause I have no idea what's going on. I'm not a mind reader, ya know.

Discussion

1. The husband's shift away from his usual cooperative behavior signals his opposition to his wife. At this point, either of them can initiate compassionate listening. What might the husband share his true underlying need with his wife? How could he do it in a way that maintains connection with his wife, instead of creating pushing her away? What might the wife have said if she revised her last message so that it reflected the two-part compassionate listening strategy?

Discussion Input

1. The husband could say, *"I'm starting to feel angry about what you just said, and I don't want to be feeling this way."* The wife could revise her message to reflect the two-part compassionate listening strategy by saying, *"I recognize you're feeling frustrated. What can I do to help?"*

Scenario

A woman says the following to her husband:

> You always huff. I can't stand it when you do that. Why don't you just say what's on your mind? You drive me crazing with your huffing.

Discussion

1. How might the husband respond to his wife if he were to respond by practicing compassionate listening?

2. How might the husband use a *true-for-me statement* to help his wife understand how he feels?

3. The wife begins her message with an *accusatory you statement (You always ...)*. Revise her message, beginning with the subject pronoun *I*, and keep the message focused on the wife's rational explanation of her own feelings, not on what the husband she perceives her husband to have done wrong.

4. Why is it important to avoid *accusatory you statements*? What impact do they have in conversation with a relationship partner? Explain.

Discussion Input

1. He could respond, *"I hear you. I have trouble expressing my feelings. Can you help me?"*

2. He could say, *"Let me tell you how I feel."*

3. *"I feel angry when I don't know what I've done to frustrate you. Do you think we can come up with a code word that signals when you get frustrated with me? Then I'll know you're frustrated and we can talk about it together before my anger escalates."*

4. When you use *accusatory you statements*, you blame a relationship partner without accepting responsibility for your own feelings. Blame causes an imbalance to a relationship dynamic, because it causes you to see your self as having "the upper hand." Blame is an emotional symbol for opposition and generates the *me-against-you* dynamic that pushes others away emotionally and encourages *negative* reciprocity (one unkindness for another).

36 "He's Got Issues, They've All Got Issues ..."

Scenario

Kate and Katrina are friends. Kate is talking about her husband and his parents over coffee with Katrina.

> **Kate:** I don't go with him when he visits his parents in Florida.
>
> **Katrina:** Never?
>
> **Kate:** No. They never come up here to see us, and he hardly goes down there. He's got issues. They've all got issues. Why do you think he is like he is?

Discussion

1. Kate makes judgments about her husband as well as about his parents. What kind of picture does she paint of them to her friend? How does she do harm to her husband, his parents, and herself by what she says?
2. What negative perceptual bias accounts for the way Kate sees her husband and his parents as "*having issues*" while failing to recognize her own?
3. Name two actions Kate could take to practice moving away from perceptual inattention when she notices that she's telling her self negative stories about her husband and his parents.
4. How would Kate's husband benefit from a change to her perceptual mind-set?

Discussion Input

1. Kate paints a negative story of her husband's parents to her friend. She does harm to her husband and his parents by creating a negative reality about them to her friend, which she invites the friend to support and extend. She also harms herself because her own negative story will make it likely that she will strengthen and extend negativity to other parts of her relationship with her husband and her life.
2. Introspection bias is one example.
3. Kate could generate a story that would position herself for collaboration with her husband. She could suggest that they visit his parents together, thinking of it in her mind as a loving act of service. She could also reach out to his parents and send them a card, letting them know that the family was thinking of them. Both actions extend love and symbolize

perception, which reflects compassionate cooperation and the feelings supporting a unifying relationship dynamic. If her husband is struggling with his own negative feelings about his parents, her negativity will strengthen his.

4. Kate has an opportunity to help her husband take responsibility for his feelings with his parents by helping him redirect his negative feelings to align with the positive and unifying attitudes and emotions of compassionate cooperation that produce a *me-and-you* dynamic. (Her alignment with his negativity only intensifies the force of her husband's opposition toward his parents and invites deeper disconnection.)

37 "She Thinks She's Coming with Us"

Scenario

In the course of dinner conversation, a woman says the following to her husband,

> "Oh, your mother called today. She thinks she's coming on vacation with us because we're driving to the North Shore. You'd better tell her, 'No way'! We haven't had a vacation together since we got married and had the baby. There's no way she's coming with us!"

Discussion

1. The husband agrees that they need a vacation without his mother. Script a *say 'no' with kindness* message that the husband might share with his mother. Make sure he clearly tells his mother that she cannot go on vacation with them and that he also generates the force of mind that is compassionate cooperation.

2. The husband's mother lives alone. What do you think the underlying issue is to her wanting to go on vacation with her son and his family? How might the son accommodate that underlying need?

3. Script an apology for the daughter-in-law to say to her husband's mother. What might she apologize for? Why might she resist issuing an apology if she allows her mind to stay in an oppositional frame? How is her apology likely to affect her relationship with her mother-in-law?

Discussion Input

- *"Mom, I hear you want to come to the North Shore with us, but we really need to have some time alone away. It's not that we don't want you with us; it's just that we need the time by ourselves. We'd love to have you come and spend a couple of days with us after we get back."*
- The mother may feel lonely and may want to be around family. The son could talk to his wife and together they could come up with some suggestions for including the mother in their life that would allow her to see the family without having to go on vacation with them.
- *"Mom, I'm sorry that we're going on vacation without you. I know it's important to you to spend time with us, and it's also important to us. I hope you'll come and stay with us for a few days after we're back."* The daughter-in-law might apologize for the fact that they are not taking the mother with them. (Not to suggest that she did anything *"wrong"* but as an act of kindness.) She might resist apologizing if she maintains an egocentric perspective, because that wouldn't allow her to see the situation from the perspective of inclusive needs and interests (hers and her mother-in-law's). If she does apologize, and if the apology reflects a sincere intent to maintain balance in their dynamic, it will invite connection in spite of their decision to take time alone as a family and exclude her. You can *say no with kindness* AND preserve power-sharing and positive reciprocity in a relationship dynamic, allowing you to maintain connection even when you are negotiating difficult topics with others and embracing their unique perspectives and interests as well as your own.

38 *"Stop Trying to Make Them Like You ..."*

Scenario

Jackie and Alison are friends. As they are driving together to go shopping, the topic of Jackie's fiancé's parents comes up. While the parents don't accept Jackie (who is divorced and has two children), her fiancé is very close to them.

> **Jackie:** His mother refused to accept the gift I sent with him. He said that she wouldn't even open it, just pushed it aside.
> **Alison:** Where's the gift? Did he take it back?
> **Jackie:** No, he left it there. We don't care about the gift. We just want them to accept our relationship.

Alison: I wouldn't bother. Screw them. You've given them so many chances. Stop trying to make them like you. You don't even live in the same country. Just go on with your life.

Discussion

1. What role does Alison play in Jackie's relationship with her fiancé's parents?
2. How likely do you think it is that Jackie's fiancé's parents will eventually come around to accept their relationship if Jackie continues to generate the force of mind that is compassionate cooperation?
3. If Jackie follows Alison's advice, how will her future with her husband's parents likely go?
4. If Jackie wants to invite connection in her relationship dynamic with her fiancé's parents, what can she do? What might be the underlying reasons for the parents' oppositional force of mind?

Discussion Input

1. Alison encourages Jackie to position herself to generate the force of mind that is opposition with the parents.
2. If Jackie tells herself stories about the parents that reflect the emotional symbols of positive perception, and continues to do so, she will invite a positive and unifying relationship dynamic with them.
3. If Jackie follows Alison's advice, her relationship with the parents will likely be negative, polarizing, and involve emotional struggle.
4. She can continue to posture herself in a *me-and-you* orientation. The parents' force of opposition may be caused by fear—that she is divorced and has children, that she may leave their son the way she left her husband. If she continues to generate the emotional symbols of compassionate cooperation, she will continue to invite connection, which will predispose the parents to eventually responding in a way that reflects *positive reciprocity* (with similar acts of kindness).

39 Don't Take the Bait

Scenario

Erin and Karin are sisters. They are talking about their brother-in-law's brother, who is a frequent topic of their conversation.

> **Erin:** He's a jerk. He's really annoying, and I hate the way he dresses. Somebody should clue him in on how to dress.
>
> **Karin:** [laughs] I know. Have you seen that green sweater? It's hideous, and he wears it *all the time*!
>
> **Erin:** Somebody should clue him in. We should send him an anonymous note.
>
> **Erin and Karin:** [both laugh]

Discussion

1. Why is the conversation between Erin and Karin harmful? How might Karin have responded differently to Erin's judgment, in a way that redirected the conversation to align with the emotional values of compassionate cooperation?

2. If Erin had created a *space for grace* before she expressed the negative judgment, taking a moment to reframe what she was thinking, how might the exchange look instead?

3. Humor can support compassionate cooperation between relationship partners, but in this case it does harm to the coworker Erin and Karin are talking about. Explain how.

Discussion Input

1. The conversation is harmful because it reflects criticism of the person-object who isn't present and creates a negative reality about him. It's also harmful because Erin encourages Karin to take the bait of opposition and aligns herself negatively against the person-object. Karin could have said something like, *"Not all of us can be fashionistas. Give the guy a break!"* which would have probably caused Erin to stop her criticism, at least in front of Karin.

2. Erin might have realized what she was doing and refrained from creating a negative alignment with Karin against him. She might have chosen to see their brother-in-law's brother from an inclusive perspective, and recognized that they each have different

strengths and weaknesses. She might have willed herself to talk instead with Karin about a book she read or a movie she saw.

3. Erin and Karin use humor to criticize their brother-in-law's brother so it has a *negative impact* instead of a positive one, strengthening their alignment against the man while drawing them closer to each other, a misguided strategy for connection.

40 *"You Never Say Anything Nice ..."*

Scenario

Derrick has just criticized the way Jen has loaded the dishwasher. Derrick's criticism leads Jen to take issue with a more general topic:

> **Jen:** You never say anything nice. You're always picking on me. Everything I do is wrong.
> **Derrick:** I don't pick on you. I don't know what the hell you're talking about.

Discussion

1. Why are Jen's words likely to provoke Derrick? Explain.
2. How does Derrick provoke Jen with his defensive response? How does his response ignore Jen's feelings and underlying emotional need?
3. What impact does the word *hell* have on what Derrick says?
4. How might Derrick shift to compassionately cooperative mental posturing?
5. After Derrick answers Jen, how might she redirect opposition into compassionate cooperation? What might it look like?

Discussion Input

1. Jen's words provoke because she uses *accusatory you statements* (*"you never," "you always"*), which point blame at Derrick. Blame causes imbalance to a relationship dynamic, which results in pushing others away.
2. Derrick defends his position by firmly rooting himself in a negative and polarizing view after Jen invites opposition. He ignores Jen's feelings and needs with a defensive response, because she invites him to support imbalance in their relationship dynamic, and he *takes the bait.*

3. *"Hell"* intensifies his defensive posturing and oppositional force of mind, pushing Jen further away.

4. Derrick might have redirected his opposition using compassionate listening even though Jen provokes him with her accusation. If he created a *space for grace*, he could have taken a moment to regroup before reacting with his own negative response. He might have said, *"I hear you. What do you need me to do to make it better?"*

Jen might say, *"Rewind. I apologize. I reacted to my own feelings of insecurity. I didn't mean to accuse you. What I really want you to know is that it will help me a lot to know when you notice I'm doing things right."*

41 "We're Not Going to Say a Word ..."

Scenario

It's about 5 p.m. on a work night. The mother is going to the basement to get the clothes out of the dryer, which she left there from the day before. Her husband is still at work. Their two children are upstairs in the house, doing homework.

> **Mother:** [Descends basement stairs to get the clothes out of the dryer]
> OH ... MY ... GOD! [Yells up the stairs to the kids] You are not going to believe this! The basement is entirely flooded! Oh my God! What are we gonna do? I can't believe this. Shit. Now, what.
> **Son:** [Comes running down the stairs]
> What happened? What happened? How did that happen?
> **Mother:** I have no idea. I can't believe this. What are we gonna do?
> **Son:** Call Dad. Call Dad.
> **Mother:** That is *definitely* not a good idea! He is going to totally freak out. Think, think, think. Let me see. Okay.
> **Son:** What are we gonna do?
> **Mother:** I'm thinking ... Dad is gonna totally freak. You know how he is.
> **Son:** Wow, this is unbelievable. What are we gonna do?
> **Mother:** Okay. Okay. I've got it. We're just gonna leave everything for now.
> **Son:** You're not gonna call Dad?

Mother: Absolutely not. We're gonna let him come home and have a nice dinner, and then we'll tell him. He'll be home in an hour and he'll be tired, hungry, and crabby. We're not going to say a word until after he's eaten.

Later, at the family dinner table, just as they are finishing their meal:

Mother: [to her husband] Now, don't freak out … We have a little problem in the basement.
Son: The basement is completely flooded!
Father: What? What do you mean? [Immediately gets up from the table to see the basement. It takes until midnight for them to remove the water and find a solution to the sump pump problem.]

Discussion

1. Why was the woman's decision to let her husband eat before learning about the problem in the basement one that supported her decision to support compassionate cooperation? Explain.

Discussion Input

1. The woman understands that when her husband is tired and hungry he is more apt to react and generate an oppositional force of mind, a result of perceptual inattention. Even if he doesn't bait her into opposition, he is likely to be less cooperative when he hasn't eaten and is tired. She also recognizes that the solution to the basement flood requires an extensive effort that will be difficult to resolve on an empty stomach.

===== 42 "Don't Keeping Doing the Same Thing and Expect Different Results …"

Scenario

Meg and Pete are domestic partners. Meg knows that Pete generally doesn't like surprises, for two underlying reasons: he feels left out in the decision-making process and he is usually unhappy with Meg's choices. Meg, on the other hand, loves surprises, is always happy with them, and also gets great pleasure out of surprising others, especially Pete. Meg and Pete have had several arguments over the issue.

On this occasion, Pete is away on a work trip, and Meg decides to surprise him by painting the bedroom and buying a dresser. Meg is so sure that Pete will be happy that she painted the room because they talked about it once. However, although Meg thinks she knows what kind of dresser Pete would like, they've never discussed the issue or agreed on buying one.

Meg goes ahead and paints the room. She also goes ahead and purchases a dresser. Meg is very excited about surprising Pete, but she is unsure that Pete will be happy with her decisions.

Discussion

1. Why might Meg's surprise not go over as planned?
2. Why do you think Meg insists on surprising Pete? What does her decision suggest?
3. How might Meg's decision to surprise Pete, even though she knows he does not like surprises, lead Pete to feel that it's more important for Meg to get her way than to include him in decision-making?
4. What might be a better alternative than painting the room and buying the dresser, based on past knowledge that Pete doesn't like it when Meg surprises him?

Discussion Input

1. Meg knows Pete doesn't like surprises. Yet she chooses to cause imbalance to their dynamic by taking her power in a way that she knows is likely to upset Pete. Since they have not discussed the issues, and Meg knows he doesn't like to feel removed from the decision-making process, her surprise might not go over as planned.
2. Meg insists on surprising Pete because of her own egocentric "seeing." She likes surprises, so she wants to force Pete to like them also. She continues to surprise Pete, knowing that he doesn't like it and that it causes arguments. This is a case of doing the same thing over and over and expecting different results. Her decision is rooted in egocentric seeing and inattention to what she knows to be true about Pete.
3. Pete might feel that Meg is not hearing him and that she doesn't care that he wants to be included in decision-making.
4. Meg could shop for dressers and take photos of her favorites to show Pete. She could also get paint samples from the store, reflecting past discussion about paint colors. After he gets home from his work trip, she could show the options to Pete and they could decide together how to proceed. Or she could send him the samples while he's away and get his buy-in and agreement so she could have her projects done by the time he gets home.

43 *"Why Do I Always Have to Be the One ...?"*

Scenario

Kim: I'm not calling my mother. Why do I always have to be the one to pick up the phone? If she wants to talk to me, she can pick up the phone.

Discussion

1. What specific negative perceptions explain Kim's opposition?
2. How is Kim's perspective egocentric?
3. How do you think Kim's force of mind influences the authenticity of her relationship with her mother?

Discussion Input

1. Kim expresses resistance to calling her mother reflects anger and resentment. Kim is not living in the present moment with her mother but through her own biased perception of past hurts.
2. Her thoughts, recollections, and imaginings about past hurts reflect an egocentric perspective, narrowing her scope of vision to her own biased interpretations of her mother, which fuels her negative perceptions. She ignores an inclusive perspective that takes her mother's perspective, needs, and interests into account.
3. Kim's self-centered view will cause her to have either *authentically negative* relationship experiences with her mother, or *inauthentically positive* ones. She will not be able to create *genuinely positive* relationship experiences with her mother unless she chooses to "see differently," in a way that generates the positive emotional symbols of compassionate cooperation.

44 *"Why did you ...?"*

Scenario

Darcy: [to her spouse] *Why the hell did you tell them we'd be there when I told you I didn't want to go?*

Discussion

1. Why does Darcy's cause imbalance to the relationship dynamic she creates with her husband? How does the symbolic value of her word choice contribute to the message? What would be a better way for Darcy to express her underlying need in the situation so she does not push her spouse away?

Discussion Input

1. The sentence pattern, "*Why did you …?*" with falling intonation at the end of the phrase is symbolically negative and a strong representation of an oppositional force of mind. The word choice "*hell*" reflects inherently negative symbolic value that strengthens the force of opposition, making Darcy's polarizing attitudes and emotions clear.

2. Darcy might say, "*I really don't feel like going over there.*" [True-for-Me Statement] "*How much do you want to go? Is there any way we could go next week?*" [Inclusive Needs and Interests/Collaborative Problem-Solving]

45 "I Completely Forgot …"

Scenario

Mara and Violet are friends who live in cities on opposite sides of the country. Violet is in town visiting family, and Mara has agreed to meet her for coffee the morning she leaves to return home. Violet has asked Mara if she can drop her suitcase off at Mara's the day before they meet so she won't have to lug it on the metro. Mara agrees, but forgets she'll be out of town on the day they planned their meeting. Another friend's email message jars her memory. She is now faced with having to say no to Violet after she has already made a commitment. As soon as Mara realizes her dilemma, she phones Violet:

> **Mara:** Hi Violet, you're not gonna believe this, but I *totally* spaced out.
>
> **Violet**: Why? What happened?
>
> **Mara:** I completely forgot that I'm not gonna be here tomorrow. You can't leave your suitcase here today. You won't be able to get tomorrow because I won't be here. I feel really terrible. I completely forgot. I'm so sorry!
>
> **Violet**: That's okay. What's going on?
>
> **Mara:** I'm going with David early in the morning, and then we're leaving for my parents'. I feel terrible. I won't get to see you either.

Violet: Oh, no. That's such a disappointment. We're gonna miss each other again.

Mara: I was thinking that you could leave your suitcase on the back terrace. That way you could still get it tomorrow. The terrace is covered so it shouldn't be a problem.

Discussion

1. How direct or indirect is Mara in the way she says no to Violet and withdraws from her commitment? Are her words effective?
2. Does the solution Mara proposes show her intention to generate the force of mind that is compassionate cooperation and to be helpful to Violet? Explain.

Discussion Input

1. Mara is very direct and takes action to *say no with kindness* as soon as she realizes her dilemma. Her words are clear and effective. They are honest and kind at the same time.
2. Mara proposes a solution that shows inclusive "seeing" and symbolizes service. She shapes her story in a way that allows her to maintain a balanced relationship with her friend, offering a way to help her solve her suitcase problem.

46 Take Responsibility for Your Feelings

Scenario

Kelly expresses her frustration and anger about her son to a friend through *negative venting*:

It really pisses me off that he never calls. I know he's busy, but we're all busy. He's such an ingrate. We'd never do that with our parents!

Discussion

1. Taking responsibility for your negative feelings means confronting them and talking about the real issues causing you to tell yourself negative stories about others and sometimes share them. It also involves using the creative force of your mind to imagine possible reinterpretations of your stories that will enable you to see others in the light of positive perception *and* get your real needs met. What underlying feelings might be causing Kelly to act out her negative feelings in the interaction described? In other words, what might be

the real emotional need she camouflages by acting out her feelings instead of confronting them and rationally explaining them to herself and her friend?

2. How could Kelly explain her feelings rationally, and what solution could she imagine to get what she needs?

3. Why doesn't her *negative venting* serve her? How does it harm her son?

Discussion Input

1. Kelly may feel a *fear* of being abandoned, not cared about, rejected, or unimportant to her son. Those fears may cause resentment, anger, and criticism that her son *never calls.* She feels entitlement to his phone calls, since she raised him and feels she devoted her life to him.

2. Kelly could explain her feelings rationally to herself (and to her son if she wanted to) by using *true-for-me statements* that would allow her to recognize and embrace her *small self* feelings without alienating her son and causing others to have negative perceptions of him. If she reframes her negative story, creatively using her mind to come up with a solution that would address her real need (to talk to her son), she might realize she could call *him* when she needs to talk to him.

3. Her *negative venting* doesn't serve her because it reinforces the force of opposition that causes her to see her son in a negative light and push him away by inviting imbalance in their relationship dynamic. It makes it likely that she will see her son as uncaring in other relationship situations as well. It also creates harmful negative alignments by unfairly influencing her friend's perception of her son.

---

47 Setting Boundaries

Scenario

Patrick and Neil are adult brothers who were raised by their grandmother in a household where Patrick was always looking out for Neil's interests. Patrick has helped his brother out financially over the years when he's overspent foolishly even though Patrick doesn't make a lot of money. He's angry with Neil for not "growing up" and being more responsible with money. But he doesn't know how to *say no with kindness* to Neil's latest request for money to cover a $1,000 charge on his credit card.

Discussion

1. How might Patrick's tendency to control and take responsibility be harming his brother and their relationship? What might change if Patrick redefined his role of with his brother? How might it affect their relationship?
2. How might Patrick *say no with kindness* to Neil the next time he asks for money?

Discussion Input

1. Patrick may be preventing his brother from growing up by neglecting to redefine their childhood roles of *caretaker* and *enabler*. If Patrick stops taking financial responsibility for Neil, he might find that Neil becomes more responsible and that they develop a more balanced relationship, like adult friends rather than the parent-child dynamic they have extended from childhood into adulthood. Patrick enables Neil to be financially *irresponsible* by bailing him out repeatedly. He also ensures that he has the dominant role in the relationship because he holds the purse strings, which causes an imbalance in the relationship and invites non-reciprocity of kindnesses, where Patrick gives and Neil accepts.
2. Patrick might *say no with kindness* in the following way the next time Neil asks him to bail him out financially: *"Neil, I hear that you need money again, and I really do want to help you out, but I don't feel I'm really helping you by enabling you to be irresponsible with money, so I'm going to say no this time. I would like to find another way to help you out so you won't keep getting yourself in these financial binds. How about if I help you work on a budget and help you manage it until you get the hang of it? I can also help you figure out what you can do about your $1,000 credit card bill."*

---

48 *"She's Controlling and Dominating ..."*

Scenario Description

Sophia sees her mother as controlling and dominating. She thinks she is always polite when she talks to her mother, since she withdraws instead of arguing with her, but the stories she tells herself about her mother reflect symbols of resentment, criticism, and entitlement. In Sophia's eyes, her mother can't do anything "right" and Sophia is never "wrong."

Discussion

1. Is Sophia's general orientation toward her mother *genuinely positive*? Explain.
2. How does Sophia's force of mind contribute to the dynamic between them?

3. What might Sophia do the next time she notices a negative thought, recollection, or imagining in her mind about her mother? What would the effect be?

Discussion Input

1. Sophia's general orientation toward her mother is *inauthentically positive*, because she invites a *me-against-you* dynamic with her that results from her negative perception of her mother, which causes her to see herself as "right" and her mother as "wrong," a consequence of egocentric "seeing."

2. Sophia's negative and polarizing force of mind generates opposition, and invites imbalance in their relationship dynamic. Her passive-aggressive tendencies "bait" her mother to assume a controlling and dominating role in the dynamic, which extends imbalance. Unless one of them restores balance, they will always push each other away.

3. The next time Sophia notices a negative thought, recollection, or imagining in her mind, she can choose to reframe it, using the paradigm of positive perception to guide her. She might use *true-for-me statements* or try *laughing at herself*, or *being humorous* with an intention to create emotional linkages with her mother. She could also take an honest look at her real emotional need so she can explain her feelings rationally to herself and maybe in conversation with her mother. By working to restore power-sharing and positive reciprocity in the dynamic, she will be able to generate the attitudes and emotions of compassionate cooperation that invite and support connection.

49 Harboring Anger and Resentment

Scenario

Krista and Kate are in-laws. Krista feels that Kate excluded her and her partner in her plans to visit mutual friends the year before and has been holding on to resentment and anger ever since. Kate has no idea what is going on, because it hadn't been her intent to exclude Krista and her partner, and neither Krista nor her partner said anything to her after the visit. Kate does feel Krista's rejection, however, because Krista refuses to go to dinner or interact with her. But, Krista's partner makes excuses for her, saying Krista doesn't feel up to dinner because *"she's working too hard, she's tired, she's busy."* Finally, almost a year later, Krista agrees to go to dinner. Halfway through dinner, she acts out the feelings of resentment and anger that she's harbored toward Kate for over a year. Kate feels she's been hit with a hard ball as Krista hammers her with a series of accusations and blame for excluding her and her partner. *"You didn't ... You could have ... You should have ..."*

Kate tries to defend by saying, "*I had no idea, It was a misunderstanding, I'm sorry.*" The result is a spiraling web of attack-and-defense that interrupts connection between them.

Discussion

1. How does Krista's egocentric "seeing" of the situation position her for opposition with Kate? How do you think it affects her own sense of peace to harbor negative feelings toward Kate for over a year? How does Krista harm herself in so doing?
2. Although Krista thinks she has been "brutally honest" with Kate, and in some way feels empowered by the confrontation and her upper hand in it, how does she do harm to the relationship?
3. What might be Krista's real issue, the source of her feelings? Does she confront it?
4. What type of relationship experience does Krista create — genuinely positive, inauthentically positive, or authentically negative? Explain.

Discussion Input

1. Krista's egocentric "seeing" causes her to blame Kate and see her as selfish. By harboring negative feelings and spinning her negative story in her interaction with her self for more than a year, she intensifies the force of opposition and the *me-against-you* dynamic she extends. Krista does harm to herself because she strengthens her own polarizing thinking, about Kate and about other relationship partners and situations.
2. Krista causes imbalance to the dynamic she creates with Kate through criticism and attack, which symbolize power-grabbing and cause negative reciprocity that can only separate, not connect.
3. Krista might feel as though Kate deliberately rejected her. If so, rejection might be a childhood theme Krista extends into her life that causes her to push others away through fear, anger, resentment, anger, criticism, and entitlement. Krista doesn't confront her real emotional issue. Instead of "owning" her *small self* needs, she attacks Kate.
4. Krista creates an *authentically negative* relationship experience because she generates the force of opposition by the negative symbols she uses to create her story of Kate, and also shares her negative story directly in interaction with Kate.

50 *"He's Always Criticizing Me ..."*

Scenario

Alexa thinks the following to her self about her domestic partner:

> He's always criticizing me. I can't do anything right in his eyes. Nothing I do
> meets his expectations. I'm so tired of it!

Discussion

1. What underlying feelings might be causing Alexa's criticism? In other words, what might be her real emotional need, the reason she acts out her feelings in her mind?
2. What *small self* part of her might be acting out? How might it disrupt balance in her relationship dynamic with her partner?
3. How might Alexa rebalance the relationship dynamic?
4. How does she harm herself with her negative story about her partner?
5. Why would *reframing* help? What steps would she take to reframe her negative story?

Discussion Input

1. She might feel unworthy or incapable to doing anything right in her own eyes. Her real need might be to hear praise.
2. She might have an *always wrong* aspect of her *small self* that engages with her partner's *perfectionist* self. She might also realize that she tends to act out an old childhood feeling, that she could not do anything right in her father's eyes. This would invite imbalance through unequal power-sharing in the dynamic.
3. She might confront her real need to hear praise (or whatever else it might be) and express it rationally to her partner instead of acting it out. She might say, *"Let me tell you what I need"* to her partner and use the creative force of her mind to come up with a solution, such as asking her partner to praise one thing a day that she does. By taking steps to create linkages with her partner, she can rebalance the dynamic and also get her need met.
4. She harms herself with her negative story by continuing to perpetuate an *Always Wrong* feeling pattern, and by strengthening and extending her own negative thinking.
5. By reframing, she would enable perceptual reinterpretation of her story, which would allow her to "see differently," in a way that is consistent with the attitudes and emotions

of positive perception, such as love, peace, gratitude, forgiveness, and service. This would allow her to generate the force of mind that is compassionate cooperation. To reframe her negative narrative, she would confront the source of her feelings, why she is acting them out, and she would tell herself a different story, one that aligns with emotional symbols of positive perception, such as love, peace, gratitude, forgiveness, and service.

Bibliography

A Course in Miracles (ACIM). Foundation for Inner Peace, 1975. FACIM edition, 1996.

A Course in Miracles. Website. http://acim.org/Scribing/about_scribes.html.

AAA Foundation for Traffic Safety. Website. http://www.aaafoundation.org/resources/index. cfm?button=agdrtext.

Adam, Hajo, Aiwa Shirako, and William Maddux. "Cultural Variance in the Human Effects of Anger in Negotiations," *Psychological Science* 21, no. 6: 882–889 (June 2010). http://faculty. insead.edu/maddux/personal/documents/PsychScienceCultureAngerandNegotiations.pdf.

American Psychiatric Association's 2011 Meeting. http://www.medscape.com/viewarticle/743024.

Archer, Dane. "Nonverbal Cues." Website. http://nonverbal.ucsc.edu.

Archer, Dane. "Social Psychology, Sociology, and Non-Verbal Behavior." Website. http://ucmedia. berkeley.edu/brochures/brochuregif/social03-04.pdf, 2005-2006.

Autonomic Digital Reflex Forum. Website. http://www.adrforum.info/index.php?option=com_ content&view=section&layout=blog&id=5&Itemid=46&lang=en.

Baars, Bernard. "Some Essential Differences between Consciousness and Attention, Perception, and Working Memory," *Consciousness and Cognition* 6(2-3):363-371(1997).

Bandura, Albert. *Self-Efficacy: The Exercise of Control.* New York: Worth Publishers, 1997.

Blood, R., and D. Wolfe. *Husbands and Wives: The Dynamics of Married Living.* New York: Free Press, 1960.

Blumstein, P., and P. Schwartz. *American Couples: Money, Work, and Sex.* New York: Morrow, 1983.

Brady, Michael S. "Recalcitrant Emotions and Visual Illusions." *American Philosophical Quarterly* 44, no. 3:273-284: (2007).

Bretherton, Inge. "The Origins of Attachment Theory: John Bowlby and Mary Ainsworth," *Developmental Psychology* 28:759–775(1992). http://www.psychology.sunysb.edu/attachment/online/inge_origins.pdf.

Burns, David D. *Feeling Good*. New York: Quill, 2000.

Chalmers, David J. "Toward a Science of Consciousness." CogNet Proceedings 3. http://cognet.mit.edu/posters/TUCSON3/Chalmers.Vision.html.

Cherry, Kendra. "The Kanizsa Triangle Illusion." *About Psychology*. psychology.about.com/od/sensationandperception/ig/Optical-Illusions/Kanizsa-Triangle-Illusion.htm.

Chopra, Deepak. "Neuroscience of Enlightenment." Science and Nonduality Conference: The Science and Mystery of Perception (SAND 13). San Jose, CA. October 23–27, 2013.

Chopra, Deepak. *The Seven Spiritual Laws of Success*. California: Amber-Allen Publishing and New World Library, 1994.

Chopra, Deepak, Menas Kafatos, and Rudolf E. Tanzi. "From Quanta to Qualia: The Mystery of Reality (part 3)." *The Huffington Post*. October 12, 2012. http://www.huffingtonpost.com/deepak-chopra/from-quanta-to-qualia-the_b_2038207.html.

Chopra, Deepak, and Leonard Mlodinow. *War of the Worldviews: Science vs. Spirituality*. New York: Harmony Books, 2011.

Crider, Major Kimberly A. "Strategic Implications of Culture: Historical Analysis of China's Culture and Implications for United States Policy." 1999. http://www.au.af.mil/au/awc/awcgate/wright/wf08.pdf.

Covey, Steven. *The 7 Habits of Highly Effective People*. New York: Fireside, 1989.

The Dalai Lama, His Holiness and Howard C. Cutler, MD. *The Art of Happiness: A Handbook for Living*. New York: Riverhead Books, 1998.

The Dalai Lama, His Holiness. "On Compassion." http://www.dalailama.com/messages/compassion.

D'Amico, Lynne. "Prince Street Practicum for Conscious Living: Course Facilitation Notes." Unpublished Notes, Alexandria, Virginia, 2002-2011.

D'Amico-Reisner, Lynne. "An Analysis of the Surface Structure of Disapproval Exchanges." In Wolfson and Judd, eds., *Sociolinguistics and Language Acquisition*. Rowley, Mass: Newbury House, 1983.

D'Amico-Reisner, Lynne. *An Ethnolinguistic Study of Disapproval Exchanges*. Philadelphia: University of Pennsylvania, 1985.

D'Amico-Reisner, Lynne. *Avoiding Direct Conflict through the Co-construction of Narratives about Absent Others*. MS presented at the American Association for Applied Linguistics (AAAL), Stanford, CT, 1999.

D'Amico-Reisner, Lynne. *Power and Solidarity in Disapproval Exchanges between Intimates: A Gender Issue?* Presented at the International Association of Applied Linguistics, Amsterdam, 1993; and, at the American Association for Applied Linguistics, Altanta, GA, 1993.

D'Amico-Reisner, Lynne. *That Same Old Song and Dance: Repetition as a Critical Discourse Feature in Disapproval Exchanges between Intimates*. Presented at the American Association for Applied Linguistics, Atlanta, GA, 1993; and, at the International Association of Applied Linguistics, Amsterdam: 1993.

De Brigard, Felipe, and Jesse Prinz. "Attention and Consciousness," *Cognitive Science* 1: 51–59: (January/February 2010).

Diener, Ed, and Martin Seligman. *A National Wellness Index*. University of Pennsylvania. February 2004. http://www.authentichappiness.sas.upenn.edu/newsletter.aspx?id=47.

Dispenza, Joe. *Evolve Your Brain: The Science of Changing Your Mind*. Deerfield, FL: Health Communications, 2007.

Doidge, Norman. *The Brain that Changes Itself*. New York: Penguin Books, 2007.

Douglas, Mary, and Aaron Wildavsky, *Risk and Culture: An Essay on the Selection of Technical and Environmental Dangers*. Berkeley: University of California Press, 1982.

Erlanger, Steven, and Scott Shane. "Oslow Suspect Wrote of Fear of Islam and Plan for War," *New York Times*. July 23, 2011. http://www.nytimes.com/2011/07/24/world/europe/24oslo.html?_r=1&nl=todaysheadlines&emc=tha2.

"Exploring Thich Nhat Hanh's Approach to the Art of Listening: Session Six." http://www.newconversations.net/compassion/cl_chap66.htm.

Fawcett, S., A. Paine-Andrews, V. T. Francisco, et al. "Using Empowerment Theory in Collaborative Partnerships for Community Health and Development," *American Journal of Community Psychology* 23 (1995): 677–697.

Feldman Barrett, Lisa, et al. *The Experience of Emotion.* Annual Review of Psychology 58:373-403: 2007..

Fineman, M., and R. Mykitiuk. *The Public Nature of Private Violence: The Discovery of Domestic Abuse.* New York: Routledge, 1994.

Fisher, Roger, and William Ury. *Getting to Yes: Negotiating Agreement without Giving In.* New York: Penguin Books, 1991.

Foster, Bev. "Music Care: Musical Approaches in Caring Communities." Manitoba HPC Conference. September 23, 2011. http://www.manitobahospice.ca/pdf/F27%20-%20Musical%20Approaches.pdf.

French, J., and B. Raven. "The Basis of Power." In *Studies in Social Power,* ed. D. Cartwright. Ann Arbor: University of Michigan Press, 1959.

Gandhi, M. K., in Bharatan Kumarappa, ed., *For Pacifists.* Ahmedabad, India: Navajivan Publishing House, 1949.

Genpo Merzel, Dennis. *Big Mind, Big Heart: Finding Your Way.* Salt Lake City: Dennis Genpo, 2007.

Gilpin, Geoff. *The Maharishi Effect.* New York: Penguin Group, 2006.

Glanz, K., K. S. Rimer, and K. Viswanath. *Health Behavior and Health Education: Theory, Research, and Practice,* 4th ed. San Francisco: Jossey-Bass, Wiley, Inc., 2008.

Hall, Edward T. *The Hidden Dimension.* New York: Anchor Books, 1966.

Hall, Edward T. *Beyond Culture.* New York: Anchor Books, 1976.

Harris, Sam. *The Moral Landscape.* New York: Free Press, 2010.

Haselhurst, Geoff. "Space and Motion." http://www.spaceandmotion.com/Philosophy-Mind.htm.

Haugh, Michael, and Carl Hinze. "A Metalinguistic Approach to Deconstructing the Concepts of 'Face' and 'Politeness' in Chinese, English, and Japanese," J of Pragmatics 25, 10/11: 1581-1611, 2003: http://www98.griffith.edu.au/dspace/bitstream/10072/14601/1/33409.pdf.

Hawkins, David R. *Power versus Force: The Hidden Determinants of Human Behavior.* Carlsbad, CA: Hayhouse/Veritas Publishing, 2002.

Heffner, K. L., J. Kielcolt-Glaser, T. Loving, et al. "Spousal Support Satisfaction as a Modifier of Physiological Responses to Marital Conflict in Younger and Older Couples," *Journal of Behavioral Medicine* 27: 233–254.

Hettler, William. "Wellness: Encouraging a Lifetime Pursuit of Excellence," *Health Values: Achieving High Level Wellness* 8:14 (1984).

Heuer, Richards J. "Psychology of Intelligence Analysis." CIA Library: https://www.cia.gov/library/center-for-the-study-of-intelligence/csi-publications/books-and-monographs/psychology-of-intelligence-analysis/art14.html.

His Holiness the 14th Dalai Lama of Tibet. "Message on Compassion and the Individual." http://www.dalailama.com/messages/compassion.

Human Emergence. Key personnel: Don Edward Beck, John L. Petersen, Ken Wilber, and Andrew Cohen. Website. *http://www.humanemergence.org/coreTechnologies.html.*

Hymes, Dell. *Foundations in Sociolinguistics: An Ethnographic Approach.* Philadelphia, PA: University of Pennsylvania Press, 1974.

Hymes, Dell. *On Communicative Competence.* In J. Pride and J. Holmes, eds., *Sociolinguistics.* New York: Penguin, 1972.

Jung, Carl G. *Collected Works of C. G. Jung.* Princeton, NJ: Princeton University Press, 1981 (originally published in 1959).

Juslin, Patrick N., and Petri Laukka. "Communication of Emotions in Vocal Expression and Music Performance: Different Channels, Same Code?" *Psychological Bulletin* 129, no. 5 (2003): 770–814.

JustUsBoys. Website. http://www.justusboys.com/forum/showthread.php?p=6482311#post6482311.

Kahneman, Daniel, and Amos Tversky. "On the Psychology of Prediction," *Psychological Review* 80, no. 4 (1973): 237–251.

Alfred W. Kaszniak, *Emotions, Qualia, and Consciousness*. Ed., Proceedings of the International School of Biocybernetics, Casamicciola, Napoli, Italy, 19-24 October 1998. Google eBook. http://books.google.com/books/about/Emotions_Qualia_and_Consciousness.html?id=TLN0793cZzkC

Kearny Datesman, Maryann, Joann (Jodi) Crandall, and Edward Kearny. *American Ways*, 3rd ed. New Jersey: Pearson ESL, 2005. [Related publication: Kearny, Kearny, and Crandall. *The American Way*. New Jersey: Prentice-Hall. 1984]

Kenny, Robert. "What Can Science Tell Us About Collective Consciousness." 2004. http://www.collectivewisdominitiative.org/papers/kenny_science.htm.

Kiecolt-Glaser, J., C. Bane, R. Glaser, R. et al. "Love, Marriage, and Divorce: Newlyweds' Stress Hormones Foreshadow Relationship Changes," *Journal of Consulting and Clinical Psychology* 71: 176–188: (February 2003).

Kiecolt-Glaser, J., L. Fisher, P. Ogorocki, et al. "Immune Function," *Psychosomatic Medicine* 49, no. 1. (January/February 1987).

Kiecolt-Glaser, J., W. Marlarkey, J. Cacioppo, et al. "Stressful Personal Relationships: Endocrine and Immune Function." In R. Glaser and J. K. Keicolt-Glaser, eds. *Handbook of Human Stress and Immunity*. San Diego, CA: Academic Press, 1994.

Kiecolt-Glaser, J., W. Marlarkey, M. Chee, et al. "Negative Behavior during Marital Conflict Is Associated with Immunological Down-Regulation," *Psychosomatic Medicine* (1993): 395–409.

Kiecolt-Glaser, J., T. Newton, J. Cacioppo, et al. "Marital Conflict and Endocrine Function," *Journal of Consulting and Clinical Psychology* 64, no. 2 (April 1996): 324–332.

King, B. "The Conceptual Structure of Emotional Experience in Chinese." Ohio State University, 1989.

Koltko-Rivera, Mark. "Psychology of World Views," *Review of General Psychology* 8, no. 1 (2004). http://www.apa.org/journals/features/gpr813.pdf.

Kopel, David. "Japan: Gun Control and People Control." December 1988. http://www.davekopel.com/2A/Foreign/Japan-Gun-Control-and-People-Control.htm.

Kovecses, Zoltan. "Anger: Its Language, Conceptualization, and Physiology in the Light of Cross-Cultural Evidence." In Taylor and MacLaury, eds., *Language and the Cognitive Construal of the World*. Berlin: Mouton de Gruyter, 1995.

Kovesces, Zoltan. "The Concept of Anger: Universal or Culture Specific?," Psychopathology 33:159-170 (2000). http://www.asc.upenn.edu/courses/comm360/anger1.pdf.

Levitin, Daniel. *This Is Your Brain on Music: The Science of a Human Obsession*. New York: Penguin Books, 2006.

MacLean, Katherine A., Emilio Ferrer, Stephen R. Aichele, et al. "Intensive Meditation Training Leads to Improvements in Perceptual Discrimination and Sustained Attention," *Psychological Science* 21, no. 6 (2010): 829–839.

Mannes, Elena. *The Power of Music*. New York: Bloomsbury Publishing, 2011.

Matsuki, Keiko. "Metaphors of Anger in Japanese." In Taylor and MacLaury, eds., *Language and the Cognitive Construal of the World*. Berlin: Mouton de Gruyter, 1995.

Mole, Christopher. "Attention and Consciousness," *Journal of Consciousness Studies* 15, no. 4.

"Music and Speech." http://blogs.scientificamerican.com/observations/2010/06/17/music-and-speech-share-a-code-for-c-2010-06-17/.

National Association of Cognitive-Behavioral Therapists. http://www.nacbt.org/whatiscbt.htm.

Nesse, Randolf N. "Natural Selection and the Elusiveness of Happiness." The Royal Society. Published online August 31, 2004. http://www.ncbi.nlm.nih.gov/pmc/articles/PMC1693419/pdf/15347525.pdf.

Nesse, Randolf N. "Computer Emotions and Mental Software." *Social Neuroscience Bulletin* 7, no. 2 (spring 1994): 36–37: http://www-personal.umich.edu/~nesse/Articles/ComputerEmotions-SocNeurosciBull-1994.PDF.

Pennebaker, James W. *The Secret Life of Pronouns*. New York: Bloomsbury Press, 2011.

Pew Research Center's Global Attitudes Project. July 18, 2006. http://www.pewglobal.org/2006/07/18/islam-and-the-west-searching-for-common-ground/.

Pew Research Center's Global Attitudes Project. July 21, 2011. http://www.pewglobal.org/2011/07/21/muslim-western-tensions-persist/.

Rappaport, J. "Terms of Empowerment/Exemplars of Prevention: Toward a Theory for Community Psychology." *American Journal of Community Psychology* 15 (1987): 121–148.

The Root. "Black Women on Reality TV." March 3, 2011. http://www.theroot.com/views/fight-night-black-women-reality-tv.

Rosenberg, Marsall B. *Nonviolent Communication: A Language of Life.* Encinitas, CA: PuddleDancer Press, 2003.

Sacks, Oliver. *Musicophilia: Tales of Music and the Brain.* New York: Random House, 2008.

Schatzki, Theodore R. and Wolfgang Natter, eds. *The Social and Political Body.* New York: Guilford Press, 1996. http://books.google.com/books/about/The_Social_and_Political_Body.html?id=Hm7dVprNu6cC.

Schermerhorn, Alice C., SyMiin Chow, and E. Mark Cummings. "Developmental Processes and Interparental Conflict: Patterns of Micro-level Influences," *Developmental Psychology* 46, no. 4:869–885:(July 2010).

Shearer, N. "Relationships of Contextual and Relational Factors to Health Empowerment in Women," *Research and Theory for Nursing Practice* 18 (2004): 357–370.

Simpkinson, Ann A. "Interview with Thich Nhat Hanh." http://www.buddhismtoday.com/english/world/facts/Bin_Laden.htm.

Sloman, Steven. *Causal Models.* New York: Oxford University Press, 2005.

Social Psychology Index: Social Factors Shaping Perception and Decision-Making. Website. http://www.trinity.edu/mkearl/socpsy-5.html.

Schwartz, Jeffrey, and Sharon Begley. *The Mind and the Brain.* New York: Regan Books, Harper Collins, 2009.

Tannen, Deborah. *The Argument Culture.* New York: Random House, 1998.

Targ, Russell. *Limitless Mind and End of Suffering: A Guide to Remote Viewing and Transformation of Consciousness.* Novato, CA: New World Library. 2004.

Tavris, Carol, and Elliot Aronson. *Mistakes Were Made (but Not by Me): Why We Justify Foolish Beliefs, Bad Decisions, and Hurtful Acts.* Harcourt Books, 2007.

Teilhard de Chardin, Pierre. *Building the Earth.* Wilkes-Barre, PA: Dimension Books, 1965:13.

Teilhard de Chardin, Pierre. *The Phenomenon of Man*. New York: Harper Perennial Modern Thought, 2008. Originally published in French as *Le phénomene humain*. Paris: Editions du Seuil, 1955.

Thích Nhất Hạnh. *Cultivating the Mind of Love*. Berkeley: Parallax Press, 1996.

Thích Nhất Hạnh. *The Miracle of Mindfulness: A Manual on Meditation*. Boston: Beacon Press, 1999.

Thích Nhất Hạnh. *Teachings on Love*. Berkeley: Parallax Press, 1997.

Thompson, Doug, ed. *A Course in Miracles Urtext Manuscripts*. Jaffrey, NH: Miracles in Action Press, 2009.

Tolle, Eckhart. *A New Earth: Awakening to Your Life's Purpose*. New York: Penguin Books, 2005.

Triandis, Henry C., Xiao Ping Chen, and K-S Darius. "Scenarios for the Measurement of Collectivism and Individualism," *Journal of Cross-Cultural Psychology* (March 1, 1998).

Tversky, Amos, and Daniel Kahneman. "Availability: A Heuristic for Judging Frequency and Probability," *Cognitive Psychology* 5, no. 2 (1973): 207–232.

US Department of Justice, Community Relations Service. http://www.justice.gov/crs/pubs/crs_pub_hate_crime_bulletin_1201.htm.

Ushakov, Y., and A. A. Dubkov. "Regularity of Spike Trains and Harmony Perception in a Model of the Auditory System," *Physical Review Letters*: 107, 108103 (2011).

Whitfield, Graeme, and Chris Williams. "The Evidence Base for Cognitive-Behavioral Therapy in Depression: Delivery in Busy Clinical Settings," *Advances in Psychiatric Treatment* 9 (2003): 21–30. http://apt.rcpsych.org/content/9/1/21.full.

Wilber, Ken, ed. *The Holographic Paradigm and Other Paradoxes: Exploring the Leading Edge of Science*. Shambhala, 1982.

Wilber, Ken. "Integral Life." http://integrallife.com/learn/levels-development/stages-or-levels-development.

Wilber, Ken. *Integral Psychology*. Boston: Shambhala, 2000.

Wilber, Ken. *Integral Spirituality*. Boston: Shambhala, 2006.

Wilber, Ken. *The Integral Vision*. Boston: Shambhala, 20007.

Wilber, Ken. *No Boundary: Eastern and Western Approaches to Personal Growth.* Boston: Shambhala, 2001.

Wilber, Ken. *Quantum Questions: Mystical Writings of the World's Great Physicists.* Boston: Shambhala, 2001.

Wolfson, Nessa, and Elliott Judd, eds. *Sociolinguistics and Language Acquisition.* Rowley, MA: Newberry House, 1983.

Yu, N. "Metaphorical Expressions of Anger and Happiness in English and Chinese." *Metaphor and Symbolic Activity:* 10: 59–92: (1995).

Yudkowsky, Eliezer. "Cognitive Biases." Singularity Institute for Artificial Intelligence. Draft 2006. http://b510.r.google.com/click?q=cognitive%20biases&lnk=http%3A%2F%2Fsinginst. org%2Fupload%2Fcognitive-biases.pdf&ref=http%3A%2F%2Fwww.google. com%2Fsearch%3Fhl%3Den%26source%3Dhp%26q%3Dcognitive%20biases.

Yudkowsky, Eleizer. A Community Blog Devoted to the Art of Human Rationality: Inferring Our Desires. Website. *http://lesswrong.com/lw/5sk/inferring_our_desires/.*